The Globalisation of Love

Wendy Williams

Dear Terri,
Thank you for being my new best friend!
Wendy

First Published Great Britain 2011
by Summertime Publishing

ISBN 978-1-904881-51-3

Book Design and Artwork by Kim Molyneaux
at www.KimMolyneaux.com

Web Design and Implementation by Niko Gaitanidis
at www.NSoulutions.com

Acknowledgements

Since this is my first book ever, this is going to be a long list of acknowledgements to include all the unwitting souls in my life who were inspirational or offered guiding light or were just plain nice somewhere along the way. (First time authors are allowed this indulgence.) Here it goes, with many, many thanks...

Jo Parfitt, my publisher, helped me 'find my voice' and overcome my passion for and excessive use of exclamation marks!!!!! Theresa Sigillito Hollema, Lois Williams and Claudia Mühlbauer ruthlessly told me when to 'edit, edit, edit' and also encouraged me with every chapter. Dr Faizal Sahukhan was warm, supportive and encouraging even when we were still strangers. Dr Claudia Luciak-Donsberger was enthusiastic and cautioned me about 'political correctness'. Michael Gates took time between flights to print and read critical early pages and he told me that I'm really funny!

Niko Gaitanidis put together 'a plan' and brought professionalism into my online world. Kim Molyneaux designed the book, wrote funny emails and exuded patience.

Frits Hermans and George New taught me about motives and managing my own. Anne MacDonald said, 'you don't succeed just by thinking about it'. Mr Gaffney showed me quite literally how to find my way around the world.

Parker Anderson helped me to find my most magnificent self. Marijke van Liemt helped me discover what things mean to me. Roswitha Kliesch has been helping me find harmony for over 10 years. Lee Paslawski and Phil Paslawski showed extraordinary kindness.

Lily and Dick, my 'Same Same' GloLo parents – when, at 18, I told them that I wanted to be an accountant, they said, 'don't be silly dear, you are a writer'.

Heimo, my GloLo husband, whipped up gourmet meals every evening when I looked in the fridge and suggested that we just eat peanut butter on toast.

Kate, my GloLo daughter, managed to escape from the nanny on a regular basis and burst into my office, Rambo-style, to declare that it is 'play time'. You were always right.

Claudia and Iza have kept the family household in tact.

Special thanks go to the GloLo couples who were candid, funny *and nice* during the interviews. Special mention goes to my GloLo neighbours, Isolde and dear Maurice (RIP), Penny and Omar, and to Lydia, Virginia and Peter, Andrea and Kurt, a.k.a. *The Gang*, and to Jan and Gordana.

A final thank you to my wonderful girlfriends who gave encouragement and screamed, 'is it done yet?' every time I saw them… for a whole year.

About the Author

Canadian Wendy Williams lives in Vienna with her Austrian husband and Austro-Canadian daughter. She has lived in six different countries and worked internationally for 18 years. She has had lots of multicultural relationships. (The exact number is somewhere between 'statistically significant' and 'not a trollop'.)

www.globalisationoflove.com

The Globalisation of Love

Contents

Foreword

When Dr Wendy Williams asked me to write the foreword of her book, though feeling honoured, I wondered how I would find the time to read the book and provide an appropriate introductory piece. Like many other healthcare professionals who have a demanding lifestyle, I was multi-tasking between counselling clients, instructing at a local university, holding book readings, giving media interviews, and spending quality time with my family and friends. I really did not think I could add more to my plate. "Besides," I thought to myself, "didn't my recently published book already critically explore the challenges and solutions of dating and marrying someone outside of one's own race and culture?" However, knowing Wendy personally, and appreciating her intelligence, determination for perfectionism and insight into relationships, I agreed to at least read her manuscript. I'm glad I did. After reading *The Globalisation of Love*, I realised that I would have to make time to pay tribute to Wendy's fresh and unique approach to the increasingly global phenomena of multicultural romance.

In my own experience as a therapist, providing 'multicultural sex and relationship therapy', I see progressively more individuals and couples (perhaps just like you), despite the many challenges they face (ie family obligations, cultural expectations, peer pressures, and sexual misunderstandings, to name only a few), who choose to be involved in a multicultural relationship. Of the various issues we deal with in our sessions, primarily, they seek validation in their relationship.

Wendy's book gives readers the validation to accept their relationships, to, in fact, celebrate all aspects of what Wendy calls a 'GloLo' relationship. This is the main of several reasons I wanted to write this foreword. Many GloLo partners feel helpless in a world that is still, for the most part, biased towards couples of similar backgrounds (monocultural couples). These GloLo couples seek guidance in the various areas of their relationship and the assurance that everything will be okay. Wendy, being in a multicultural marriage herself for over 12 years, and having interviewed dozens of people from around the world, satisfies this need. She, in her friendly, respectful manner, takes readers on a journey, from what they can expect dating a GloLo partner, to the intricacies of getting married, to how to get settled as a married couple.

Wendy immediately captures her readers' attention, questioning: "What is a multicultural relationship, anyway?" There doesn't appear to be an easy answer, right? It is for this reason that Wendy creatively pens her own definition, categorising such relationships into three simple, yet profound groups – Same Same, Different Different, and Same But Different. To find out which one you belong to, read *Chapter 1*. And what type of person is a candidate for multicultural romance? Wendy, from her exhaustive anecdotal research, has also created a GloLo profile: nice, savvy, culturally unique, strong sense of self, chummy lover and having the GloLo gene. Believe me, it gets even better…

I love how Wendy, in *Part 2*, fearlessly addresses potentially challenging issues as religion, race(ism), language, the mother-in-law factor, and so on. By exploring these intricate and once taboo subjects in a light and approachable manner, Wendy shows her readers that relationship complexities can be prevented if couples are aware of the dynamics associated with dating and ultimately marrying a GloLo partner.

I also love that even though Wendy strategically guides her readers to the proverbial altar, she does not stop there. In fact, she, much like a therapist who offers a follow-up session even after therapy has successfully terminated, seals the deal by equipping her readers, in *Part 3*, with the knowledge of what comes after the "I do's", or the walk around the ceremonial fire, or obtaining parents' blessings. You get the drift. In this final leg of the multicultural journey, Wendy thoughtfully relates her readers to the decisions they will need to make regarding where to live, the types of foods to eat, how to raise their GloLo kids and which holidays to take, where, and with whom. Yes, this lady has managed to skilfully cover it all.

When I first met Wendy, she was an aspiring author-to-be, and she demonstrated all the related qualities – hopeful but uncertain, eager yet cautious. Now, years later, it gives me great pleasure to regard Wendy not only as a friend, but a colleague, someone who has captured my professional respect through her work. *The Globalisation of Love* is not a recipe book. It will not instruct you on what actions to take; rather, it encourages critical thinking and offers options. It is my hope that this book, the most recent in a short line of existing literature related to multicultural romance, creates dialogue and fosters understanding between GloLo partners, among therapists seeking to obtain cultural sensitivity in their own work, and within the general reader who is curious about the global appeal of multicultural romance. Now, let the adventure begin…

Faizal H Sahukhan, PhD

Couples Counsellor & Clinical Sexologist

Author of *Dating the Ethnic Man: Strategies for Success*

www.multiculturalromance.com

Vancouver, BC, Canada, 2011

Introduction

One of the most profound effects of globalisation is that people from everywhere are falling in love with people from everywhere else. There is a world of romance happening out there and it is called the globalisation of love.

When you think about it, the globalisation of love is nothing new actually. There are references to multicultural romances in the bible starting with Egyptian Moses and Zipporah, his Ethiopian wife. Shakespeare wrote *Othello* in the early 1600s and had 'the Moor of Venice' marry 'Venetian' Desdemona. Movies starting with *Guess Who's Coming to Dinner* in 1967, which portrays a Black-White couple, to *NY I Love You*, a collection of multicultural stories that take place in New York City, demonstrate what is happening in multicultural melting pots like the United States. Disney is following the globalisation of love trend and in 2008 created *The Princess and the Frog*, their first interracial romantic fairytale, with American Princess Tiana, Disney's first Black princess by the way, and Maldonian Prince Naveen.

Celebrities like German Heidi Klum and British Seal, American Johnny Depp and French Vanessa Paradis, British Elton John and Canadian David Furnish, for example, give multicultural relationships *panache*. Additionally, there has been a flurry of royal weddings in recent years where the crown prince has chosen a foreign bride to rule the land with him.

It's funny that when I met my husband on New Year's Eve of 1996/97, I did not know that I was about to begin my own multicultural journey through life. After all, his English was passable as I scraped by in

German, so we could communicate. Austria seemed to be civilised enough, and Vienna is rather more glamorous than my native small town Canada. Obviously we got on well, and get this, our 'world views' were amazingly similar. Other than the fact that he could not ice skate, he did not seem so very different from the hockey playing Canadian boys with whom I exchanged first kisses while growing up in snowy Canada.

During the course of my marriage, our worlds and 'world view' have moved and merged, and clashed and connected. I starting thinking to myself, this is noteworthy stuff, maybe we should be on *Oprah*.

What I also did not think at the time is that there are 'others' like us. Like magicians and 'muggles' in the Harry Potter books, I did not know that you could divide the romantic world into 'multicultural' and 'monocultural' couples. These 'others', the protagonists of *The Globalisation of Love* are called 'GloLo' couples (yes, just like JLo). And GloLo couples have GloLo weddings, GloLo children and even go on GloLo vacation. GloLo couples experience the multicultural phenomenon of bringing together in addition to two personalities their two worlds.

There are patterns. There are issues that arise in seemingly every multicultural relationship, regardless of lands of origin and whatever colourful combination of culture, language, religion, ethnicity and colour the couple bring together. And they are unique because no two people are alike, and no two couples are alike, particularly when one is from way, way over there and the other is from way, way over here. I started thinking to myself, this is noteworthy stuff, maybe someone should write a book about it.

How big is the GloLo trend, anyway?

There are 195 different countries in the world, which allows for 18,915 potential combinations of national mixing and cultural matching and moving here and there to marry and share multicultural lives together. But how many couples are there out there who are truly multicultural? How big is the GloLo trend, anyway? Well, to be honest, I have no idea. Statisticians the world over, forgive me this next statement as it is likely to offend your professional dignity when really no offence is intended. Statistics are deceiving and 'multicultural statistics' are even more deceiving. First of all, how do you measure a multicultural marriage? Is it by nationality, ethnicity, religion, language or colour or some of the above or all of the above?

Existing research statistics tend to focus on one issue of a GloLo relationship, usually race or religion. A 2008 Pew Research Center report, for example, found that one in seven new marriages in the United States is 'interracial or inter-ethnic' and that the multicultural trend has *doubled* since 1980. Yet doubling still means that only 14% of new marriages in the US are GloLo marriages and who knows what it is elsewhere in the world. Even if I am actively looking for GloLo relationships, like when you buy a red car and suddenly you see red cars everywhere, I still have to say that there seems to be some media sensationalism around the GloLo phenomenon. One frustrated sociologist writing about her observations on biracial relationships blogged, "Given that such unions are 'flourishing', 'common', and at 'an all time high', I might assume that the people I know are unusual because they are *not* in interracial relationships."

Not every new car on the road is red, and not every new relationship is a GloLo romance, but you do tend to notice red cars more than other cars, don't you? Red cars have panache. Similarly, you do tend to notice GloLo partnerships more too. Sometimes you see it in biracial couples, or you hear it when they speak, with foreign accents, mixed languages and sometimes even hand signs and charades.

Like red car ownership, I think too that GloLo couples have a sort of GloLo-radar that helps them to quickly identify, and befriend, other GloLo couples. When I look down our short street I see, in addition to my own GloLo household, a Hungarian woman with a Ghanaian-born English man, an Austrian man with a Mexican woman (his ex-wife is from Morocco), a British woman with a Croatian man, and a German woman with a French man. Who would know that we are in Austria? Well, there is a United Nations headquarters down the street so maybe that has something to do with it. Not every neighbourhood is so GloLo diverse.

What about the divorce rate?

During the writing of this book, several people asked me, "What about the divorce rate? Is it, like, off the charts?" There seems to be sort of an *urban myth* out there that GloLo relationships have a lower success rate and that they tank more frequently and faster than monocultural relationships. Once again, I do not know.

I did read a bit about how the split rate for GloLo marriages is *lower* than monocultural marriages. It makes sense. A GloLo relationship is often hard won. As you will read in the chapters of this book, GloLo couples have to overcome language and cultural barriers, religious differences, immigration issues, perhaps social stigmas or family pressure, relocation to a new country and subsequent 'living abroad' issues. GloLo couples therefore get 'deeper' into the relationship and therefore the tendency to get out is lower and divorce rates are *lower*… some say.

Others say that GloLo couples have a *higher* divorce rate. One survey I read, for example, reported that interfaith marriages, just one aspect of a GloLo marriage mind you, are *three times* more likely to end than same faith marriages. That makes sense too. Multicultural couples have all the issues that exist in monocultural relationships, you know, money, sex, and laundry, *plus* language and cultural barriers, religious differences, immigration issues, perhaps social stigmas or family pressure, relocation to a new country and subsequent 'living abroad' issues. It is a lot to deal with in addition to being madly in love.

Whose idea was this, anyway?

This book is about multicultural GloLo couples from around the world. I even included a few stories about me and my husband, but just the really good ones. Dozens of GloLo couples shared their stories, their laughter and their tears and provided me with rich content and wonderful anecdotes for this book. They told me how terribly terrific (and sometimes how terrifically terrible) it is to share your love, your life and your refrigerator with a cultural stranger, never mind having children together. They come from 48 different countries. The interviews were in English and German. Sometimes accents were strong (in German, that would be mine) and I therefore took editorial liberty and polished up the non-native English speakers. Sometimes the accents were absolutely too adorable to edit. It gave the story *authenticity*, so I kept the original language as much as possible. Names and identities have been changed too, except for me and my husband of course.

The Globalisation of Love is about the ups and downs, the whirls and twirls, and the fun and frustration of a multicultural relationship.

"Leave your expectations at home," many GloLo spouses told me.

"Accept that every day is a new learning experience," said others.

It sounds exciting, doesn't it? That is why I decided to write a book about it. When you and your GloLo spouse are laughing about cultural *faux pas*, debating the religious figures in your life, stumbling over each other's language, flying around the world to visit in-laws, you might ask yourself, in jetlag and culture-shock induced frustration, 'Who's idea was this, anyway?'.

The answer was given to me by Jacqueline who has a Black-White, Muslim-Jew, Middle Eastern-European and Arabic-French GloLo marriage.

"You do not choose a multicultural relationship," she stated. "You choose a person. Only later do you realise that you are part of the globalisation of love."

Dear reader, enjoy this world of romance and the globalisation of love.

Wendy Williams PhD
November 2011

www.globalisationoflove.com

wendy@globalisationoflove.com

♥

Top 10 clues that you have a GloLo relationship

1. Your partner does not recognise the tune when you whistle the theme song to your favourite childhood TV series.
2. 'Driving home for Christmas' involves passports and other official travel documentation, international flights, time zone changes, and climatic differences.
3. When you share childhood memories, the stories may sound similar but where one of you says 'sand', the other says 'snow'.
4. The day you consider to be the most significant spiritual holiday of the year, your partner calls Tuesday.
5. You sneeze "AHH – CHOO" and your partner sneezes "ACH – EEH".
6. You learned drastically different versions of history, particularly relating to WWII.
7. Your partner is deeply passionate about the upcoming World Series for a sport you had previously never heard of.
8. Of the 100 million active Skype users, you were the seventh to join.
9. When you come home from work in the evening, your home smells like the Tandoori Kitchen although you are a strictly meat and potatoes kind of guy.
10. The household computer requires two keyboards – one in your language and the other one covered in hieroglyphics.

Part I
The GloLo Beginning

1. Global Alliance Strategies
2. When Heinrich Met Saanvi
3. Profile of a GloLo
4. Meet the Parents
5. The Wedding

Love

1

Global Alliance Strategies

What is a multicultural relationship, anyway?

During the writing of this book, the world, or my social network at least, divided itself into two distinct camps. There were those who were *really, really* interested in the subject matter and were keen to delve into the nitty-gritty details of multicultural love. Then there were those who *really, really* wanted nothing to do with the book and they scoffed, yes *scoffed*, that the nitty-gritty details of multicultural love are the same as in every relationship. Something about sex, money and power, but I don't remember the rest.

The first camp, The Flashers I called them, was absolutely desperate to be included in the book, and indeed almost begged to be interviewed. They saw in me a chance to reveal, flasher-like, their intriguing love stories and gain their Andy-Warhol-fifteen-minutes-of-fame. When I resisted their offers to expose their multicultural affairs because, according to my armchair psychologist assessment, they did not have the right profile, they would ask, "What *is* a multicultural relationship, anyway? We are *all* different, aren't we?" and then insist that their story was juicy and newsworthy.

The second camp, The Scoffers, would ask, derogatorily I might add, "How do you *define* a multicultural relationship, anyway?" indicating that 'multicultural' is a pretty loaded term for an armchair psychologist. They were usually the snooty intellectuals who were somewhat sceptical about my patent cocktail party answer, when asked about my profession, that I am writing a book. It was obvious that they thought 'writing a book' was a cheap euphemism for 'unemployed' or 'finding myself' or 'spoiled housewife', not to say that any of the aforementioned labels are unworthy, or even untrue.

Both camps provided good questions though, so that is where my research began. I set out to answer, "What *is* a multicultural relationship, anyway? And how *do* you define it?

Exogamy, outbreeding and the globalisation of love

What became immediately apparent in the research process was that there is a lot of talk *about* multicultural relationships, with an emphasis on the growing trend in this romantic phenomenon, the unique challenges that daunt the cross-cultural star-crossed lovers, and the ethnically rich, multilingual, globally aware offspring resulting from this 'social trend'. Very little attention, however, is given to the definition of a multicultural relationship.

There is a vague mention of the core components of multiculturalism, such as nationality, language, ethnicity, race and religion. Single issue terms like 'interfaith' and 'biracial' are bandied about as the hallmark of the modern day marital trend. There is also a bit of a 'bi' versus 'multi' discussion. Since there are only two people in an intercultural relationship, at least in theory, is it not therefore *bi*cultural rather than *multi*cultural? Some then suggest that *cross*-cultural is more appropriate, but are we then really *crossing* cultures, like bridges, or is it *inter*cultural, which is sort of *between* cultures, or are we *merging* them, which brings us back to *multi*cultural, doesn't it?

There are also a few racy terms that social scientists would use to describe the observed behavioural patterns of their research subjects, such as 'exogamy' and 'outbreeding'. To be honest, when I first saw the word exogamy, I thought it was a board game that kids might play on a rainy day, yelling "EXOGAMY" when all the plastic players, miniature men and women of different races wearing varied ethnic costumes, are successfully paired off. In fact, exogamy is not a board game but the 'custom of marrying outside of your own group'. It reminded me of my friend Cindy, a high school cheer leader, who quit the squad and dumped her football player boyfriend in our final year. Soon after this first 'scandal', she was caught in the library kissing the nerdy smart guy. Cindy had left the group, so to speak, and her exogamous incident was reported in the high school gossip newspaper as 'Cindygate'. Apparently it was the bestselling issue ever. Exogamy sells.

Outbreeding, by contrast and perhaps paradoxically, refers to the '*inter*breeding of individuals or stocks'. It sounds kind of titillating, doesn't it? This free love flair, however, did not provide me with an answer to the cocktail party question, "what *is* a multicultural relationship?" or at least not for the kind of cocktail parties I usually attend.

Most of the discussions on and definitions of these terms that describe a multicultural relationship would suit the plot of a film noir, all dark and moody and loveless. It seemed that multicultural relationships are not quite the *globalisation of love* I was thinking about when I chose the title for this book. I wanted exotic love between ebony and ivory, war brides nursing foreign soldiers back to health *and then marrying them*, East meets West love at first sight with no common language 'but the look in her eye' kind of thing. Outbreeding just didn't cut it.

Well, I had always fancied myself to be a closet snooty intellectual anyway, so I set out to create the *ultimate* definition of a multicultural relationship. Like black high heels in a woman's shoe closet, however, the definition of a multicultural relationship also requires more than one version.

According to my research, three distinct global alliance strategies could be identified:

- Same Same Relationships
- Different Different Relationships
- Same But Different Relationships

You can see already that these definitions will provide more useful information than the term 'outbreeding'.

Same Same

For anyone who has been to Thailand, you will know the meaning of Same Same. For example, Same Same is when you want to buy a white T-shirt in size small and the street vendor holds up a blue T-shirt in size large and says, 'same same'. And the street vendor is right to some degree because a T-shirt is the same as a T-shirt, right? Same Same partnerships are similar.

A Same Same relationship is based on the *obvious* cultural characteristics of the two lovebirds involved, such as nationality and language. Technically, Same Sames are not really *multicultural* because they bear the same nationality and have matching passports, so they are both T-shirts so to speak. Their cultural reference points, however, may vary remarkably. This is easy to understand in very large countries like the USA, Canada, Russia, India and China. East Coasters and West Coasters, and those millions and millions in the middle, may well have different worldviews and cultural reference points. Variables ranging from the local weather to the political climate will influence how the indigenous population live their lives and, perhaps more importantly, how they think. Hence regional differences abound.

It is not only large countries that have Same Same couples however. Smaller countries also have regional differences. The Romeos and Juliets from the northern Italian province of South Tirol (Bolzano-Bozen), just south of the Austrian border and historically a part of Austria, may have little in common with their romantic counterparts from the southern islands of Sardinia and Sicily. The landscape and climate are different. The language is different. Industry and the work ethic are different. They are rather different actually, but also Same Same. They are both Italian, right?

Family culture

Another breeding ground for potential Same Same partnerships is within family culture, particularly in high immigrant countries like Canada and the USA, where everybody is from somewhere else. Second or even third generation families are still strongly influenced by the tradition and culture of their forefathers, often completely unaware of it. With a focus on the future and enjoying the fruits of peace and prosperity in the newfound land, or struggling and scraping by to establish a decent life in the newfound land, entrenched family values and behavioural norms influence how they interact with their partners.

Culture clash in the Canadian kitchen

My parents are Same Same. On the surface, they seem very much alike and very *Canadian* for that matter. They love canoeing and have a deep respect for nature and a Canadian flag waves in their backyard. They both believe in a liberal immigration policy and they watch the hockey match together on Saturday night. The stage for a culturally harmonious marriage seems set.

Below this veneer of Canadian-ness however, is a world of difference. My mother grew up in a Ukrainian neighbourhood, eating *Perogies* (potato dumplings) and *Borsch* (beet soup). My father grew up with English parents in a strong British community, and he still warms the pot first before preparing his tea. When they married, during the height of the Cold War no less, the first thing my 'foreign' mother was taught was how to make a proper Shepherds' Pie (a casserole of ground beef, potatoes and vegetables).

My mother excelled at pie making and thereby earned herself accolades as a good housewife and homemaker. It was the 1950s remember. Her mastery of the Shepherds' Pie, however, meant the death of *Perogies*. Again, it was the 1950s, and *Perogies* were for *Communists*.

Along with other cultural indicators such as language, dress and customs, my Canadian-born 'foreign' *Communist* mother was culturally squeezed into a British Canadian *Capitalist* family. And Capitalists eat Shepherds' Pie, not *Perogies*.

While President Truman and Joseph Stalin were cooking up hydrogen bombs in their boyish quest for global hegemony, the real consequences of the Cold War were being played out in my mother's kitchen. Supper was decidedly British, and this was long before Jamie Oliver brought British cuisine into *cuisine* territory. It was only with the fall of the Berlin Wall and the collapse of Communism that the *Perogie* was de-politicised and became culturally neutral. The household *Perogie*-ban was lifted.

Same Sames sometimes have difficulty recognising that they are multicultural because they are from the same country and therefore may not expect cultural issues to surface in their everyday lives. In *Intercultural Marriage Promises and Pitfalls*, Dugan Romano writes that at the beginning of the relationship, and often well into it, couples are not aware that they are 'operating from within two different value systems that are not in agreement'. Since Same Sames share the same nationality, it may not even occur to them to consider cultural issues in their relationship. They tend to label culturally based differences as personal preferences, or they eat Shepherds' Pie and ban *Perogies*.

The young and the culturally restless

Often at least one partner in a Same Same relationship has lived abroad for many years. Children of expatriates, diplomats, and 'army brats' are what David C. Pollock and Ruth E. Van Reken call *Third Culture Kids* in their book with the same title. Third Culture Kids, or TCKs, tend to have Same Same relationships. Their experiences living abroad changes their fundamental cultural coding and even if they return to their home country as adults, their early experience in other countries alter their basic cultural framework. Their exposure to new cultures, education systems, and lifestyles teaches them that the way things are done is not the only way to do things, and they tend to pick and choose cultural bits and pieces along their international journey.

One of my first romantic relationships was very Same Same, although I did not recognise it as such at the time. He was from an expatriate family who had moved around the globe. He had lived in more countries in more far flung places on more continents by the age of twenty than most people will see in a lifetime. I was like George W. Bush when he became president. I did not have a passport.

My born-in-Brazil-Canadian boyfriend could not name the past five Prime Ministers of Canada, but he could list the United Nations Director Generals like they were his uncles. While I spent my youth learning the best snow shovelling techniques (it's all in the knees) and tending to first degree frost bite on my cheeks, he was frolicking on the beaches of the Great Barrier Reef. It hardly seems fair to call us both Canadian, does it?

We once went to London together. It was my first trip abroad and I was ecstatic with anticipation – Buckingham Palace! Big Ben! Harrods! He was quietly grumbling, "London, *not again*". It was not just this variance in our knowledge of world capitals that made us fundamentally different though. If you think of cultural behaviour and abiding by cultural norms as a kind of unconscious mimicry of the people who surround us, I 'mimicked' the Canadian world in which I was immersed, and that included unbridled enthusiasm for all things foreign, whereas he 'mimicked' his international world, where the concept of 'foreign' hardly exists. Well, let's say that we were in different cultural zones and went our separate ways. I still *love* going to London though!

In summary, Same Sames are multicultural couples with matching 'his and hers' passports. Whatever else matches is sheer luck.

♥

Top 5 clues that you and your partner are Same Same

1. You and your partner sing your national anthem in two different languages.
2. When you first met, one of you had to ask how to spell the other person's name.
3. The in-laws, who live in the same country, are five time zones away.
4. Family parties look like the opening ceremony of the Olympics, just without the flags.
5. You cheer for the arch enemies in your country's professional sports league.

Different Different

For linguistic efficiency and because the term is impressive in its original context, I will refer to Different Different multicultural pairs as Double Ds. Double Ds are what most people think of when the term multicultural is mentioned. Double Ds do not share the same nationality, ethnic base, or language and are possibly of a different religion and race. You can hear or see their differences more readily.

Double D relationships are highly romantic. Just the chance, nay the *fate*, that you, from way, way over there happen to be way, way over here, and from the *billions* of potential people to meet, your paths cross and you have the opportunity to fall in love. Well, it is destiny written in the stars, Paul Coelho philosophy and the plot of a Bollywood romance all rolled into one.

The good news is that Double Ds do recognise that they are different and they therefore expect cultural diversity within their relationship. The bad news is that, well, I would not have much of a book if it was that easy, would I?

Even if Double Ds know *cognitively* that they are different, they are still blinded by love. They focus on the similarities in personality, such as "you won't believe it, we met at an airport and he *loves* to travel, just like me" or "he *also* cried when Bambi's mother died, we must be soul mates". Furthermore, Double Ds delight in cultural distinctions such as "he's 35 and lives with his mother, isn't he a *devoted* son?" or "he carries a ceremonial dagger with him, I feel so *safe*". The differences add to the romantic glamour and magic of the situation.

When I started writing *The Globalisation of Love*, it was the Double Ds I had in mind. Proudly, I am a Double D myself.

Ambassadors for world peace

My husband is Austrian and I, as you will hear repeatedly throughout this book, am Canadian. Well, an Austrian and a Canadian seems like a good match, doesn't it? We both love the great outdoors, and we love to ski, and hike and climb. We both cried when Bambi's mother died. We must be soul mates!

Well into our second decade together, we have learned, sometimes by coincidence and a good laugh and sometimes by painstaking trial and error, that we are not always soul mates and occasionally not even a good match. Some days, it is all we can do to avoid an international incident.

Although this is not reality TV, I welcome you to take a look into our private lives for a moment. (Sorry darling, just think of the royalties.) On the surface, our likes and dislikes are strikingly similar, thankfully along with our sense of humour. However, how we *communicate* our likes and dislikes and how we *deal* with our likes and dislikes is rather different.

Some dissimilarity can of course be attributed to personality. We are not twins after all. Undeniably though, the non-overlapping spheres of our behaviour often get back to culture. The disparity between our attitudes toward life and our expectations of daily living wouldbe a sociologist's research dream. How we define and express fundamental emotions such as happiness, anger and sorrow would make an easy PhD thesis. Dealing with our 'high involvement – low involvement' and 'linear–reactive' communication styles would keep a counsellor's family well fed for years. Where we fall on the optimism – pessimism scale is further apart than Mars and Venus. Power hierarchy, respect for authority, blaming, cheating, concepts of time, leisure and cloth versus paper napkins at the dinner table, again are all starkly different.

Our epiphany was our first wedding anniversary. Dear reader, brace yourself for this ghastly account of a GloLo meltdown. As the memory is still profoundly painful, I will stick to the main detail(s) of the story: There was no Happy Anniversary gift. Now I have said it for all the world to hear. My fairy tale romance with a charming Euro-man came to a sudden and screeching halt. In *my* fairy tale, you see, the husband 'surprises' his wife with a lavishly expensive gift, even though they cannot really afford it, because he thinks she is worth it.

Why, I asked myself repeatedly, and eventually him, after 365 days of *more or less* wedded bliss, was there no gift? Had I not demonstrated my continued love and commitment by 'surprising' my husband with a big, juicy steak barbecued, *medium rare*, just the way he likes it? Note to readers (and to husband): I am vegetarian. Well, I wished I had burned it.

Obviously I spent the day in tears. I could not imagine that the beautiful tradition of gift-giving, as a symbol of continued commitment and love between a husband and wife, was not universally practised around the world. The absence of a gift could only indicate one thing: he loved me no more.

Heated discussions ensued, *after* he finished his steak, and commenting that it was 'perfectly cooked' I might add. There were reckless accusations of forgetfulness, cultural insensitivity, and being a tight-fisted cheapo. There were nasty refutes. "I did not *forget* to buy a gift, I simply *did not* buy a gift", "North American imperialist consumerism is the plague of modern society" and "if I ordered something from EBay now, would it still count?" to quote just a few.

As you can well imagine, my heart was in tatters, although the sparkly earrings I picked up at the jewellery store around the corner, *as a symbol of our continued commitment and love*, did cheer me up somewhat.

After this harrowing first anniversary, which very nearly became our last, we started to look deeper into the fault lines of our relationship. We recognised that there was more to 'me and you' than just 'me' and 'you'. We are products of our collective cultures. We are not only from Austria and Canada, we are the Austro-Hungarian Empire and the British Commonwealth, we are the old establishment and the new frontier. We are practically rewriting history just by being together. We are Double D, Different Different.

We, we decided, are ambassadors for world peace. If we cannot get along, with our shared passion for alpine sports and our common tears for Bambi, how can we expect nations and empires, with their nuclear weapons of mass destruction and imperialist ambitions, to manage the world over? Our diplomatic misunderstandings and occasional border skirmishes are now analysed and reviewed with a level of precision and expertise that would make a NATO General proud.

And isn't it just lovely how, once a year, on the anniversary of this treaty, the Austrian ambassador gives the Canadian ambassador something shiny and sparkly in a small velvet box, *as a symbol of their continued love and commitment to world peace*, and she barbecues him a big, fat juicy steak, cooked medium rare, just the way he likes it?

Global village

My husband and I have cultural differences, but we are veritable *twins* compared to Jacqueline and Fred. I met them at a hotel lobby in London. They had arrived ahead of me and I observed them for a few moments before introducing myself. They have a sort of Heidi Klum-Seal flair to them and did seem to attract second glances just by being there.

Jacqueline began our conversation by ticking off their contrasting identities on her fingers.

"We are Black-White, Muslim-Jew, Middle Eastern-European and Arabic-French, so we cover most of the sensitive topics in world culture and politics today. Thankfully I am not American. It would be too much of a cliché," she added.

"Our children are British and therefore different from either of us," Fred continued. "We are also 18 years apart in age, so there is a generation gap. Our household is a little global village of nations and three generations."

"Over the past 15 years, we have negotiated on everything," Jacqueline provided further detail. "There is language and religious holidays. Obviously we are both liberal, but we are still products of our upbringing. When we got married, there were so many discussions and compromises. The only thing we really agreed upon was that we were getting married."

I could not help but ask if it was not too much of a burden for them to have such a diverse household or if they would have preferred a partner with whom they share more commonalities.

"No," Jacqueline stated vehemently. "Maybe it would have been easier for our parents, but it would have been boring. We learn so much from each other," she beamed.

"I agree," said Fred, "our marriage breaks down a lot of stereotypes. I hope other people learn from us too."

In summary, Different Different relationships are between partners who are, well, different. Some of the variances are banal and meaningless, and also can be sources of enlightenment and laughter. Some differences are deep and historical and even difficult to recognise as cultural diversity. Double Ds create little global villages within their own household and, perhaps inadvertently, become ambassadors for world peace.

♥

Top 5 clues that you have a Different Different relationship

1. When you cross international borders with your spouse, customs officers ask, "Are you travelling on business together?"
2. Your neighbours think your spouse is the housekeeper/ nanny/gardener.
3. Your family has never been to the country where your spouse grew up and would have difficulty locating it on a world map.
4. The marriage certificate was preceded by travel visas, immigration documents, blood tests and a criminal record search.
5. When you hear a CNN newscast about two warring states, you think, "yes, we had the same problem last year..."

Same But Different

The Same But Different relationship, or SBD for acronym lovers, is a third category of multicultural relationship that is a close cousin to the Same Same relationship. Remember how my parents are Same Same because they grew up in the same country but have a fundamentally different culture? Same But Different couples grew up in a *different* country but have fundamentally the *same* culture.

A SBD relationship is one that is defined by the *dominant* socio-ethnic trait which defines them most as a person, usually religion, race and ethnicity, and usually at least one partner is in a minority context. Hence we have such terms as French Canadian, Russian Jew and African American. The French, the Russians and the Africans are not minorities *per se*, however they represent a minority population in the particular socio-cultural mix where they are living. Let's look at the French Canadian example first.

Pierre grew up in a French Catholic family near Montreal, Canada.

"I am French Canadian, not Canadian French," he explained. "So when I met Joelle in Lyon, it seemed natural that I would have a French girlfriend. I did not think, 'she is not Canadian'. I thought, *c'est bon*, she is French, like me."

"Pierre is different from French men," Joelle joined in. "In some ways he is more charming and sometimes less charming, but I like it. He speaks like my grandfather did. It reminds me of the past."

SBDs recognise the similarities in each other, which is typical at the beginning of any romantic relationship, but often do not recognise the power of the differences. Since their language and religion are usually the same, communication is not considered a problem, and they share the same value system. Their skin colour is the same, so they share a common heritage and history. Despite different nationalities and passports in different colours, they are often not even aware where they are the same and where they differ.

There are, for example, many Turkish immigrants in Vienna, Austria and now so-called 'second generation' Turks. The second generation Turks live within the Turkish community however they attend Austrian schools and are influenced by their birth country. When these second generation romantics marry new immigrants from Turkey, they have fundamentally difference perceptions of both their ethnic background as well as their host country. They have different levels of comfort and understanding within the host country as well as practical issues such as language and understanding the local systems.

Drinking *Balli Süt* (milk with honey) in Vienna's Turkish district, Güner, a thirty-something dental hygienist from Istanbul, explained her situation with Fahri, her Turkish-Austrian husband.

"I came to Vienna from Istanbul when I was 27. I am educated and modern although it was always clear that I would marry a Muslim. Fahri came to Vienna when he was six years old. But he is more traditional than I am. There were debates about head scarves and education for our daughter. My decision to work was a big issue for him. Perhaps because he lived outside Turkey for so long, he holds onto the old values and traditions that he knew as a boy. I am 100 per cent Turkish. Fahri has Austria in his veins."

When I pointed out the contradiction of their situation, that she in fact seemed to have more of Austria in her veins, Güner continued.

"Turkish women, particularly in the capital, are changing. Fahri is not there to see the changes. He thinks of traditional Muslim wives. I am a modern Muslim wife but that does not mean that I am Austrian."

Güner and Fahri share a common history and heritage. What they miss together is a common present. Their ethnicity and religion are the same, but their modern day interpretation of it is different.

A third SBD couple, African American Diana and Nigerian Omar, had a similar experience, this time based on skin colour.

"My family was happy that I chose a Black partner," explained Diana, "and I was happy too. I did not want to marry out. I am proud to be Black. Marrying a White man would betray my Black heritage. We need to stick together," she added solemnly.

Her husband, Omar, from Nigeria, saw things differently.

"Diana says she is a Black woman or an African American. Why? Before she met me, she had never set foot on the African continent. I am from Nigeria. I grew up in a rural area where everyone is Black. I did not know that I was 'Black' until I came to the United States. Suddenly I am a 'Black man', not just a Nigerian or a man. Diana and I have the same skin colour, but our experience being Black is very different. If I was Caucasian or Asian, Diana would not have chosen me."

"You see," Diana lit up, "it is good to be a Black man."

What defines Diana in her home setting is being part of the Black minority in the USA. The history of slavery, oppression, bigotry and racism is internalised and is a strong component of her character. On the outside, Diana and Omar might seem similar, but on the inside, they are culturally different. As Omar put it, their experience being Black is entirely different. They are the same, but different.

Top 5 clues you have a Same But Different relationship

1. You have different passports (see, you really are different).
2. One of you thinks that your partner is too liberal, too orthodox, too traditional, too modern, or too Western.
3. Your parents were pleased with your choice of partner *before* they had actually met your partner.
4. Your children have dual citizenship.
5. You and your spouse have the same faith/ethnicity/colour/language, but visiting the in-laws still requires international travel.

So, let's get back to the original question at the beginning of this chapter: what is a multicultural relationship, anyway? It is a relationship where fundamental values and norms are based on different cultural frameworks. The balance of power between the two cultures expresses itself in language, food, religion, and family traditions and may be in constant flux between his, hers, theirs and others. At the risk of sounding like a snooty intellectual, the answer is, a multicultural relationship consists of partners who are the same, or different, or the same but different, who have inadvertently signed a pact and are on a lifelong mission for world peace.

In the next chapter, we will look at profiles of these multicultural relationship ambassadors.

2

When Heinrich Met Saanvi

In this chapter, we will take a look at how multicultural couples meet. Before we continue though, I would like to make a distinction between *how* GloLo couples meet and *how to* meet a GloLo partner. This chapter is about *how* they meet. If I knew *how to* meet a GloLo partner, or any partner for that matter, I would be so busy consulting my single girlfriends through the process, not to mention flying to Oslo to pick up my Nobel prize for ending worldwide singledom, that I would hardly have time to write a book. If I do crack the code on *how to* meet a partner though, I promise to share it with you. For the time being, the focus is on the cosmic arrangement of time and events that leads people from around the world to meet and marry other people from around the world.

As a starting point, let's take a reference from the place that practically invented romantic beginnings – Hollywood. Remember the 1989 movie *When Harry Met Sally*? Apologies to all you youngsters out there who have never heard of it, but it *is* considered to be one of the greatest romantic comedies of all time. Here is the summary. Harry and Sally live in New York City. Over a period of 12 years, they meet each other via common friends, then by coincidence in an airport and in a bookstore, and they become friends, then lovers, then they split up and then they get back together again. Yes, to all you youngsters out there, the plot does sound lame, but it *was* the romantic *Zeitgeist* of the 1980s, and undoubtedly has the most famous orgasm scene, in a New York diner no less, in movie history. Now that I have your attention...

If Cupid, you know, the guy with the bow and arrow who inspires love and romance, played any role in the Harry and Sally story, clearly he was being paid by the hour, so he took his time and maximised his billing potential. By contrast, on a GloLo assignment, *When Heinrich Met Saanvi*, for example, Cupid cannot rely on sloppy, random meetings. With issues like geography, culture, language, and *timing*, Cupid has a limited window of opportunity to introduce Heinrich and Saanvi, ignite the spark, inspire them to fall in love, and then plan and roll out a future together. Being friends of friends and relying on the whole fancy-seeing-you-again scenario is *not* an option. Therefore Cupid, on a global mission, has to be results oriented and is clearly paid on a success rate basis rather than by the hour.

Let's look at the cosmic constellation of *When Heinrich Met Saanvi* another way. There are almost seven billion people on our planet, so that means that at any given time, there are maybe a quarter of a billion singles, of marriageable age, who are eligible and *looking for love*. (My apologies to statisticians and demographers for this random, and perhaps reckless, calculation. I am just trying to demonstrate a point.)

Some of the quarter billion swinging singles out there, that is 250,000,000 people, will fall in love with the girl/boy next door, or will follow the Harry/Sally scenario and eventually fall in love with a friend of friends or the blind date Aunt Martha arranged or someone from, *ooh taboo*, the workplace, or maybe the tennis club. GloLo couples, by contrast, have little to no overlap between friends, family, career or even continents.

According to the sparse and frequently contradictory research on this topic, 90 to 97 per cent of all couples are monocultural, depending on where the study is done and how multicultural is defined. Remember how Same Same couples share the same nationality but are culturally quite different and Same But Different couples have the same culture but different nationalities? It is difficult to capture real and perceived categorisations in a study. The main point is that although multicultural couples are increasing in society, they are still a small minority of the population.

When monocultural couples meet, they usually share a common framework for everyday life, so where they live, family and friends, place of work, and so on, are part of their existing cultural reality. It is therefore easy for the new partners to relate to or identify with each other. When you ask them, "What's new?" they answer, "Nothing much. Well, I did meet this cute guy and we're absolutely *soul mates*." The new thing in life is therefore singular, a new boyfriend or girlfriend, while other variables such as job and home remain the same.

In a multicultural meeting, by contrast, at least one of you is not on home turf, and therefore outside of your cultural reality. The situation or circumstances are not really the norm, and so you have issues like temporary job postings, expiring visitor's visas, and return plane tickets quickly getting tangled up in the web of romance. So when you ask them, "What's new?", their answer is something like, "Well, I met this cute guy from ______ (fill in exotic, far away country here) and we're absolutely *soul mates*, but his visa expires in three weeks so we might get married so he can stay or I will move with him to _____ (fill in exotic, far away country here) but I don't speak the language so I'm not sure." Therefore meeting the new boyfriend or girlfriend essentially turns their entire lives upside down. Obviously this is a job for experienced Cupids only.

Let's take a systematic look at how GloLo relationships begin. Based on the couples I interviewed, there are five clear paths to the globalisation of love. They are:

- Vacations and mini-breaks
- Jetsetting
- Mail Order Brides
- Hugh Grant syndrome
- The Noble Cause

Vacations and mini-breaks

Sometimes it does happen just like in the movies. You wake up one day *single* and *lonely*, you empty your savings account and book an all-inclusive vacation package to a tropical island, you pack your bags, fly to the exotic location and meet the man/woman of your dreams, and you come home arm in arm, without a suntan. Nudge, nudge, wink, wink.

In general, people are more relaxed on holiday, aren't they? It may be that most of us just look way better with a bit of a suntan, or the, oops, one too many *Mojitos*, or even the delirium following a sunburn, but there is definitely some kind of vacation *drug* that makes people more open and friendly, as well as more adventurous and willing to live for the moment. You never know when living for the moment ends up lasting a lifetime, do you?

The best story I heard was from a couple who met on an island that is literally called *Magic Island*.

"It's in Southeast Asia and it really is paradise," Richard, a diving enthusiast from England told me about meeting Marijke, his Dutch wife.

"The diving is beautiful, the sunsets are golden, and the only thing crowding the sandy beaches is driftwood. With a beginning like that, it was pretty hard not to think that this was our destiny."

"After finding out my boyfriend at the time was actually married, I decided to take a year off," Marijke explained. "I sold my car and had enough money to travel for a year. I wanted nothing to do with men actually! But the setting was so beautiful, the dives together were amazing, and it really was a magical beginning," she gushed. "I fell in love with Richard very quickly."

"I am from the south of England and Marijke is from the north of Holland," Richard continued, "so we are practically neighbours. We didn't think that we are different. We thought how much alike we are and how the setting was the perfect beginning for us. We go back every two or three years."

So *Magic Island* really is a vacation destination that keeps its promise, and Richard and Marijke have managed to keep the magic in their relationship alive.

Prince in castle scenario

Even though it sounds like I am trying to compete with Richard and Marijke, and monopolise the book with my own stories of romanticism, how I met my husband was quite magical too. We met in a castle, *yes, in a castle*, on a weekend get-away to Austria. I was living in Germany at the time, so that made it a weekend get-away rather than a big holiday from Canada. A lucky thing too, because travelling and jetlag always gives me terrible dark rings under my eyes which would have been a deal threatening disadvantage for sure. But back to the story…

The scene of our meeting reads like the set directions for a kitschy romantic Hollywood movie starring Julia Roberts during her blond phase. There was, and this is not a word of embellishment or exaggeration, a 500-year-old castle in a dense, snow-covered forest, and it was on New Year's Eve, and he came to me with a flute of Champagne and we danced the Danube waltz and at midnight he kissed me, all without saying a word. *I know*, it sounds too much like a 12-year-old girl's fantasy to be true. But it *is* true and it is our story, and with that kind of beginning, we sort of felt *obliged* to marry (didn't we, darling!).

Obviously for both Richard and Marijke as well as for me and my husband, such preposterously romantic beginnings can hardly be maintained long-term. Good old reality must kick in at some point.

"It's been downhill ever since," my husband likes to say of our meeting.

He is just *joking* of course. *Of course* he is just joking. Ha ha. Ha. *Anyway*...

GloLo couples who first meet in a vacation-like setting are faced with the challenge of the transition from the Caribbean island dream or prince-in-castle scenario to "it's only an eight hour flight from my place to yours, I'll sell my stock options and we can visit every third week for a year" kind of thinking.

In the early thrills of love and lust, GloLo couples will go to extreme measures to continue their holiday romance, and many do this without knowing that behind the coconut rum inspired connection, there may be deep cultural differences. Any would-be trouble spots and incompatibilities are glossed over in the frenzy of accumulating frequent flyer miles, the haze of jetlag, and trying to build a relationship based on phone calls, Facebook, text messaging and nightly all-night Skype sessions. (All snickering references to cyber sex are being *ignored* for the time being.) A lot of time and concentration is spent on getting together, making the most of the sweet hours together, bemoaning the scarcity of those hours, and then planning the next romantic escapade when more hours can be snatched together, with the whisper of "I miss you" playing in the background like elevator music.

Between proclamations of love and memorising the International Air Transport Association (IATA) flight schedule, reality and other cultural issues have little place in the heady first flush of post-vacation love. Newly coupled GloLos scarcely have time or opportunity to ask "Have you seen the cat today? Mmm, that stew smells good. What's your secret?" or "Why does your mother think she will be moving in with us?" that would otherwise unveil major cultural indicators of compatibility. It is so exciting too, who would even want to bother with real life?

After meeting my husband, *in a castle* remember, we continued to *rendezvous* at the equidistant point between our respective places of residence which was, as Cupid so brilliantly arranged, the ski resorts of Austria. I literally did not recognise my husband if he was not wearing a ski suit, unless he was, well, *not* wearing his ski suit, until the end of ski season. Fortunately, other than that one relic T-shirt from his university days, he looked as dashing and dapper in street clothes as he did in ski wear. There was no 'wardrobe shock' so to speak, but we still had a lot to learn about each other though, and a few surprises too.

Richard and Marijke had 'wardrobe shock' when they left *Magic Island* and returned to Holland to set up a life together.

"We met on the beach so Marijke was always wearing a bikini and maybe a sarong in the evening," Richard told me.

I was impressed that he knew the word 'sarong' but it just goes to show how people can learn and grow when they travel, doesn't it?

Richard continued. "When we returned to Europe, we rented a small flat in Utrecht. Her clothes took up all of the closet space and half of the flat. I did not know that this bikini girl living out of a backpack was actually a clothes horse. I mean, it's not a problem. It was just a surprise for me." He laughed a bit.

"Yes," Marijke laughed with him. "I said that I sold everything I owned so that I could travel for a year. Everything does not include clothes however, so Richard was surprised that I had so many boxes in storage."

Clothing may be a superficial indicator of personality and character, however it represents the tip of the iceberg of social markers that help us to identify and understand new people we meet. The basic exchange of information that takes place between monocultural couples, such as the neighbourhood where you lived as a child, your university *alma mater*, and your current place of work lose real meaning in an international context, particularly on a beach or on the ski slopes where a third cultural codex exists. Language and the way you speak, your manners and etiquette, and even how you treat other people are indicators that help strangers determine what type of 'clan' you are from and essentially if they want to become friends. The usual signs are confused in a multicultural holiday setting. Therefore GloLo couples who meet on vacations and mini-breaks will need to introduce their non-vacation personalities, in addition to their cultural selves, to their partner. So you see, it's a bit more complicated than just picking up a seashell souvenir at the airport gift shop, isn't it?

Jetsetters

Jetsetters is a term that once described the fabulously wealthy and the fabulously aristocratic who led a life of permanent glamour by jetsetting from one exotic location or hip metropolitan city to the next, such as Jacqueline Onassis Kennedy, leaving Ari's yacht, the *Christina* I believe, in the Aegean Sea to attend a gala event, a charity fundraiser let's say, in New York after she stopped off in Paris, staying in a suite at George V of course, to pick up her designer outfit. And that was just a typical week. Fortunately she married a Greek shipping tycoon, after the US President that is, which secured her a life of privilege and jetsetting.

The original GloLos

Jetsetters were the original GloLos. Their love lives have never been restricted by such mundane elements as geography and waiting for the next Lufthansa seat sale. Jetsetters attend the same posh parties, regardless, or even because of its remote location, their yachts are harboured side by side in St. Tropez making them *neighbours* in a sense, they have the same interests, like Champagne and caviar I guess, and without the necessity of having to work 40 hours a week to pay the rent, they have the time and energy to jetset about in pursuit of love. It is a *socioeconomic* thing.

Since jetsetters already live a very international life, enabled by private jet, never *coach*, and have multiple homes, London, Cote d'Azur, and Dubai would be considered a good start, they are somewhat 'culture-free'. They wander the globe with other jetsetters, their overwhelming wealth is the dominant cultural characteristic, and it may take several couture seasons before they even realise that they were born in different countries.

My dear friend, the Begum Aga Khan, is a jetsetter, and she explained things to me clearly. Okay, the Begum and I have never actually met and I had to rely on Google for most of the story, but she looks like a nice lady and I can imagine that if we ever do meet, we will become best girlfriends.

The Begum, who was born in Germany as Gabrielle Honey, married Prince Karim Aga Khan IV. Prince Karim, who was born in Switzerland, is the Imam of the Ismaili Muslims, and he lives in France. Gabrielle, I mean, the Begum, first married Prince Karl-Emich zu Leiningen, in Venice, which gave her a new name, Princess Gabrielle zu Leiningen.

It was only when *Princess* Gabrielle zu Leiningen married the Aga Khan that she became Muslim and changed her name to Inaara and became Begum Inaara Aga Khan.

Do you think, when they were courting and travelling to his many houses 'all over Europe' according to *Hello!* magazine, or going to the Ministry of Transport to have the name changed on her driver's licence that Prince Karim ever asked, "So Gabi, wher'ya from anyway?" When you own the world, so to speak, where you are from simply does not matter.

Sadly, the Begum and the Aga Khan have split up. The Begum now lives in Berkshire, according to *Hello!* magazine. Maybe they had cultural differences after all. When the Begum and I become best girlfriends, I will definitely ask her.

Jetsetters, bless 'em, started the GloLo trend. With their enthusiasm for frequent partner exchange however, they do not seem to be the best examples of multicultural relationships. What really furthered the globalisation of love, however, is the *nouveau* jetset, what we will call second and third tier jetsetters. Not everyone has an unlimited trust fund, but you can still get around the globe with impressive frequency these days.

Career gypsies

Second tier jetsetters are the working class jetset. International companies, management and communication consultants, and a flurry of other world-class experts have created careers for themselves based on a connection of international airports, frequent flyer miles and hotel loyalty programmes. Worldwide travel has decoupled itself from income or inheritance and has become as normal as taking the 7:47 to Paddington Station or the 8:03 to Gare de Nord. Rather than sipping Dom Perignon all day, hunting pheasants with Charles and Camilla, or organising 'charity auctions', this new class of career gypsies are working 12 hours a day minimum. Armed with an internationally recognised MBA or a PhD in a groovy and cutting edge topic, they create restructuring strategies, they merge and acquire, they coach and counsel, and lecture at conferences on expert subjects from global warming to stem cell research. They work with other world-class experts from all over the world with fraternity-like commitment and zeal. Hence business trips and international conferences have become ripe breeding grounds for the globalisation of love.

Essentially, the sailor 'with a girl in every port' has been upgraded, educated, supplied with a corporate expense account, a Blackberry and WLAN, and a travel schedule comparable to the Minister of Foreign Affairs. And often *she* is better paid than the Secretary of Foreign Affairs too. The high disposable income is reinvested in the airline industry for weekend sojourns around the globe and fuelling the flames of international romance and intrigue.

This whirlwind of travel can add to the glamour and flair of the new love interest. The challenge for career gypsies is to ground their relationship and transition from a long-distance weekend relationship to something a bit more pedestrian and normal.

Austrian Christian and Spanish Salma were dual career gypsies. They both worked for consulting firms that required 100 per cent travel to locations that changed weekly. They met in the business lounge of Zurich Airport. After a brief pre-flight exchange, they started a series of text messages.

"Salma's texts were so funny," Christian began, "I just had to meet her again. So I invited her to dinner."

It took several more messages to determine his schedule and her schedule and where they would actually meet for that dinner.

"Our first date was a weekend in Paris, and our second date was in Nice. It was only after eight months of meeting on weekends that we spent one full week together and we were not in a hotel. It was a disaster actually. Cooking and making up the bed was just not part of our dynamic. The fantasy was over," Salma explained.

"We split up. It was only when Christian stopped travelling a few months later that he missed me. He invited me to his new flat in London. It was sparsely decorated and the fridge was empty, but it was still lovely to be in his home. I knew we had a chance."

"We are still dependent on take-out food, but at least we can be together on a daily basis," Christian continued.

"Will you get married?" I asked.

"That's a good idea," he said with a smile. "We will keep you updated."

Three weeks later, Salma wrote to say that she and Christian are engaged. He proposed to her at home on the sofa while eating Chinese take-out. They had officially landed.

Company team building

Second tier jetsetting can be less peripatetic too. One of my very dear friends, originally from London, met her Austrian husband at the annual corporate sailing event. It was the *only* contact they had in the international company for which they both worked. They sailed on the same boat *three years in a row*.

"The third year I saw Stephanie getting on the boat, I decided that she wasn't getting off the boat until I had a date with her," Alex told me enthusiastically. "From more than 10,000 other employees, I was three times lucky! It was definitely a sign for me!"

Through their mutual employer, relocation to Vienna was possible.

"We were strangers in different countries and now we drive to work together," said Stephanie happily. "We even work in the same building. How's that for company team building?"

Both of the career gypsy stories show a common 'high stakes' theme in the globalisation of love. The meeting is exciting and even glamorous, but then the couples have to find a way to bring the fantasy into reality.

"It was not easy for us to get things right," Salma explained. "We had our jobs and our travelling lifestyle. It required some degree of reprioritisation."

"Any regrets?" I asked her.

"No, none at all. But every birthday, Christmas and anniversary gift is a plane ticket to somewhere."

And that, ladies and gentlemen, is why they are called jetsetters.

Destiny

Sometimes career gypsies experience the first flutter of love not so much as the joy of meeting a soul mate but more because he is the only person within a 2000 km radius who speaks the language. Carla, who was in a small town near Socci, Russia on a three month work assignment, told me how she met her husband Andrei.

"I was there to teach English," Carla told me "but I did not know before flying there that no one even spoke beginner English. When I met Andrei, I literally fell at his feet. I was so happy to meet someone I could talk to without using a dictionary and a charade of sign language. It was only after a few weeks that I recognised the person in him."

Sometimes the gratefulness you feel toward a kindly 'native' is confused with passion and love. It can be difficult to ascertain under these circumstances how you would react to the same person in your home environment. The end result might not lead to happily ever after.

"I know," Carla admitted, "that I probably would not have met and befriended Andrei back in Chicago. But because I was stranded on a language island, I had the opportunity to get to know him, and I am thankful for that. It changed my life obviously."

Andrei had been very quiet throughout the interview, so I asked him how he felt about meeting Carla on her language island.

"I knew that I did not have any competitors for Carla," he said in a strong Russian accent. "The others are better looking and stronger," he said, putting his shoulders out in a strong man hold, "but only I spoke English. So you see, it was meant to be this way, for me and for us."

I asked Andrei where he learned to speak English so well.

"My grandfather was a translator. He taught my father. My father taught me. It is historical in our family."

Andrei's children will also speak English.

Poor students

Students are also jetsetters. With scholarships, exchange programmes, study abroad and learn a language requirements, work placements and partner universities, and probably a few jetset parents too, students today are positively *nomadic* in their education. As a result, they are pairing off like animals on Noah's Ark in new and colourful combinations.

Sarah is a confident 17 year-old high school student from a small town in Austria. Given her age and geographic location, you would more expect her to be dating the boy next door. Sarah met her Canadian boyfriend two and half years ago. Although pleased with the country of choice, I *swear* I had nothing to do with it. We met at her parents' house.

"I went to Canada for an exchange semester. I lived with a family whose daughter Kylie is the same age as me," she started telling me, with just a touch of German accent still hanging in her speech. "I spent six months there, then we were apart for six months, and then Kylie came here."

"Who is the guy?" I asked, noticing the *Roots* logo on her sweatshirt, a distinctive Canadian brand that Canadians, and Japanese tourists, purchase with fire sale enthusiasm.

"Austin is his name, he's Kylie's neighbour," she explained. "We met at school but were just friends. We kept in touch on Facebook and then things changed. Now we Skype every day."

"*All day* every day," I could hear her father in the background saying, and Sarah smiled bashfully.

"We meet in the summer and at Christmas. We both applied to the same universities in London so we can finally be together," she continued.

So Sarah poached *Kylie's* boy next door. I asked if Kylie had an Austrian boyfriend.

"No," answered Sarah. "She did for a while, but it didn't work out."

"Do you think it was due to cultural differences?" I asked her.

"No," she answered patiently, "they were only 16 years old."

Boyfriends are everywhere

High school and university is normally a good time to learn about love, and related activities, and generally have the time of your life. Studying, socialising, and cheering for the varsity team, along with the requisite hormonal fluctuation, can fill the days and nights of students quite adequately. GloLo students have the additional thrill and challenge of a budding romance and learning about love, and related activities, on a long-distance basis. On the one hand, it is exciting and opens a new dimension to the existing reality that goes beyond the student pub. On the other hand, living in one country and loving in another has the risk of distracting lovelorn students from enjoying the present and living their lives fully.

Technology has enabled round-the-clock connectivity and that may give young lovers the feeling of being more connected than what is actually possible from remote locations. It is a delicate balance to manage a long-distance, not to mention multicultural, relationship on the one hand, and still live in the real world. Italian Sylvia and German Torsten met during an exchange semester in Heidelberg, Germany, and then lived apart for one year before Sylvia could return to Germany to complete her university education.

"We ate most of our meals together during that year," Sylvia explained. "We would have our computers open on the breakfast table and eat together, probably more frequently than now. But it was still a difficult year. It was depressing."

Torsten agreed. "Sylvia was always with me in my pocket," he said, patting his jeans pocket where he carried his telephone, "but I still missed her. When she finally returned to Germany, it was like having a new girlfriend. People are different in person."

"How was she different?" I asked.

"Well, she can't cook. We ate our dinners together but I never had to eat her food. I taught her how to cook," he claimed.

"Is that true?" I asked Sylvia.

"I cannot cook well, and Torsten likes good food. We did not discuss our meals. I only noticed that his meals took more time. It is a funny way to learn about someone," she said of the online relationship experience.

Students-in-love are crossing borders, altering, or even stopping, study programmes, and realigning their lives to enable them to be with their one and only GloLo. These are tough decisions to make, with potentially tough consequences, for a 21 year-old student.

I asked Sylvia, now a worldly 24, what she would do if the relationship with Torsten did not work out.

"What do you mean?" she asked, sounding confused. "If it doesn't work out with Torsten, I find a new boyfriend. Boyfriends are everywhere."

Oh. Well, then on to the next topic.

Mail Order Bride

Another common way of meeting a GloLo partner is through mail order or, in today's parlance, 'international marriage broker'. Perhaps this method of falling in love needs some explanation. It is simple supply and demand economics actually. There are lonely hearts out there, usually men in rich western countries, who are lonely and looking for love, or lonely and looking for someone to cook and clean, or lonely and... you get the point. They are the demand side.

Then there are the other lonely hearts, usually women from poor developing countries or emerging economies, who are also lonely and looking for love, or lonely and looking for someone to transport them out of their poor developing country or emerging economy to a better life in America or *anywhere*, or lonely and looking for a place to cook and clean and send every possible saved penny back to their home country to support parents, siblings, cousins, and build a new school for the community. They are the Mail Order Brides, or MOBs for short. MOBs represent the supply side.

Supply and demand lonely hearts meet on websites such as sexywifewhocooks.com or chambermaidwife.com or even bikinibride.com. Their star crossed meeting is not so much written in the stars as it is written on the website under their personal profile, with provocative poses and clever self-marketing pitches such as, "I am kind, sensitive and warm, and I like to read the classics". It impressed me that so many 25 year-old women today like to read the classics.

But who's to be judgemental? Is it really any different than meeting in a bar? Isn't it just using the technology of today to expand the dingy local bar to international dimensions? And who doesn't say about their partner, 'He/she changed my life' or 'They opened a whole new world for me'? In the MOB sense, we are speaking a tad more literally is all.

Oksana Kornienko Leslie is a Mail Order Bride from Uzbekistan. I use her real name because she wrote a book about her story called *How to Survive in International Marriage*. In her book, Oksana describes, in wonderfully Russian accented detail, why she wanted to leave Uzbekistan, which was for both economic and political reasons and how, with the help of a friend in the US, she flew to Moscow to meet an American, Mr. Keith Leslie. Within three days, the deal was sealed with promises and plans for marriage and for Oksana to move the United States. Like most MOB relationships, Oksana's relationship to Keith started on a very pragmatic basis and yes, let's admit it, there was a strong economic incentive. However it does not take long before emotions are involved and issues of culture evolve.

"Both partners have expectations of marriage, and how they live together as a couple and as individuals, all of which is culturally loaded. We receive our 'relationship education' by observing our family and our relationships in our country and culture of origin," explains

Dr. Claudia Luciak-Donsberger, intercultural relationship expert. Their expectations of each other are only revealed once they are living together, which usually means they are already married or are dependent on a pending marriage to secure an immigration visa. What appears at first to be a pure economic exchange is of course a deeply emotional situation. Oksana and Keith have a marriage which sounds just like any other GloLo marriage, fraught with family issues, a job crisis, moving house and the death of a close family member. What is salient through the chapters of Oksana's book is a mutual growing of love between them. Thank you Oksana and Keith, for your generosity of spirit and for sharing your story of love and learning.

Hugh Grant Syndrome

A fourth way for GloLo couples to meet, and a close cousin to Mail Order Bride, is what I call Hugh Grant Syndrome. I use Hugh Grant to represent a man who is dashing in looks and charming in character, and Hugh Grant, or at least his onscreen characters, represents this personality profile. Maybe Cary Grant resonates more with you of the silver generation, or Justin Timberlake, I mean Justin *Bieber*, to you girls who are just a tad younger than me.

It happens frequently that some lonely hearts, again usually men from rich western countries, are sent to work in poor developing countries or emerging economies. Now, how shall I put this politely? Without wishing to offend anyone, most of these men look nothing like Hugh/Cary Grant or Justin Timberlake/Bieber. That is not to say that they are not really nice guys. They are just not pop stars or Hollywood legends. They are ordinary guys working ordinary jobs, often something technical and *maybe* a little bit dangerous, like nuclear weapons inspector or mafia endorsed importer/exporter.

In the global marriage market place however, being a nuclear weapons inspector or mafia-endorsed importer/exporter, or just being a Westerner in a poor developing country or emerging economy, is a highly sought after partner. In the astutely observant words of American country music singer Chris Cagle, "Chicks dig it".

I asked my Canadian friend Colin, who lives in Ukraine, if he felt uncomfortable with the swarms of local women vying for his love, not to mention his passport, which they would need for their own visa application to live in Canada.

"Are you kidding? I never got this kind of attention at home. I love it here!" he exclaimed.

"I am like a celebrity," he continued matter-of-factly. "You think women love Donald Trump because he is so handsome? No. It's a package deal, and part of the package is money. My status here is similar. I can offer the women something that most Ukrainian men cannot. Some money but also hope and opportunity. Is that bad?"

Through geography, and let's be frank, economics too, Mr. Average Nice Guy is transformed into Hugh Grant, or even *The Donald*. The usually economically disadvantaged women see in 'Hugh Grant' a lottery ticket to middle class. The globalisation of love is therefore also the globalisation of hope and opportunity.

As with Mail Order Brides though, cultural issues creep into the relationship after the celebrity status has waned. This may take place as soon as the bride and groom leave her poor developing country or emerging economy and go to live in the 'land of opportunity' from whence said Hugh Grant came.

In both the Mail Order Bride case and with Hugh Grant Syndrome, expectations and reality sometimes do not match. Meeting someone in the high stakes to-marry-or-not-to-marry lottery without knowing their background, without seeing them in their home environment, without meeting their family and friends, and basing the relationship at least partially on economic variables (and hey, who doesn't?) can easily lead to misunderstandings and disappointment. A middle class Westerner in a poor country may give the impression of being wealthy, even if unintentional, whereas in his home context, he is simply middle class or *average* or even not that much of a good catch. Stories of Russian mail order brides arriving in the US to discover that their 'rich American husband' lives in a shack, or has the hygiene standards 'less than a dog' are not uncommon.

It is important in both cases to establish realistic expectations of, for starters, life in 'the West'. Through worldwide popularity of American TV and movies, where even a waitress in New York City has a 150 square metre loft apartment with floor to ceiling windows overlooking Central Park, MOBs can be very disappointed with the reality of daily life in the West. The dream of living like the *Desperate Housewives* on Wysteria Lane may become a bit of a nightmare and the globalisation of love quickly turns into the globalisation of bitterness and resentment.

So what is a MOB to do? And is there a cure for Hugh Grant Syndrome? Well, until the day comes when there is economic parity between all countries in the world, in other words *never*, there will be international brides and grooms who are looking to capitalise on their respective areas of 'comparative advantage'. As with any international business deal, cultural awareness and a good management team can lead the organisation successfully into the future. A background check and thorough due diligence are important for building trust. That may include references from friends, photos of the family, and checking out your new home address on Google Earth. (Don't laugh, I met one MOB who did it.) Sufficient funds for a plane ticket home, stored somewhere safely, provide an exit strategy. A true Hugh Grant will understand the inquisition and admire his MOB for her intelligence.

Unlike an international business deal however, an international marriage is a highly personal decision that requires a lot more than a nine to five commitment. The rules for finding Mr. or Mrs. Right still apply. It is a package deal, remember, and it is still a marriage.

Noble Cause

A fifth way to meet a GloLo spouse is via the Noble Cause. This could be a category of the jetsetters, the working class jetsetters that is, but it earns its own title because it has something unique about it. Noble Cause GloLos meet on location and on assignment in a distant land, where they are both foreigners, under conditions of duress or threat. They are there for a purpose, and usually a purpose that is noble and selfless. Noble Causes may be the likes of journalists hooking up in war zones between reports on the rebel forces, or missionaries spreading the love of Jesus, or humanitarian workers, building schools and building hope for the poor and the destitute.

Noble Causes are special because they have a common *mission* in life. Their cultural background may be vastly different but how they choose to live and work in their daily lives, amongst dropping bombs, intense poverty, or other situations of risk and danger is very similar. Within the context of their meeting point, they are two peas in a pod. Only when they leave their war zone and the focus of their attention broadens to include 'normal' aspects of life, do they become a multicultural couple, with distinct personalities, and often much to their surprise.

American Mark and German Katharina are both doctors who worked for an international medical aid organisation in the Sudan.

"When we met in Sudan, I was impressed with Mark's commitment and dedication to the children," Katharina began. "He worked so hard and he just seemed fearless. Now in California, he is different and his focus is gone."

Mark explained his position.

"My focus is the same. The Sudan was part of my mission as a doctor, but just for a period of time. My mission continues in the US. I practice medicine and want to be an excellent doctor," he said.

"I would like to do another mission," Katharina explained, "whereas Mark wants to settle, buy a house, and have children. Part of me is still in Sudan with the children there."

She looked at Mark pleadingly, and I have to admit I probably broke all professionalism and looked at him pleadingly too.

The Noble Cause that first bonded them together, bringing medical care to the poor, now risks driving them apart. In the same way that meeting someone on a vacation or mini-break dilutes the power of your respective cultures, meeting within the context of the Noble Cause also puts a cultural framework around the couple. It defines their personalities to be living in a war zone or impoverished or godless place. Without the Noble Cause, one or both partners may seem like a different person.

"We talk a lot about priorities," Katharina explained. "And our priorities have changed. Well, mine haven't but Mark's have."

"Maybe it's a cultural thing," Mark offered. "I've done my bit in Africa, whereas Kat has more of a life mission. She feels a responsibility to others. I feel a responsibility to myself."

Maybe Mark is right, that it is a cultural thing. Long-term commitments, career changes, living abroad, living without running water, these are issues that are based on cultural orientation. A noble cause for one is not the same as a noble cause for another.

So that covers the five main paths to the globalisation of love. It does seem more exciting that falling for the boy next door, doesn't it? (No offence intended to the boy next door. I do know some cute ones.) To put it succinctly, whether at work or at play, the globalisation of love can happen anywhere and everywhere.

Wendy Williams

3

Profile Of A GloLo

So far we have discussed what a multicultural relationship is and how a multicultural relationship gets started. In this chapter, we will talk about the lovebirds that pair off in international constellations. I have been referring to them as 'GloLos' throughout the book. What is a GloLo, anyway? Let's find out.

Despite the proliferation of TV shows dedicated to 'profiling', from *CSI: Miami* to *CSI: New York* to *The Profiler*, and so on, there is an absence of prime time 'profiling' of people who have exotic partnerships. In our increasingly multicultural society, it could be a real market niche if you think about it, a sort of romantic thriller, without the corpse of course. There is international intrigue, sex, romance, loads of hidden clues in cultural coding and cryptic foreign languages. Viewers would tune in weekly to find out, "Who is this international man/woman of mystery?" Catching, isn't it? But first I need to finish writing *this* book.

A lot is written about the *issues* in a multicultural relationship however relatively little is written about the *people* in the relationships. It is a typical problem in globalisation to 'de-personalise' the phenomenon and forget about the people, isn't it? As the main premise of this book is about the globalisation *of people* in love, it became clear that I better get cracking and poster a GloLo theory or two. Who knows, it could even become a TV series.

No profile

Now, maybe I am biased, but aren't GloLos somehow special? A kind of rare bird that flies an alternate migration route? A lemming that doesn't jump? A sheep who says, "No thanks, I'm not hungry right now, I'll skip this grazing session"? Don't we *deserve* a profile of our own? Assuming that you, dear reader, answer "Yes" to each of these questions, you will likely share my disappointment in the following.

Dugan Romano, author of *Intercultural Marriages Promises and Pitfalls*, one of the bibles on multicultural relationships wrote, on *page four already*, that "there is no such thing as a fixed profile of the intercultural spouse..." It was a bit crushing to read this and visions of my Emmy awarding winning TV series on profiling multicultural couples, *GloLo: Miami* I would call it, faded fast, and some basic truths became apparent. Since the globalisation of love is a *global* phenomenon and people anywhere and everywhere are doing it, it would imply that the range of personalities, in both character and culture, would be so broad as to make a generalised 'profile' impossible. We are not like serial killers, after all, 'of medium height and weight', with those beady eyes and 'mommy issues'.

The power of "there is no such thing as a fixed profile of the intercultural spouse..." left me with three choices. It could have been a mercilessly short chapter that started and ended with the quote "there is no such thing as a fixed profile of the intercultural spouse..." However the idea that a GloLo does not have a fixed profile seemed contrary to the whole 'rare bird' theory, so that led me to the second consideration.

In Romano's book, the sentence right after "there is no such thing as a fixed profile of the intercultural spouse..." is a list of six personality *tendencies* of people who marry internationally. Romano categorises GloLo individuals as 'non-traditionals', 'romantics', 'compensators', 'rebels', 'internationals', and 'others' and these categories explain why or how GloLos become GloLos. I reflected on existing research and considered the interview couples I met with from all over the world. There were some non-traditionals, some romantics and compensators, a few rebels, several internationals and a few others too. But these categories *differentiate* GloLo individuals from another. Worthy though the analysis is, and I encourage readers to read Romano's book, I was looking for a common identity and a bit of kindred spirit. Maybe we were all good in geography and poor in math, or our favourite ice cream is macadamia nut brittle, or we can touch the tip of our nose with our tongue. There must be something common to all GloLos other than the title of 'international spouse', something worthy of a prime time TV series.

GloLoTini

In the interviews I conducted for this book, for example, a personality trait I noticed in the GloLo couples I met with was that they were very nice. Well, that does seem like a cheap plug to write about how 'nice' the GloLo couples are so that they buy the book and tell all their GloLo friends to buy the book, which I hope they do of course. But we did seem to enjoy ourselves during the interview, or at least I did, and there was an air of peace and harmony on earth kind of thing. So 'nice' goes on the GloLo profile list.

Further, most interview participants seemed reflective and usually had good humour about their GloLo relationship. They were already deeply philosophical about their relationship even before I stirred up the fire on multicultural marriage. I shamelessly tried to ply them with alcohol, my famous GloLoTini, to improve the chances of hearing gossipy cultural clashes that required UN peace keepers to settle, but usually it only resulted in scribbled hand-written notes that were difficult to read the next day. So that might be another conclusion about GloLos. They are not boozers or they can handle alcohol much better than yours truly. But they were still a nice bunch, even if that does not sound very scientific.

So that led to the third and final option which was… more research. Thankfully, other GloLo researchers use more scientific methods than the GloLoTini and determined that intercultural spouses do in fact have a thing or two in common, a *profile* of sorts. You know, I think *GloLo: Miami* is really going to be a big hit after all.

Smarties

GloLo couples are smart. Actually, who can say who is really smart, right? GloLo couples are well educated, which is different from being smart. Mary Alupoaicei, author of *Your Intercultural Marriage*, found that intercultural couples, in America at least, are more likely to have an advanced degree at Master's or PhD level than monocultural couples. Remember the jetsetters who are consultants and global experts and so on? Education seems to be at least a partial ticket to jetsetting and ultimately the globalisation of love, so they are smart in that sense at least.

The GloLo couples with whom I met are very well educated. I thought they were smart too, but without testing their IQ, which we all know is *culturally biased* anyway, who is to say? The caveat to this conclusion however, is that my sample study of GloLo couples was derived from friends, friends of friends, and friends of other GloLo couples who are part of the consultant / global experts group who can wallpaper their WC with their degrees, diplomas, certificates and other indicators of higher learning. Couples who volunteer for interviews have some kind of connection to the researcher or are at least literate in the language advertising the search for interview couples. It is called a 'statistical bias'. So, as with many scientific conclusions, we can say that GloLos are *generally* well educated and *probably* a smart bunch too. They speak multiple languages, can navigate their way through a new country and culture, they know when to book flights to get the best seat sales, and how to adapt cooking recipes to local ingredients. Maybe that is not smart but savvy. So I would like to add that to the official list of the GloLo profile. They are nice and they are savvy.

Feeling a bit marginal today

Jane Khatib-Chahidi, Rosanna Hill and Renée Paton, authors of *Chance, Choice and Circumstance: A Study of Women in Cross-Cultural Marriage*, write that another shared experience of many GloLos is that the poor dears have often had "feelings and experiences of marginality – of being different from others, of not belonging, or of social isolation". It certainly makes *the globalisation of love* sound like balsam for the socially marginalised soul, doesn't it?

Further, Romano writes that generally "people who enter into an intercultural marriage have already distanced themselves somewhat from a strict adherence to many of the predominant values of their own society." So it is kind of a reinforcing cycle whereby a GloLo feels alone or marginalised and, as a result, tend to distance themselves from the source of the alienation, their very own culture. It is a complex psychological phenomenon and I can share my very personal experience of marginalisation in Canadian society.

As a Canadian, it is just sort of expected that you love hockey. It is kind of a *national duty* to love hockey. Along René Descartes' line of 'I think, therefore I am', it follows that, 'I am Canadian, therefore I love hockey'. Well, undoubtedly this will break my father's heart to hear, but it is time to come out of the cultural closet on hockey and admit, gulp, I just never got into it. I prefer *soccer*. Yes, I have even 'gone native' and refer to it as 'football'. Maybe it has to do with poor eyesight and it is just easier to watch a large white ball bouncing off a player's head than it is to follow a tiny black puck zinging around the ice rink somewhere below the *black* skates of the team. I mean, that puck is *tiny*. At the risk of sounding like a sex craved pervert, it is also more aesthetically pleasing to watch the well-toned bodies of the football players running around in shorts, and even *shirtless* on a hot day, than it is to watch big hockey players covered up in padded toddler pants and helmets and mouth guards and 'protectors' everywhere. I mean, most hockey moms cannot even recognise their own sons on the ice without the big numbers on their jerseys.

Since leaving Canada, I live a relatively hockey free life. Sometimes I have to fake it on the phone with Dad when he asks if I watched the game last night. "Yeah," I say, "just the last goal," which I actually saw on the sports channel. I was too embarrassed to tell him that I married a guy who can't even skate. I have kept this fact secret from my family. It would be akin to a drug problem.

So in this sense, I have really distanced myself from 'an adherence to the predominant value' of Canadian society, which is a love of hockey. Gosh, I can hear the scribble of my father's pen writing me out of the family will already.

Died and gone to heaven

Several women I spoke with felt marginalised and frustrated in their birth country due to gender relations. Just as I did not get into hockey, Martha did not get into gender relations in her native Mexico.

"Even as a young girl," Martha told me, "I would look at my mom and my older sister and see how they were treated by their husbands. The kitchen was like a restaurant for the men. They sit, they eat and they leave, and they don't even have to pay!" she exclaimed.

The existing cultural value system in which she lived was contrary to her own individual value system, so she distanced herself by non-cooperation at home, with many nasty scenes in the kitchen apparently, and eventually studied abroad and married a Swedish man. Sweden, in case you do not know, is the world role model on gender equality.

"When I first met Björn," Martha told me, "he cooked for me and cleaned the kitchen. I was like, what are you doing in the kitchen? Did I die and go to heaven or something?"

We all laughed and Björn continued. "A Swedish woman would expect this and consider it normal. Martha was very appreciative and impressed with my cooking."

"That was it for me," Martha concluded, "I knew I would marry Björn or another cooking Swede. I could not go back and marry a Mexican man."

It was getting near to lunch time, so I jokingly asked Björn if he had cooked Swedish meatballs.

"No, it was a stir fry actually," he answered and described it in mouth-watering detail. It is the ratio of garlic to ginger apparently that makes it so good.

"I told you," Martha repeated, "I thought I had died and gone to heaven."

Many men and women applaud Martha's rejection of stereotypical gender relations in Mexico and congratulate her on her choice of a 'gender equal husband'. This is not a feminist rant however. Women can also feel alienated in a culture where gender equality is the norm.

Chivalry is chic

Bea, a Danish girlfriend, told me how she did not understand the 'gender neutralisation' in Danish society. Similar to Sweden, Denmark is at the forefront of gender equality. However she longed for a swash-buckling partner who would 'treat her like a woman' and 'take care of her'. She found that in her Spanish husband, Enrique from Barcelona.

"There is a different dynamic between men and women in Spain. I am not saying that Danish men don't treat women well," she explained, "but the sexual tension has been rationalised away. Spanish men are more flirtatious."

Her mother, a law professor, is heart-broken.

"She thinks I am betraying women everywhere," Bea said, "particularly women who struggled for gender equality in Denmark. But I like how Spanish men treat the women. It is not political, it is personal. I just did not find the attraction in a Danish man."

In a society where 'everyone is a feminist', and where gender equality is the dominant social norm, Bea simply did not fit in. Hence she found cultural asylum in a foreign partner and something that she missed in her own culture.

"Chivalry is chic," she stated.

Both Martha and Bea felt marginalised in their home cultural environment and had their own ideas about social gender issues, whether inspired by Gloria Steinem or Harlequin romance novels is irrelevant. For each woman, the 'social norm' clashed with her individual and personal norm, leading to a cultural island. So in addition to being 'nice' and 'savvy', GloLos are also 'culturally unique'.

I just wanna be me

Similar to feeling socially marginalised, I mean *culturally unique*, many GloLos said that reaching their goals and 'self actualisation' in their own country was not possible. The cultural setting was not just contrary to their personal preferences but also a barrier to their personal aspirations.

Gender

Gender again, you might ask sceptically. Did I mention that this is not a feminist rant? Gender is a topic that was mentioned frequently in the GloLo interviews, regardless of the level of GloLoTini consumption. Several women had jobs in traditionally male dominated professions, such as marine biology and engineering, and simply could not survive in the workplace because of sexism and role definition in their home country. A foreign partner helped to create an 'entry strategy' into a job market where working professional women can thrive.

"The irony of my situation in Sweden is that I blend in," explained Martha. "No one notices that I am a *female* engineer. I can pursue my career without the gender based restrictions I faced in my own country."

"Marriage was not the solution to my problem," Martha continued, "but it did help facilitate the solution. I still have to be a competent engineer, but at least being a woman is not a disadvantage."

For Martha, a career as an engineer was more important to her than living in the country where she grew up and where her family still live. I asked her if it was a difficult choice to leave Mexico and her family.

"You know," she answered, "I would love it if I could work in Mexico and be with my family. I miss the sunshine too. But I had to pursue my own life without problems and being called a feminist, like it's a dirty word. I just wanna be me, you know."

Sasha is another woman who left her home land to pursue her own business. In her native Nairobi, she worked as a logistics strategist in what she described as 'a man's business'. She was discouraged by frequent discrimination toward women in her business and 'not being taken seriously' as well as by the corruption in the business community and even in the police force. Sasha recognised, or at least believed, that she would not be able to make an honest living for herself if she stayed in the country. For Sasha, having a foreign partner was a convenient 'exit strategy' from Kenya to a new country where she could continue her career.

"It was a coincidence that shortly after I met Willy," she told me referring to her German boyfriend, "my business ran into trouble or trouble ran into my business. It was clear that as a woman, I would not overcome the political business environment in Kenya. When Willy asked me to join him in Europe, I saw it as a chance for our relationship and a chance for me."

Sasha could not continue working in logistics in Germany so she started her own catering business, called EthnoCat, which specialises in international 'fusion' food.

"I consider a job to be more than just a way to earn money," Sasha explained. "I always want to enjoy it and to be proud of my work. My business is doing well and I am grateful."

Like Martha, Sasha's pursuit of a meaningful career overrode national and cultural alliances or even proximity to family.

Sexuality

Nabhi, a gay man from India, shared his story of 'just wanting to be me'.

"Until 2009, it was a crime in India to commit a 'homosexual act'," Nabhi started. "Sex and sexuality is not openly talked about in our culture. It is difficult to be gay and to meet gay men. A few years ago, a royal prince was disinherited by his family because he publicly announced his homosexuality. It was a scandal. India is not Kama Sutra you know."

Nabhi was referring to Prince Manvendra Singh Gohil who created media headlines both in India and internationally, by publicly declaring that he is homosexual. The prince was even on *Oprah* apparently, although I did not see that episode.

Nabhi was transferred to Amsterdam with the international company he works for and that opened up a world of gay relationship freedom.

"I don't really think about the cultural differences between me and Stephan," Nabhi continued, referring to his German partner. "I have also had relationships with Dutch men and culture was not such an issue, other than dinner time. I like to eat 'Indian' food every day. Of course, I call it 'dinner' but they would say, *'not Indian food again'*." He laughed a bit.

"It would be nice to have an Indian partner, but that is not likely. I am just happy right now that I can be myself," he concluded with a smile.

What Martha, Sasha and Nabhi have in common is the desire to be themselves and not be hindered in their personal or professional lives by external societal norms. They also share a strong sense of self. The desire to 'just be me' led them across borders and into GloLo relationships, or sometimes in the reverse order. It is the globalisation of self actualisation and fulfilment.

The GloLo profile is building. They are nice, savvy, culturally unique and have a strong sense of self.

I'm different, just like you

Not surprisingly, when these savvy 'wanna be me' spirits meet nice, culturally unique like-minded individuals, they place a strong value on the relationship. In a sense, they find a home within their relationship.

I remember one of the early interviews I conducted for the book when I was a real 'Newbie' to say the least. I met with Sheida and András. Sheida is an African American from Chicago. Andràs is Romanian and from Transylvania, which is Hungarian speaking. Together they are multicultural, biracial, interfaith, multilingual and intercontinental. They will practically write the book for me I thought. I sat with my pen posed and ready to capture their cultural clashes in the prose of a bestselling exposé.

Then they started to tell me how much *alike* they are and how they have not really noticed big cultural differences between them. The interview continued for almost three hours and there was not a cultural conflict to be heard. Visions of my bestselling book and Emmy award winning TV series burst like a red balloon at a children's party.

The common thing that defined Sheida and Tamàs, and where they found a strong personal connection with each other, was their experience as a member of a minority group within their own country. Sheida's cultural experience is as a Black woman in a predominantly White society, and a society with a brutal history of slavery and oppression toward Blacks. Tamàs' personal culture is as a Hungarian member in a Romanian speaking country and from a region which historically did not belong to today's Romania.

Sheida and Tamàs have their respective patchworks of cultural norms and values, practices and beliefs, traditions, customs, language, and religion which is part of their *national* cultural profile, but what defined them most as individuals with respect to their native culture was a feeling of 'not belonging' and even of discrimination. Feeling 'different' all your life and then meeting someone who is 'different', just like you, can be an intoxicating basis for a romantic partnership. Sheida and Tamàs found in each other a cultural homeland, and this creates a powerful bond.

Amongst all the nice couples I interviewed, there was, with a high degree of consistency, a strong commitment to 'making things work'. Perhaps because they do not feel strong ties to their own culture, GloLo partners look for a sense of belonging within their relationship and a 'my marriage is my homeland' type of security.

My mission to find reliable statistics to support the theory that GloLo partners have a stronger bond than their monocultural counterparts was unsuccessful. It is not a to-divorce-or-not-to divorce style of question. Marital satisfaction and being all chummy with your spouse is a *qualitative* variable, which is difficult to measure.

Based on my sample study, I am going to risk it and say that GloLo spouses are more committed to their relationships. Even if it is only because the stakes are higher, a topic we will explore in another chapter, a GloLo relationship is not that easy to get into and not that easy to leave. Hence another trait for the GloLo profile is a strong bond and commitment to their partner, what I will call 'chummy love'. So an international spouse is nice, savvy, culturally unique, has a strong sense of self and has chummy love.

The GloLo gene

Joel Crohn, author of *Mixed Matches*, another bible, or Koran or *pre-eminent publication* on multicultural relationships, found in his research that many multicultural couples were "very aware of their attraction to others from distinctly different cultures *before* they met their partners."

I thought about my long and colourful romantic history and other than the Same Same boyfriend mentioned in *Chapter 1*, there was hardly a Canadian to find in the whole lot. (I married late remember, so let's just say that 'the whole lot' is sufficient in number to be 'statistically significant' if you know what I mean.)

This led me to theorise that maybe there is a 'GloLo gene', as yet undiscovered, that predisposes people to be attracted to foreign partners, like being left-handed or having big ears. The GloLo gene might appear in some but not all related offspring. Sometimes the GloLo gene skips a generation, like the twins gene, for example. My parents, remember, have a Same Same GloLo relationship, so my theory started making very good sense.

If you were born with the GloLo gene, that would mean that even if the boy/girl next door was really, really cute, you would not be attracted to him/her. Maybe this is why Hugh Grant is still single. Hugh probably has the (as yet undiscovered) GloLo gene and is simply looking for love in all the wrong British places. Again, I would theorise that Hugh just needs to expand his recruiting territory and give some non-British gals a chance. Hugh, if you are reading this, I have several very cute single girlfriends from all over the world. *Call me*.

There is also evidence of the (as yet undiscovered) GloLo gene in language schools. In *I Always Wanted to Marry a Cowboy*, Ingrid Piller writes that some people who are learning a new language will "desire to become a member of the community of the speakers of that language". They learn the language and associate strongly with the culture, like Francophiles who love France and all things French. But really, with all that great food and the lovely wines, who *isn't* a Francophile?

A Canadian friend, Sal, has had a fascination with Japan since her teens. She has visited Japan five times and speaks Japanese with some degree of fluency. She has had several relationships with Japanese men. She married a Canadian man in the end, but a Japanese-Canadian.

"He's only half Japanese actually," she told me when their relationship started.

Honestly, I think she was disappointed. They married in a Japanese ceremony. Sal's Japanese mother-in-law, who has lived in Canada for 35 years, was delighted with the wedding and said that Sal's wedding was "more Japanese than in Japan". It was the best compliment Sal heard on her wedding day.

So I really think this GloLo gene is something for researchers to consider carefully. Just imagine, if we could locate the GloLo gene, politicians could include it as part of their election campaign qualifications. With a high concentration of the GloLo gene in global leaders, we would probably have world peace in no time.

The GloLo profile expands: nice, savvy, culturally unique, strong sense of self, chummy love, and the GloLo gene.

Global citizens

Another common characteristic of GloLo partners is their personal global positioning system, what I call P-GPS. Because so many GloLo citizens felt on the margin of their own culture and distanced themselves from their home environment, as well as the likelihood of having the (as yet undiscovered) GloLo gene, there is a strong penchant toward being a 'global citizen'. The cultural labels they attach to themselves tend to follow a reverse order of specificity. Whereas a non-GloLo citizen from Munich would say, for example, that she is Bavarian, then German, and then European, identifying herself first with the local culture, then national and then international culture, a GloLo citizen will identify herself in the reverse order and start with the larger and broader cultural and geographic identifier.

"I am Asian, I am Taiwanese, I am from Hsinchu County," my friend Melinda says.

It is perhaps no surprise that she lives far from home, in Singapore with her American boyfriend Mike. He could not meet for an interview so I asked Melinda about his 'global position'.

"Mike is a New Yorker. He loves New York City," she said, bursting my P-GPS theory.

"Your theory still works," Melinda consoled me a bit, "just not with Mike and not with New York."

Because the GloLo citizen has distanced his or her self from their home culture, they tend to have loose cultural ties and a broader sense of a 'universal culture' as well.

"First and foremost, I am human," Veronika stated. "It sounds better in German, *ich bin ein Mensch*. Then I am European and then I would say that I am from Austria."

She is a global citizen. Not surprisingly, *global* citizens find refuge or cultural asylum in other *GloLo* citizens. Therefore, in addition to being nice, savvy, culturally unique, and having a strong sense of self, chummy love, and the GloLo gene, the seventh and for now final characteristic of the GloLo profile is being a global citizen. The profile of an international spouse is not bad at all.

Conclusion

So it seems that GloLos are primarily a nice bunch of people. They are smart, or well educated, or let's say savvy, and they feel marginalised and even oppressed in their home country, but not so marginalised where they are foreigners, and they are different because they are alike and culturally unique. They are global citizens, committed to their partner and, pending further research, may be born with the (as yet undiscovered) GloLo gene. Why there is not yet an Emmy award winning TV series about this is beyond me. So please, pour yourself a GloLoTini and check your TV listing for *GloLo: Miami* soon.

GloLoTini

- 75 ml sparkling wine or sparkling water
- 75 ml cranberry juice
- 35 ml orange juice
- Twist of lime

Serve in a large white wine glass.

Share with friends and lovers.

Refill frequently.

Meet the Parents

Meeting your partner's parents for the very first time is usually a bit nerve wracking, isn't it? You want them to like you, of course, and you hope that your partner will present you with pride, signalling to his family that you are quite simply the light of his or her life, his or her reason for breathing, and your common destiny is, quite frankly, irrefutable, no matter what they think. It is quite likely that you will be hanging out, at least metaphorically speaking, with these people for the rest of your life, after all. You do not always know the long-term future of your romantic relationship when you meet your partner's parents, but usually GloLo couples are well on their way to marriage, or to add a bit more spice to the introduction, are already married, by the time the first meet-the-parents meeting takes place.

In a multicultural relationship, whether you are interfaith, interracial, or of a different ethnic background, meeting the parents is a bit like an international summit meeting on global peace. Various family representatives come together, hopefully in a peaceful manner, knowing that there are things about the other faction that are different, maybe not desirable, and sometimes downright weird, yet the goal is still the same: peace, harmony and the globalisation of love. You become an ambassador for your faith, race, or culture. Suddenly that little cross you wear around your neck, the one you thought was no big deal, is a symbol of how your most fundamental belief system differs from the family who stand before you. If you have never given much thought to skin colour, suddenly a few shades lighter or darker on the colour palette are read like a history and geography encyclopaedia. Even speaking the same language with a different accent tells everyone within hearing distance that you are not from here and you are not 'one of us'.

When a GloLo partner is introduced for the very first time as 'the GloLo partner', reactions range across the gamut from 'a welcome addition to family' to a 'cultural invader' or 'cultural thief'. Sometimes your role is set before you even walk into the room. History, politics, culture, bigotry, biases, and even innocence may all determine your in-laws' perception of you long before you met the GloLo love of your life. Joel Crohn writes "... whether out of racism, prejudice, ignorance, or the desire to protect religious or cultural continuity, mixed matches often find themselves confronted with intense negative reactions to their relationship."

Just because your partner is a groovy GloLo kind of guy or girl does not mean that his or her parents are equally groovy to foreign ideas and the globalisation of their son or daughter. No degree of charm, kindness and cultural sensitivity on your part will convince your partner's family otherwise. (You still have to be charming, kind, and culturally sensitive though.) The past 500 years of religious and ethnic developments and three generations of world politics are all compressed into those first few moments of introduction. They may need time to figure out how a charming, kind, and culturally sensitive person like you fits together with their current world view on people from your culture, religion or race.

On the other extreme, your partner's family may heartily welcome you into the family precisely *because* of your ethnicity, colour, faith or language. Positive stereotypes can help you win a quick place in your mother-in-law's heart however, just as with negative stereotypes, may hinder acceptance of you as an individual. You may be held in high regard as a card-carrying member of your clan with little room to manoeuvre outside the expectations of your new family.

In both cases, meeting the parents is an important threshold to cross in a GloLo relationship. Like all things GloLo, it therefore requires further examination.

In this chapter, we will look at:

- The Setting
- The Greeting
- The Meeting

The Setting

The setting can determine the success or failure of the first meeting of the parents, as we will see in this chapter. Whether you drive across town or fly half way around the world, GloLo partners have several variables to consider. The setting for the first GloLo meet-the-parents meeting includes geographic considerations, location choices, and time of year, all of which make this meeting special and memorable.

Geography

Since GloLo partners are usually from different countries, and when not, often from different regions within a country, meeting the parents usually means that someone is travelling. It may be a solo flight, just you flying in to meet your future family, for example, or it may mean that a whole *delegation* has arrived to meet you, the future bride or groom or often the new wife or husband.

It can be a bit overwhelming. Firstly, someone has probably spent a significant sum of money just to be able to get all relevant parties into one room together. In addition to this financial investment, flying, what with the crowds and delays and random acts of terrorism, not to mention having to walk *barefoot* through airport security, is making travelling these days very unappealing. Secondly, when inter-continental travel is involved, there is jetlag, that soul-destroying, bone weary tiredness resulting from the time zone changes. My theory is that jetlag is a top killer in society, but no one is willing to admit it, however I shall leave my conspiracy theory for another book. Back to this book: jetlag means that someone looks awful with dry, flaky skin and feels even worse. Jetlag makes you dehydrated *and* oily at the same time. None of this helps to make a good first impression. One likes to feel confident under situations of potential duress and not be worrying about dermatological problems.

Anyway, bedraggled and broke, everyone arrives at the destination of the first GloLo family summit, and then there is the issue of accommodation. Given that everyone is still just one degree of separation away from being total strangers, the anonymity of a hotel seems appealing. However that adds extra costs to an already pricey journey and can be perceived as highly impersonal and inhospitable in many cultures and within many families.

If we ignore that option for the moment, that leaves us with the house guest option. If it has been a long journey, then it is likely to be a long stay too. It is a tough commitment for both parties to live together under one roof, share a bathroom and eat breakfast together every morning without first having had the time to get to know each other. There is a lot of reality TV potential, with family drama, tension and comedic relief, in this arrangement. Further, some families simply do not have any space for house guests, or they have a different concept of space for living. One GloLo friend was horrified to learn that the 'guest room' she was staying in was actually the bedroom of her fiancés' parents. They had generously given her their bedroom and were sleeping on the floor in the second bedroom.

Every family has their own household culture as well. American Jennifer, a conservative East Coaster, was a bit shocked that her German boyfriend's parents were very liberal concerning their state of dress or undress while at home. She was upset when her future father-in-law entered the bedroom she was sharing with her boyfriend wearing only his boxer shorts.

"It just seemed too familiar," she said, "we had only met for the first time the day before. I was just wearing a T-shirt myself. And I could not help thinking that what stood before me was a preview of my boyfriend in 30 years."

She physically shuddered at the thought, poor dear.

Like the fast-tracking that is common in the GloLo relationship itself, meeting the parents can be an intensive crash course in getting to know your sweetheart's family.

Over the rainbow

Whoever does the travelling has probably taken vacation from work and is using treasured free time for something that is really not a vacation in the conventional sense of rest and relaxation. It is also safe to bet that at least one person in the meet-the-parents set-up is outside of his or her cultural comfort zone. If you are the traveller, maybe you have never been to the host country before, or maybe it is the in-laws who have never even left their home country before this trip to meet you. Somebody in the meet-the-parents scenario is likely feeling a bit like Dorothy in *The Wizard of Oz* and that first recognition she shares with her dog Toto that "we're not in Kansas". Whether it is you, your partner, or your future mother-in-law, going over the rainbow for the first time can be unsettling. When too many things, from food to language to climate, are different all at the same time, it leads to a kind of sensory overload, and a feeling of being overwhelmed. As if meeting your future monster, I mean mother-in-law is not already emotionally charged enough.

Hit the beach

Feelings of nervousness about 'meeting the folks' are mixed with a feeling of excitement and expectation. Travelling can be amazing, right? Seeing new things, trying new foods, and enjoying the different climate are all part of travelling with your GloLo partner, right?

Ryan, a mining engineer from a small town in northern Canada, was very excited about going to Brazil to meet his future parents-in-law in January simply because 'it's Brazil, baby' and therefore hot and sunny, and not freezing cold as it is in Canada 'in the dead of winter'.

"I brought my swim suit and frisbee," Ryan told me. "I was ready to hit the beach. But then we went from one relative to the next, every single day, from the air conditioned car to the air conditioned apartment. In nine days, we went to the beach once. It was gruelling. I would have had more fresh air and sunshine at home."

The idea behind 'meeting the parents' is to actually meet the parents, and other family and friends. It is not really a vacation, even if it is Brazil, baby.

Mozart versus Shania Twain

The first time I took my husband to my hometown to meet my parents was like a state visit. I think my parents were so grateful that he married me (more on that later) that they wanted to confirm that he had made the right choice by selecting a bride from this lovely northern town. They were determined to show him that small town Canada was just as worthy and could offer a tourist just as many riveting attractions as Vienna, a cultural capital of the world.

Anyway, we were met at the airport with balloons. It is the kind of airport where they wheel the stairs up to the airplane and then the passengers descend the plane and *walk* across the tarmac to the airport. It has a very 1960s-Jackie-O kind of flair to it.

Anyway, we were driven through town, along the scenic route, and my father seemed to be driving *very slowly* although that could just be his age, and several neighbours *waved* as we drove up our quiet street. After a quick lunch at home, the sightseeing began in earnest. We were deep, deep down in the damp, pitch black corridors of the local gold mines, we were face to face with a 600 kg moose on a wildlife safari, and we visited the hockey museum and saw the jerseys of the gap-toothed hockey players who made us proud by playing professionally in the national league. The highlight of the visit, according to my mother at least, was the visit to the Shania Twain museum. In case, dear reader, you live under a very large rock and are not familiar with the name Shania Twain, she is a country and western superstar, the highest selling female musician in any genre *of all time*. There are more impressive statistics, but suffice it to say that she is a legend in her own time. Never mind that Ms Twain currently lives in New Zealand, on the exact opposite side of the globe from her hometown, she did spend her formative years in this wild Canadian frontier, just a scant few kilometres from my childhood home I might add, and therefore sheds some of her limelight on our humble, working class town.

"You may have Mozart," my father addressed my husband competitively, "but we have Shania. Who do you think has sold more albums and sells out more concerts? Shania or a man in a wig?"

"There's her wedding dress," my mother said breathlessly pointing to Shania's modest bridal ensemble.

"She is definitely prettier than Mozart," my husband conceded diplomatically.

As we were being shuttled from one museum/monument/look-out point to the next, my husband, jetlagged and exhausted, and not prepared for the frosty minus 25 degree temperatures, realised that he had lost his hat and mittens.

"I'm cold," he shivered.

"You're in Canada now, son, you'd better get used to it," my father encouraged gruffly.

"Wear these," my mother said with somewhat more sympathy, offering him a pair of lilac woollen mittens, which he immediately put on his blue-ish looking hands.

Inevitably at this point, an ex-boyfriend of mine, a big ex-hockey player of course who now coaches future champions, appeared and short introductions were made. It was very cold, remember.

"Is that what men wear in Europe?" he asked, pointing to my husband's pastel mittens, "lady colours? Funny, you'd never get caught wearing those things around here, eh," he said with mild amusement.

My husband's cheeks were bright red with cold anyway so I have no idea if he was embarrassed and I certainly was not about to ask him. He was particularly quiet during the ride home, although I attribute that to jetlag.

Ultimately, meeting the parents, and miscellaneous others, on your vacation may well leave you feeling like you need a vacation.

Location

Once you have worked out which country to meet in, and sorted out accommodation ahead of time, you have to choose a location where the first meeting should take place. Sometimes the meeting just happens naturally, such as at the airport or train station, as happened with my husband and my parents. Both make good meeting places because there is usually a lot of activity and bustling about and finding luggage and so on. In other words, there are a lot of distractions, so you can meet the parents and then immediately shift attention away from staring at one another trying to think of something to say toward locating luggage, dodging other frenzied travellers and reuniting families, and finding the car in the gigantic parking lot. The danger of the airport / train station meeting, however, it must be said, is the The Long Drive Home as well as the potential Even Longer Traffic Jam. The front seat / back seat conversational set-up makes it awkward to engage in polite conversation and keep it flowing. Even where to sit is culturally significant. The front passenger seat of the car is reserved for the 'guest of honour' in some countries whereas it is considered to be 'the death seat' in others. Imagine putting your future mother-in-law in the 'death seat'?

Further, the airport meeting leaves no time to transition from one world to the next and to recover from the journey before being propelled into the spotlight of family attention. My friend Gina, who works as a human rights lawyer for an international NGO, had just completed a long haul flight and a 25 degree temperature increase between Canada and India, when she was packed into a tiny little car, without a seatbelt, and driven across Mumbai for an hour and a half to her fiancé's parents' home.

"Traffic was so slow, I didn't care about the seatbelt, but I was dehydrated from the flight and feeling nauseous. There was no air conditioning, the windows were open, and it was hot and sticky. I was melting and nearly vomited several times. His parents' first impression of me is being pale, silent and occasionally heaving."

It is a tough image to overcome.

A second option is, therefore, to give the travelling party a bit of time to adjust to the new environment and meet at the family home. If you or your partner represents the travelling party, the front door of the parental home may be the first point of contact. I try not to make recommendations in this book, but this is one situation where I will make a breach. Since you and your partner are the ones in the multicultural relationship, you are likely already quite open and culturally ready for new things, whereas other family members may still live in a 'monocultural world'. By meeting them within their own comfort zone, the only challenge they face is you. It is easier *for them*, and ultimately that makes it easier *for you*. Plus it gives you a chance to snoop around and see which way your mother-in-law hangs her toilet paper, not to mention witnessing the daily household dynamic between ma and pa-in-law. You can learn a lot about your GloLo partner and his or her kinfolk just by sitting an hour in the parlour.

If your family or your partner's family are the travelling party, and they have come to your comfort zone, again I will share this tidbit of advice on the wisdom of hosting the meeting at your GloLo love haven: don't do it.

There is no need to combine meeting your mother-in-law with her first visit to your home. Houses, housekeeping, decorating, and when to use the good linen are things that are culturally determined. If your partner's parents have never seen a typical _____ (fill in your nationality here) home, it might be better to acclimatise them gradually to you, to your relationship with their son or daughter, and then to your home.

Lindsey, a linguist in London, no alliteration intended, was living with her GloLo boyfriend when his parents came to visit from Japan. Mahito, although over 30, had 'forgotten' to tell Lindsey that his parents did not know that he was living with her and that if they did know, it would be 'shameful for everyone concerned'.

"I had to pretend that I did not know where the tea was," explained Lindsey, still sounding exasperated about the experience. "Mahito had not told his parents that we were living together so I had to move my shoes and coats from the front closet. I felt like a cheap tart. When Mahito drove them to their hotel, thank goodness for small mercies there, I had to drive with them and there was a lengthy debate about driving me home first, which Mahito's parents thought would be most polite. It was a total charade and I was in a foul mood for their entire visit."

Despite Lindsey's vexation, I could not help but ask if Mahito's parents liked the flat.

"Yes," she exclaimed. "They said it was a 'good' flat and that Mahito has become very domestic. Ha, what a lark. That's my potpourri in the WC."

Time of year

Perhaps even more important than the country and the location of the meet-the-parents event is the time of year. There are climatic considerations, religious holidays and national ceremonies to consider.

American Vanessa, a skiing enthusiast and outdoor adventure girl, fell madly in love with Adrian from Costa Rica. He went to university in Colorado and now works there in the tourism industry. After a year together, Adrian proposed to Vanessa and it was time to go to Costa Rica to meet his parents.

"The only time of year we could both go to Costa Rica was at Christmas," Vanessa began. "I really love Christmas with my family, and being from Colorado, I have always celebrated a classic Bing Crosby white Christmas, but I agreed to go so that I could meet Adrian's family before the wedding in the summer. In a nutshell, it was hot, windy, dusty and heartbreaking. There was a plastic Christmas tree with tacky, faded ornaments. Even though his family was very friendly, I was terribly homesick the entire two weeks and cried every day. His family thought I was insane."

"No, no, not insane," Adrian consoled her. "They thought you had too much sun. They were worried."

"Well, that was another problem," Vanessa agreed, referring to a nasty sun burn she got while walking along the beach. "I look like a puffy-eyed red lobster in all of the pictures."

Another GloLo traveller went to Tunisia during the Muslim Ramadan fast when neither food nor drink is consumed between sunrise and sunset. It was October, and not particularly hot, but still 25 degrees and much hotter than Lyon, where Natalie had started her journey.

"Riadh's family was very welcoming and friendly. When we got to his mother's flat, they asked, 'How are you? How are you?' All I said was, 'I am so thirsty' and this odd silence fell across the room," explained Natalie. "I felt awkward, like a 'sinner' because everyone was thirsty of course. It was sort of an involuntary indoctrination into Ramadan."

"Poor Natalie," Riadh continued. "We are liberal in Tunisia and we do not expect non-Muslims to observe the fast. Mama offered Natalie a glass of juice, but she refused it."

"If I drank the juice, I would have felt guilty," Natalie explained. "If I didn't drink the juice, I knew his mother would feel like a poor hostess."

It was a real cultural conundrum even if everyone was trying to be sensitive and tolerant. I asked Natalie what happened next.

"I said I would drink the juice at sundown," she answered.

I commended Natalie on her diplomacy and strong will.

"No," she said with a cringe, "I went to the bathroom and drank water from the faucet. I was so thirsty."

The message in these stories is that there are certain times of year when it is simply easier to travel and causes less emotional strain and less adjustment. Meeting the parents is enough by itself.

The Greeting

As you can see, meeting the parents requires as much forethought and planning as a military operation, although rarely with the same consequences. So far, we have looked at the *strategy* of considering geography, choosing the location and visiting at the right time. This next part of the chapter is about *tactics*. If this were a film or documentary, we would roll this section in slow motion so that viewers could see what happens in the sphere of language and communication when a GloLo couple bring their families together.

Language

In the past few pages, we have watched different meet-the-parents scenarios go ever so slightly awry without even considering that the key actors even speak the same language. There is an entire chapter on language coming up, so I will stick to meet-the-parents related issues. It is very simply actually. Either you have a common language with your GloLo partner's parents or you do have not a common language. Either way, there may be surprises.

When Vanessa was in Costa Rica, she thought she would get by on her self-proclaimed 'high school Spanish' but homesickness and sunburn left her on the language sidelines.

"Sometimes Adrian and I speak a bit of Spanish," she said, "so I thought I would understand his family, but they seemed to all speak at once. I could not join in the conversation and Adrian was constantly translating for me. It made it difficult to get to know people and I could not be myself."

Even Canadian Kevin, a junior diplomat in London, who speaks the same language as Carole, his British bride-to-be, could not prevent some international cultural jesting.

"When I met Carole's parents for the first time, they said, 'Oh, his accent, it's so cute, so colonial.' I know I don't sound posh," he said, "but I am educated."

"Darling," Carole said, dripping in poshness, "they were just teasing. Don't be such a Hooray Henry."

Kevin and I, fellow Canadians, just looked at each other in doubt. What's a 'Hooray Henry'?

Name and title

I found out about 'Hooray Henry' and it is not at all flattering, although I am sure Carole meant it purely in fun. It does lead to the next point however, which is what to call the parents of your GloLo partner.

I think every couple faces this question, even in monocultural relationships. On the one hand, you are family! You and their son or daughter have shared intimate family details and will spend your lives together and probably bear children together. On the other hand, you just met these people, and being too familiar can be, well, *too familiar*. How do you find the right balance?

Indian Arvind approached his German girlfriend's parents with a high degree of reverence and respect.

"In India, parents and elders are treated with deep respect. I knew that Claudia's parents were not thrilled that I was from India, and I thought I knew how to handle the situation. I said, 'Herr _____ , it is a pleasure to meet you'. His stony response was, 'You mean Herr *Doktor*'. Titles are very important in Germany and I had not considered his academic title."

Claudia laughed. "Arvind was shocked but I knew my father would be difficult. It's just his way," she said.

I asked if the formality still existed.

"Oh no," Arvind said proudly. "It only took three years before he said to me, 'that's enough of Herr Doktor, you are my son now'."

The Meeting

Since parents might not yet be attuned to the whole globalisation of love trend going on, and were hoping that your choice of life partner might be someone from closer to home, like the boy/girl next door or at least someone from 'within the clan', they may not understand your choice of the love of your life. Hence, upon hearing the news about your GloLo partner, any number of scenarios can be expected.

In the worst case, parents can refuse to meet 'the heathen' with whom you are besotted. Alternately you may be 'the heathen', bringing shame to your family, your partner's family, or both families. It can all be very dramatic and stressful for GloLo couples with divided loyalties and divided families.

The non-meeting

Some parents are just not ready for the globalisation of love between their son or daughter and you. Hence the planned meeting becomes a sort of 'non-meeting'. In The Big Bad Blonde Bahu blog, written by an American woman who is together with an Indian man, she writes that following a 14 hour train ride, she met her mother-in-law who refused to speak or even look at her, despite the offering of flowers, Gerbera daisies if that has any meaning. She was also deposed from her boyfriend's bedroom for the duration of the stay and had to sleep on the floor in the living room. With a bit of a vengeful spirit, she wrote in her blog, "Now, in addition to trying to control my emotions around the MIL [mother-in-law], I try to have more sympathy for what my husband endures at her hands." (April 13, 2010)

I do hope her mother-in-law is not on her mailing list.

More communicative than no meeting, and less passive aggressive than the non-meeting, is a series of possible meeting moods. The following is a list of potential labels that parents might give their son or daughter's choice of GloLo partner.

The thief

Rather than a welcome new addition to the family, a GloLo partner may be perceived as a thief, or sometimes even a 'cultural thief'. Since geography often plays a strong role in a multicultural relationship, meaning that one or both partners will live far away from their families, the other partner is seen as the one who is responsible for 'taking our little girl half way around the world'.

Dutch Jelle, a big, broad-shouldered computer sales representative, had been living and working in Asia for three years when he met and fell in love with Malaysian Laila. Within a few months, plans for marriage were made and they bought a flat together. While talking to his parents on the telephone every week, Jelle sensed that his mother was not as much in love as he was with the idea of a Malaysian wife. His mom recognised that Jelle's Asian girlfriend meant that he was 'not coming home'. When Jelle brought Laila to The Netherlands to meet his parents, his mother was rather frosty toward Laila.

"Laila became the symbol of my defection to Asia," Jelle explained. "Even though I love living in Asia and would have stayed even if I had not met Laila, my mom blamed her. The rift is still there.

Ultimately, Jelle's mother labelled Laila as a thief. Laila had stolen her grown son and kept him far away in Asia.

The traitor

Jelle and Laila also faced difficulties with Laila's family. Laila, who looks small next to Jelle even though she has an athletic build, was criticised for her choice of a Dutch partner from a 'former colonial power'.

"Jelle became a representative of former colonial times," she told me. "My family is upper middle-class and my father and grandfather were insulted that I would choose a partner that had 'controlled our family'. It is seen as a betrayal to the family and the country. Jelle is a caring, wonderful, responsible partner, but they are disappointed with him and with me."

In interracial relationships, where the cultural difference is obvious for the world to see, GloLo partners may face criticism not just from family but from society in general. Karyn Langhorne Folan, author of *Don't Bring Home a White Boy*, wrote in *The Washington Post* article 'What Mildred Knew': "White people stare (and then usually try to pretend that they didn't), Asian people stare, and Hispanic people stare. But none stare more than my fellow Blacks. To many African Americans I'm a traitor to the race."

We will further look into this colour-specific GloLo issue in *Chapter 7 GloLo Colours*, but here is one more example of the same problem.

The prostitute

The prostitute label also arises occasionally, or frequently, depending on who you talk to, in interracial relationships, particularly between White men and non-White women, whether Asian, Black, Latino or Indian. Somehow the colour mix leads to an automatic assumption that a premium has been paid.

Cho, a 'sexy preppy' Korean graduate student at New York University and Jeff, also a student, faced some odd assumptions about their GloLo relationship.

"Shortly after I returned from a holiday in Thailand, Cho and I got together," Jeff began. "I had not told my parents anything about her, just that I would be bringing home a friend for Thanksgiving. You should have seen my mother's face when Cho walked in the door. She was like, 'When did you come to America? How can you afford university here? New York is very expensive, isn't it?' It was so embarrassing."

"Although New York is multicultural," Cho added, by way of explanation, "most people can't tell the difference between Asians. A lot of people think I am from Thailand, and assume that Jeff picked me up at a bar or bought me or something."

"Even though Cho looks younger than me, she is older and better educated. She has almost finished her PhD and I am just finishing my Master's degree," Jeff stated proudly.

"He's my toyboy," Cho joked.

The lottery ticket

Very much in contrast to the label of thief is the label of lottery ticket. The lottery ticket label is earned by virtue of the economic disparities between the representative countries in the GloLo relationship. It was mentioned in the section about Mail Order Brides, for example, that one partner from a rich country, usually the man, is perceived as rich as well as able and willing to cover the financial costs for his lovely new MOB as well as her entire family.

"My family expected my spouse, who never met them, to be caring and generous to their needs," writes fellow GloLo author Oksana Leslie.

The lottery ticket GloLo partner enjoys a celebrity-like status when visiting his or her in-laws and is usually given the best cut of meat at dinner, whether or not he or she has the financial backing and willingness to fulfil the obligations implied in this role.

The Green Card

Another assumption that parents and friends can make about multicultural couples, particularly those who plan to marry, is that the relationship is based on 'administrative ambitions' such as to enable the foreign partner to obtain a residence permit in the host country, known in the USA as the Green Card.

When Vanessa, remember sunburnt and homesick in Costa Rica, first told her parents that she and Adrian would soon marry, they assumed it was to help Adrian obtain a working permit in Colorado.

"My parents didn't know that Adrian already has a Green Card," Vanessa told me. "It was so embarrassing. I was like, 'Mom, I really love this guy, okay'."

The humanitarian

Similar to the Green Card assumption is the idea that your multicultural marriage is an act of humanitarianism. Again, this assumption is most frequent when the GloLo partners have a rich country / poor country mix.

Jelle and Laila experienced the humanitarian assumption when they were in Holland for Jelle's best friend's wedding, not so much from his parents, who had already labelled Laila as a thief remember, but from his friends.

"It was great to see all my friends from university again," Jelle said. "But some people had the misconception that our relationship was somehow a great humanitarian gesture. I married a local peasant and 'saved' her from dire poverty or something. When I told them that Laila is a product manager and travels a lot for work, their bubble burst."

It's a phase

Since many GloLos partners have a strong interest in other cultures, their parents sometimes assume that the representative partner from the country is simply part of the fad.

"My parents thought my relationship with Arvind would end when my 'India phase' also ended," Claudia said. "I had travelled extensively in India long before meeting Arvind. Perhaps that helped me to understand him better when we met. I don't think I had an 'India phase' as much as a general appreciation and love of Indian culture and art. A few posters on the wall and my parents call it an 'India phase'," she laughed.

Even when Arvind talked to Claudia's parents about marriage, they still thought that the phase would pass.

"I went to Claudia's father and expressed my desire to marry Claudia," Arvind said. "His answer was, 'I don't think that's a good idea'. He thought that our relationship was fleeting."

The show case

Some parents of GloLo children try desperately to accept their future son or daughter-in-law.

When White Austrian Tanja started dating Black Gambian Lamin, her parents tried very hard to overcome their negative racism and prejudice.

"I am from a part of Austria that does not have many foreigners, and certainly no Blacks. When I brought Lamin home the first time, my parents, who had probably never had a non-Austrian in their household, treated him like an exotic animal. They invited some neighbours over to see Lamin, the 'foreigner', the 'Black man', as if to say 'we are not racist, look at our son-in-law'. But they are racist, and strongly opposed our marriage."

The snob

Sometimes family and friends take a personal offence to your choice of GloLo partner because by choosing someone from outside the clan, they interpret it that you are therefore *rejecting* a potential partner from inside the clan. Therefore they call you a snob.

A Canadian friend I met here in Vienna who comes from a small town, even smaller than my home town, met a French exchange student during her final year at university. She was hurt by how her family reacted to the happy news that they planned to marry and go to France.

"They said, 'You always thought that you were too good for us'. I never thought that. I just fell in love with someone from France. And believe me," she emphasised, "I gave the Canadian boys *plenty* of chances."

Hmm, I also gave the Canadian boys plenty of chances. If I had succeeded, I would not really be writing this book, would I?

The welcome new family member

Despite the lengthy list of nasty labels a family may give a foreign spouse, the most common label is 'welcome new family member'. Sigh. My parents were calling my husband 'son' before the ink on our marriage certificate was dry. (I was a 30plus bride, remember.)

Most of the dozens and dozens of couples I spoke with shared positive experiences when they introduced their GloLo partner to their parents. Ultimately, meeting the parents of your GloLo partner is like meeting the parents of any partner, just with jetlag and a language barrier. There may be some nervous mamas out there who are worried about 'losing their baby', but then it is time to cut the apron strings in any case, regardless of your cultural profile. Some parents will be extraordinarily kind to their new son or daughter-in-law, if only so that he or she is not whisked away, along with the grandkids, back to a foreign, alien land. There can be acceptance and groovy integration, or non-acceptance, and familial disintegration and isolation. It sounds just like family, doesn't it?

One GloLo wife, who initially had not been well received within her husband's family, told me how she had left behind her own close-knit clan and was distraught and saddened that her husband's family did not even celebrate birthdays together. A talented baker who knows that a pretty cake is the secret ingredient to a successful family gathering, she provided the fragmented in-laws with the opportunity to spend time together and to rebuild bonds that had been broken long before she arrived in her GloLo partner's life. She said she bakes nine cakes a year and invites everyone in the family to their GloLo home. Due to the increased frequency and yummy, tasty nature of the parties, her husband's family overcame their grudges and grumpiness and now share wonderful times together. Over the years, her 'label' within the family changed from Invader to Angel. That's the globalisation of love.

♥

Top 10 clues met your GloLo parents-in-law

1. Your future father-in-law wore military medallions and a beret, he eyed you suspiciously and asked what regiment your father was in.
2. Your future mother-in-law speaks loudly for several minutes, waving her hands and seems on the verge of tears and your GloLo partner who is translating for you says, "she says she is pleased to meet you".
3. Your mother-in-law gasps loudly when you hand her the bouquet of flowers you painstakingly chose for her; your GloLo spouse later tells you that leaving on the fancy coloured wrapping paper, which you paid extra for, is rude, the number of flowers you brought brings bad luck, and the colour of the flowers means 'death'.
4. It was amazing how during the course of just 10 short years, they really warmed up to you and stopped referring to you as their son or daughter's 'foreign fling'.
5. Even after 10 years, they still call you 'Yo-hawn' when your name is John and 'Pin-leepy' when your name is Penelope.
6. You have flown half-way around the world to a country you have never been to and you are met at the airport with a 'Welcome Home!' banner.
7. Your GloLo partner's mother has prepared a special traditional dinner in your honour; you smell it and see it and suddenly feel very queasy.
8. When you told your parents where you were going to meet your new inlaws, they looked panicked, told you about a story they had heard on CNN and said to be 'very careful'.
9. When your new parents-in-law ask you personal questions, they ask about 'your people'.
10. When they pour you a cup of tea, offer a glass of water or place a knife and fork in front of you on the dinner table, they say loudly, 'your people may not be familiar with this custom'.

The Wedding

But first, the proposal

Before delving into the wedding itself, it is worth mentioning a bit about the pre-wedding phase of the multicultural couple, and the proposal in particular.

Well, dear GloLo readers, although I have gone on in great detail in the previous chapter about the thrill and excitement of a budding multicultural romance, this next section has the potential to truly disappoint.

For the moment, let's forget fifty years of feminism and the equal rights movement. A proper proposal of marriage, at least for this Anglo-Saxon girl, includes a prince riding in on a white horse, gallantly dismounting, dropping to one knee, and eloquently popping the big question. A lifetime of exposure to commercial advertising sponsored primarily by the jewellery industry and Hollywood movies promoting high romance and girlfriends screaming, "Yes! Yes! Yes!" once the request of marriage has been proffered has also led to a broad, if culturally specific, conviction that a respectable proposal includes a flashy diamond engagement ring equivalent in price to three months' salary, and we are talking net salary here, of the requester.

Enter the GloLo proposal. Rather than a surprise couple of carats sparkling at the bottom of a Champagne flute, or a "Lucy, will you marry me?" electronic message on the JumboTron screen at a world series football match, or other Hollywood-style romantic proposal of marriage, a GloLo proposal is usually a bit of a letdown. For blokes who have never seen the ads or movies and don't know about the *diamonds-are-forever* culture, the risk of disappointing their GloLo girlfriend is significant.

Will you, like, marry me?

You have already heard the lovely way in which I met my husband. How is this for an anti-climatic follow-up?

Already passionately in love with my charming European prince, I was in the process of moving to Austria and had been offered a job in Vienna. So far, so good, right? In order to accept the job, I needed a work permit. Bureaucracy was not on my side. With the recognition that the paperwork would take several months, and the realisation that I would probably lose the job opportunity, my boyfriend – note, not fiancé – said in an Arnold Schwarzenegger "I'll be back" sort of way, "Oh, I guess, like, we should just get married then." And this was over the telephone. So that is exactly what we did, we just got married.

Due to complicated legislation and uncooperative immigration authorities, the multicultural couple often resign themselves to marrying. In our case, we would have married anyway, probably a bit later in the game and possibly with a bit more fanfare, and the ensuing years of marriage since then have proven that it was not the wrong decision… fortunately.

When American Stella realised that she was in a similar predicament in Switzerland, she said that the proposal was "… more of a semantic debate than an expression of desire to be together forever. We had agreed to marry only when we felt ready, and not to expedite working papers. When we hit a roadblock in the processing and my boyfriend suggested that we marry, I reminded him that we did not want to take that route. He insisted that his motivation was love only and I would not believe him. How unromantic is it that I did not believe him? I was negating his proposal!"

For some shy guys, however, the bureaucratic scapegoat is ideal. They do not risk their pride and their hearts by falling to one knee and presenting their three months' salary in a small black velvet box.

A few lucky GloLo partners already live in the same country, whether his, hers, or a new third country. This eases the transition from strangers to living together in holy, or at least legal, matrimony as husband and wife. Presumably one or both partners have ironed out the paperwork and visa requirements for the current place of residence. The wedding can then be centred around celebrations and cake rather than learning the legalese of immigration, translating birth certificates, taking health exams and proving that your love is love.

So many of the multicultural couples I interviewed during the writing of this book laughed when I asked about their engagement proposal. For all the jetset glamour and mystique of a multicultural relationship, the proposal itself tends to be a pragmatic exercise in immigration.

As in my own case, there was no declaration of everlasting love or seeing our initials carved into the bark of a tree on a walk in the woods. No Champagne and, darn, no jewellery. So it may not have been The Grand Proposal that I might have dreamed of when I was 12 – okay, *since* I was 12 – but the most important thing to remember is that I still married my prince!

♥

Five things to know about a multicultural trip to the church/mosque/synagogue/registry office

1. Decision-making is fast-tracked

When multicultural couples first meet, the concept of dating, 'taking things slow' and going to dinner and a movie once in a while, is not usually an option. One or both partners have an expiring visitor's visa and/or a non-refundable plane ticket in their pocket, so there tends to be real time pressure on the falling in love process. Frequently GloLo couples say, "We knew right away that this was the real thing". Of course, because if they had dilly-dallied about the issue, one or both of them would have flown off into the sunset and back to their home country, and that would have been the end of it, right? GloLo couples are faced with an almost immediate choice – if they want a relationship, they need to take it to the next level, and fast.

2. The stakes are higher

In a monocultural relationship, when boy meets girl, they usually have one decision to make, which is, 'do I want a relationship with this boy/girl?' The answer is a simple 'yes' or 'no'. In a multicultural relationship, the decision about the boy or girl also includes a broader question that goes something like, 'do I want to give up my job, sell my flat, leave my family and friends to fly half-way around the world to a country where I don't speak the language to pursue a relationship with this boy/girl with whom I have spent two weeks on vacation and Skyped with for a month and on whom I will be financially dependent?' The decision about the romantic relationship is made in conjunction with many other life factors.

Consider the list of the 10 most stressful things in life. The list varies, but things like moving house (never mind moving countries), wedding planning, and not working are constants. It is perhaps worth noting that serving time in jail is not on most lists, so maybe that is a real indicator of the significance of the GloLo stakes.

3. The globalisation of isolation

The irony of the globalisation of love is that it often leads to a certain sense of isolation for one or both partners. On the one hand, at least one partner is not in their native country and may miss having contact to their own social network and the reference point they provide. As a GloLo partner integrates into the new world into which their new lover introduces them, they may long for people and practices, not to mention the humour, of their home country and culture. They are making a huge decision about their life and may long for comfort and advice from friends and family. It would help if they even knew the guy, right?

On the other hand, the local partner may not even know any of their imported partner's family or friends, so they are proposing marriage without knowing what is behind the package of their foreign lover. Internet technology has done wonders to close the communication gap between families, assuming of course that there is some sort of common language, but it cannot compensate for experiencing regular family dynamics. After all, you never really know a family until you sit with them at the dinner table, do you?

4. Spontaneous and untypical behaviour is common

The majority of GloLos with whom I spoke during the writing of this book declared that their decision to marry was spontaneous even though they, as people, are not spontaneous. I find it amusingly ironic that the one time these conservative risk-avoiders the world over decide to be a little carefree and have a little fun, they do it not with a bold new hair cut or a visible tattoo, but with a presumably life altering lifelong decision like marriage. Love really does conquer all, doesn't it?

5. Bureaucratic love

Another oddity in the globalisation of love story is the frequency of 'green card marriages'. Green card marriages refer to American marriages conducted solely for the purpose of a foreigner acquiring a green card or unlimited work permit in the US. Andie MacDowell and the perhaps oddly cast Gerard Depardieu made a movie in 1990 about two people who marry for a green card ... and then fall in love. Typically, GloLos are already in love, but they still marry for a green card, or equivalent working visa, simply to allow them to get on with their lives, both living legally in the same country. GloLos really are in love, but in the end, they often don't marry for love, but for the green card. Ironic, isn't it?

In summary, the GloLo proposal and engagement period tends to be a mix of whirlwind romance meets expatriate reality and pragmatism. You have all of the elements of meeting The One, with the lovely heart palpitations and that butterflies-in-your-tummy feeling, the joy of *finally* finding your soul mate and exiting the tiring singles game, finishing each other's sentences and delighting in your differences, having a permanent date for all future office Christmas parties, and there is also the enormous relief in knowing that now you will not die alone in a public housing estate with nine cats for roommates. Ah, love's first blush.

While the sweet elixir from Cupid's arrow is pulsing through your veins, with the head-spinning emotional and physiological consequences, a few other things are also happening too. For example, you are also moving to a new country, seven time zones away from home where the climate is an average of 20 degrees hotter, or perhaps colder, than what you are used to and for which your wardrobe is inappropriate. While you learn a new language, drive on the *other* side of road, find a new job, you still have to figure out where to buy new foods for new recipes in the Metric, or perhaps Imperial, system in shops and markets or shopping malls that little resemble the retail environment of home. Amid this adjustment and just when you thought that things were all becoming a tad overwhelming, something new is added to your To Do

List. The wedding of course! In the next section, we will look at the different possibilities for a multicultural wedding.

The Wedding

It is probably fair to say that most people feel rather emotional about weddings, or as one recent bride put it, *intensely primeval*. Whether the nuptial ceremony is defined as the prosperous union of two families, the happiest day of a girl's life or a Big Fat Greek Wedding, it is bound to raise emotions in a miscellaneous range of family and friends.

The bride and groom do play in the starring roles on Wedding Day, however as with any big budget Hollywood/Bollywood production, it is more likely to be a result of the collective influence of assorted mothers and mothers-in-law, priests and preachers, family traditions, tips from the latest bridal magazine (despite conflicting trends between the French and English editions of *Vogue*), as well as a host of miscellaneous relatives and friends who feel that the marriage is somehow all about them. Each of these creative partners brings in their own set of expectations based on a colourful framework of cultural norms and values.

Hence, the multicultural wedding could, or perhaps even should, be its own industry. Just think of the variables. On a grand scale, we have religion, ethnicity, and cultural tradition, which determine how things could, and once again perhaps should, be done. On a smaller scale, we have seemingly endless decisions to make concerning invitations, flowers, *The Dress*, the guest list, food, the ceremony, the music, not to mention the location, all mixed with family traditions. Each of these wedding component variables is a cultural minefield just waiting to be triggered, and can turn the bride-to-be into an intercultural Bridezilla.

All of these 'creative differences', and hence opportunities, in the multicultural wedding can be categorised into four main wedding options for the bride and groom-to-be:

- The Cultural Merger Wedding
- The Double Wedding
- The Secret Wedding or
- The New Fangled Wedding

As you will not find definitions of these terms on wikipedia.com, let's discuss each option in more detail.

The Cultural Merger Wedding

The Cultural Merger Wedding makes perfect sense for a culturally merging couple... *in theory*. The idea of mixing religions, traditions and languages into one ceremony does have a Ghandi-esque harmony to it, doesn't it? If the United Nations can pull off an annual Christmas party, why shouldn't two people bring together two sets of family and friends to kick up their heels for a day in celebration of love? Well, did you ever notice the security at a typical United Nations get-together? This is not without reason – these multicultural experts recognise the plutonium potential of a multicultural shindig.

As with any marriage celebration, the creative possibilities of a Cultural Merger Wedding are limitless. For every wedding variable, from the flowers of the bridal bouquet to the wedding vows to the receiving line etiquette, attention to detail allows brides and grooms to express their personality, their style, their humour, their spending power, or at least their credit card limit, their family customs, and of course their own unique culture.

Did the bride wear white?

As a woman, my natural instinct is to immediately ask what is probably the most fundamental question relating to any type of matrimonial ceremony anywhere in the world, which is, "WHAT WAS THE DRESS LIKE???" In the Cultural Merger Wedding, the answer to this can vary. Does the bride wear white or red or purple? Do the guests wear white? Is black okay? Does the sacred ceremony take place in a church, a synagogue, a mosque, in the backyard or on the beach? Are live animals involved? Is it a morning ceremony, taking advantage of the great lighting for photos, or all afternoon, including tea, or something cocktail-ish in evening? Who will walk up the aisle, and when? And what if there is no aisle?

To some couples, these may seem to be banal choices that have lost their cultural significance in our globalised world, or are perhaps just a matter of good and poor taste, but to other families, these rituals and rites of passage are an important part of family and cultural tradition, and the continuity of these practices is as significant as the continuity of the family institution.

When John and Lajita married, they made a conscious choice to include elements of his American Irish Catholic heritage and her Indian background. At Latija's henna party, a shamrock was included in the henna design on her hands. John and his groom's men secretly had their hands hennaed too, also with the shamrock.

At the Catholic church ceremony in Minnesota, the mothers of the bride and groom made their pledges to accept and protect their new son and daughter-in-law respectively, an important ritual in a typical Hindu ceremony.

Lajita laughs when she talks about choosing the banquet food.

"I have been vegetarian my whole life but there was no way we could serve our Minnesotan guests a vegetarian buffet, so we had a variety of meat dishes. To the untrained eye and pallet, many Indian dishes are similar, and it was funny to hear John's Uncle Bob, a farmer, raving about the Punjabi Korma dish which is pure tofu."

Ideally, the Cultural Merger Wedding takes the best of both worlds and fuses together the elements to create a wedding ceremony that both partners respect and appreciate.

The advantage of the Cultural Merger Wedding is that it recognises the marital union for what it is – a cultural merger of two individuals. It is perhaps a microcosmic demonstration of how your life together will combine personal histories and backgrounds into a cultural family mosaic. The bride and groom can cherry pick from both cultures and create a wonderful collage of tradition, mixing incense with holy wine, breaking bread and breaking plates, tossing coins, rice and rose petals, and mixing verse and song of poets and pianists from around the world.

If I can just refer back to the dress topic again, the most exquisite wedding gown I have ever seen was at an Asian-Indian wedding where the bride wore a dress – gentlemen, bear with me here for a moment – with a sequined red bodice and an explosive purple meringue skirt, all in brushed silk. It gave a whole new meaning to wanting to be in the bride's shoes – anything for that dress! But I digress. The point is that she took the traditional approach from both cultures and created something new, possibly *even better*, than the original, much to the pleasure of both her mother and her new mother-in-law, who both felt that she was respecting the significance of tradition.

I will – ich will

The disadvantage of the Cultural Merger Wedding is that it requires loads of compromises, and therefore often disappointments. Inevitably, there will be some hushed 'if only' regrets and other subtle and not so subtly expressed wishes about how the wedding was conducted.

Virginia from Sussex, a backpacking globe trotter since the age of 17, thought she was being 'culturally generous' by marrying in Stephan's hometown in Germany rather than her own. She rallied up a number of family and friends who were happy to share in a multicultural wedding 'on the Continent', as they put it. The wedding ceremony, based on Protestant and Catholic values, was conducted in two languages. In an attempt to charm the international crowd, traditional Stephan said his vows in English while Virginia gave her vows in German. Both sides of the family later complained that they did not understand what was being said, either due to not understanding the 'foreign' language or, perhaps even worse, not understanding the strongly accented language each partner spoke in their non-native tongue.

"When I watch the wedding video, I can actually hear the Germans grumbling to each other during the English language segments and the English guests whispering to each other during the German language segments," Virginia told me.

"It was all sort of anti-climatic for the guests," Stephan added. "They were given pieces of the story, but due to the language confusion, never got the full feeling that the service was complete and that we had married properly. They felt a bit cheated actually."

Fidelity and the flaunting floozy

On a similar note, mixing customs within one ceremony can sometimes be misinterpreted, as Susie and Kassim experienced. Susie, a cheerleader for the university football team and as American as apple pie, surprised friends and family when she brought home Moroccan-born Kassim as her new boyfriend and eventually fiancé. Kassim had lived in the United States since his late teens and somehow maintained the smouldering charm of a character from *1001 Arabian Nights* with the savvy of an internet business owner. Family tradition rang strong on both sides so the wedding planning required intricate negotiations.

Three brides in Susie's family had worn the borrowed blue garter belt at their weddings, and three times, the garter belt had been caught by a family member who then married within a year. As a bride, it was family *duty* to wear it. Kassim's family had lived in the United States for over a decade and were considered liberal Muslims. Kassim had explained to his immediate family members that the blue garter belt was a symbol of fidelity and that Susie might 'show a bit of leg' at some point during the evening festivities. Apparently the warning was not well understood and one of Kassim's aunts loudly expressed her disapproval at Susie's playful removal of the garter belt, to appreciative whooping and laughing amongst her own guests, as provocative and vulgar, declaring it a striptease of a common floozy. His ancient grandmother almost fainted and it took Susie and Kassim several months to regain good graces with certain family members who referred to her as 'floozy Susie'.

International business mergers require a team of bankers, lawyers, and management consultants to fairly, legally, and smoothly complete the transaction. Cultural merger weddings require no less consideration and guidance from third parties. Seeking out a broad range of opinions and ideas for the wedding not only helps to avoid any cross-cultural mishaps, but may also lead to the creation of a spectacular cultural mosaic of tradition, hope and love.

Location, location, location

Just as in real estate, one major factor affecting the success of a Cultural Merger Wedding is location. In a multicultural relationship, and probably in all weddings actually, the location is a major decision for the couple. In the multicultural context, there is one guarantee and that is that any chosen location is going to be wrong for someone.

When Brazilian Anna Lucia and Portuguese Pedro announced their intention to marry, Anna Lucia experienced family rivalry concerning the wedding location.

"On the one hand, both families were pulling to have the wedding in their home country, with the promise of hosting a lavish event," she remembers. "On the other hand, they claimed that they could not afford to fly to the other country. The suggestion to use the proposed wedding budget to fund flights overseas was like suggesting embezzlement. All logic vanished and it was a competition to prove who is the poorest."

Once the first hurdle is passed and a location has been chosen, it hopefully leads to the second hurdle, which is hosting the wedding guests.

There will likely be international guests which means travel arrangements, overnight stays, often time changes and climatic adjustments, language issues, and, as with any international travel, forgotten medication, food intolerances, lost travel documents and confusion with the new currency. In summary, international guests mean *more stress* for the bride and groom.

Pascale, a French political reporter, remembers her wedding.

"My wedding was tough work. I spent three consecutive days, including my wedding day, translating for my parents," she told me.

Her parents came to Poland for her wedding to Derrick. Her common language with her betrothed is English, so she was mixing French, Polish and English the entire time. Fluent in all languages, however unaccustomed to simultaneous translation, Pascale, usually easy-going and relaxed, developed a screaming headache, which continued throughout the entire wedding ceremony. She admits to saying her vows a bit faster than she usually speaks so that she could ask her sister, the one with a handbag, for a couple of pain relievers. Once she had some Champagne, which her parents had brought with them, the day was rescued. Derrick completed the anecdote nicely.

"Pascale is usually happy and bubbly. It must be from the Champagne, which is where she grew up in France, and my special name for her is Bubbles. On our wedding day, Bubbles needed the bubbles." He laughed gregariously.

"Don't worry, Bubbles." He turned to take her hand in his, "I needed the bubbles too."

The Montagues meet the Capulets

The seating arrangements at the Cultural Merger Wedding, an art in itself at any social function, even when the guests know each other, is like negotiating a global peace treaty. There are two extremes to pursue. One option is to simply code the guests according to ownership and nationality, and keep the groups separate. Forget that a marriage is the lifelong union between two families – sometimes it's just easier to keep separate the Hatfields from the McCoys and the Montagues from the Capulets. This sectioning of bride and groom families will lead to both the bride and the groom skipping between each group for the duration of the ceremony and party, but it will keep to a minimum the need for translating and those long, awkward silences that follow when perfect strangers who do not speak a common language are forced to smile politely at each other over a five course meal, *plus speeches*. The other possibility is to mix and mingle and create your own little global village in the wedding hall. With a bit of common language and a few interactive introductory games, this can actually be quite good fun.

A wedding-appropriate icebreaker is the game *Great Romances of History*. Each guest is given a piece of paper with the name of one half of a famous couple, such as Romeo or Juliet for example. Before guests sit down for the long meal, they circulate through the room looking for their great love. It encourages guests toward good-humoured mixing and mingling without the need for deep discussions on global politics. Within minutes, the guests, not to mention the bride and groom, may even feel that there is a merging of families taking place.

If done well, and probably more so if done poorly, the Cultural Merger Wedding is memorable. It is up to the cultural sensitivities of the bride and groom or other wedding planners, and the cultural willingness of the guests, to make the event memorable for the right reasons. Daunting? Yes. Impossible? No. Just think of the UN Christmas party.

The Double Wedding

The Double Wedding is a very pragmatic solution for a bride and groom from wildly different cultures where a Cultural Merger Wedding would require an intimidating level of international diplomacy. Perhaps there is no common language on the part of the families or geographies strongly influence wedding attendance for one party. History can also play a role in the Double Wedding if the marrying nationalities were once, ahem, not so compatible, and one or more fathers say something like, "Over my dead body will I set foot in that land of cannibals." You get the picture.

The Double Wedding involves marrying twice, usually in two different locations, and according to the culture, religion and tradition of one partner in one location, and then the other partner in the second location. It must be commonly understood and accepted by both partners that each wedding is meant to recognise and satisfy the cultural dispositions of each partner and their family and friends. Hence there is a kind of 'No Meddling' rule that applies to the visiting bride or groom.

Cole and Ritu chose the Double Wedding. They met in Washington, where they both worked at international NGOs. Despite the temptation to import his Scottish clansmen and her Indian family to the US for a local ceremony, which might have been easiest for the soon-to-weds, Cole and Ritu decided that it would be better to outsource the whole project to their respective mothers.

"A local wedding would have meant excluding many dear family members, including my ageing granny and my sister who was pregnant at the time and therefore was not allowed to fly. We realised as well that we would be the only two people at the wedding without jetlag," Cole explained.

"If we really wanted our guests and families to enjoy themselves, we needed another location... or two. So that's what we did," added Ritu.

Wedding tourism

The advantage of the Double Wedding is that the couple can afford to be culturally indulgent. This is not the time to set a precedent or stand your ground on issues of tradition, religion or language. As long as no live sacrifices are made, most brides and grooms-to-be simply go with the cultural flow and immerse themselves into their partner's world of wedding ritual. The local family is inevitably pleased, usually the new mother-in-law in particular, that they are able to host a gala event, unencumbered by pesky cultural conflicts and international political correctness.

And visiting guests, when sufficiently briefed on the importance of cultural acceptance, usually delight in the exotic experience of wedding tourism. The less they are catered to, the better, unless it is the voice of David Attenborough narrating in the background.

No one has pulled off the Double Wedding with as much flair and panache (not to mention CO_2 output) than Elizabeth Hurley in her marriage to Arun Nayer in 2007. In the meantime, she has had the gall to leave Arun for another man, an Australian by the way, so still very *GloLo*, but then he left her and now she wants Arun back, but this is *not* the tabloid press here. Let's just get back to the wedding in 2007.

Elizabeth had multiple ceremonies in multiple dresses, from a 15th century English castle to a palace in Rajasthan. Granted, Liz sold the photo rights to the lavish ceremonies for a couple of million euros, which would have provided her with ample budget for the festivities, not to mention her own personal fortune and that of her multi-millionaire betrothed. But the Double Wedding is still a realistic option even if you and your betrothed are not majority share holders in several Fortune 500 companies.

Probably the key to success in the Double Wedding is outsourcing. Why not let the host family plan, and even pay, for the local bash? Even Liz probably Skyped a few times with Arun's mom to discuss table settings.

The risk of the Double Wedding, other than the very obvious issue of the Double Cost, is confusion within the marriage and amongst families. Questions arise such as, "which wedding did you enjoy more?" (Do NOT answer that question!) and "which ceremony is the real wedding?" Let's be honest here, most men have enough difficulty remembering one wedding anniversary in one country in their native language, never mind presenting them with multiple options. (A clever multicultural wife will, of course, use this to her favour, but that is perhaps the subject matter of another book.)

Upon seeing Cole and Ritu's wedding photos from Mumbai, Cole's Scottish mother thought that her son had married his Indian bride 'wearing his pyjamas' she said, referring to the *kurta churidar*, a loose-fitting outfit of white cotton.

"The lack of cultural context can lead to misunderstandings and some family and friends just don't get it," Cole told me. "The Indian wedding was supposed to be *an Indian wedding*. It was not intended as a compromise." In the meantime, Cole's mother has two wedding photos on the fireplace mantle at home. One of Cole in a tuxedo and Ritu resplendent in a white floor length bridal gown that would make Bridal Barbie envious, and the second photo, where Ritu wears a regal red sari, once again a dress that Barbie would envy, and Cole is wearing his white Indian wedding 'pyjamas'.

As much as the international guests may enjoy wedding tourism, the bridal pair themselves may also want to hear comforting text by David Attenborough. A Thai bride, Kamala, said how strange it was to feel like a guest at her own marriage to her Indonesian husband.

"In Thailand, the wedding ceremony *rod nam sang* is for family and close friends only," she explained. "This gives the ceremony a certain intimacy as well as *gravitas*. In Indonesia, *everyone* is invited, including business associates and hardly neighbours we hardly know."

Adhi and his family thought it would be rude not to invite everyone. Kamala said it was less like a wedding and more like a village festival, but it was great opportunity to get to know the people of the city where she would be living.

In summary, the Double Wedding offers the couple a wonderful opportunity to learn about each other's family and culture without the threat of imposition or change and refreshingly without the need to negotiate. There will be plenty of time for cultural compromise once the marriage has commenced.

The Secret Wedding

Consider the Secret Wedding to be the multicultural equivalent of eloping, the somewhat dubious City Hall or Registry Office Wedding, the Shotgun Wedding, only without the pending pregnancy, or even the Elvis Wedding in Las Vegas. Sometimes the choices and the obligations of creating a wedding that is suitable to both cultures, religions, parents, families and friends is simply overwhelming. This is particularly so if there is family resistance or negative pressure concerning the choice of bride or groom. Therefore the couple avoids the risk of making *some* people unhappy by not having the appropriate wedding and (often) make *everyone* unhappy by simply avoiding a big wedding altogether. The couple just runs to the local city hall and unceremoniously ties the knot via a legal document. Often the newlyweds will splurge on a fancy lunch and then hurry back to the office, possibly sporting a shiny new ring, which few people notice. If that sounds excessively pragmatic for those with a more romantic heart, think of the scene in *Robin Hood: Prince of Thieves* (1991), where Kevin Costner's Robin Hood takes time out of his fight against tyranny to marry Lady Marian in a misty Sherwood Forest in the dark of night. It has something, doesn't it?

The advantages of the Secret Wedding are obvious. Firstly, it's cheap! Other than the registration fee, and perhaps a tip to the security-guard-turned-camera-man, the whole deal can be conducted for less than the price of a new pair of tennis shoes, leaving the wedding slush fund available for other financial pursuits. Mr and Mrs can start their married union without the usual avalanche of bills from florists and caterers.

You may kiss the bride

The Secret Wedding is my personal favourite, and in fact the route that I myself chose, much to the delight of my tuxedo-averse husband. We wed in a small town in Austria in an even smaller civil ceremony. All of the photos of 'the happiest day of our life' (in all honesty, it was pretty darn hectic) have a clock in the background. The wedding begins at 11:00 and the you-may-kiss-the-bride scene shows 11:15. We hardly had time for cold feet! We did have a nice lunch together afterwards, and then went to Venice for a long honeymoon weekend, including the kitschy gondola ride. I sent a postcard to my parents to share the good news.

We were perfectly happy with our nuptial union and rather pleased with how efficiently we had covered a marriage, a name change and a work visa for Austria, all in the matter of a day. So that was the upside of the Secret Wedding. Now here is the down side of our experience.

Some family members, who shall remain nameless, were disappointed, hurt, and possibly even resentful. They felt insulted that they were not included in the happiest day of our lives. Our wedding may not have been a big deal for us, but it certainly was for them. They had had visions and dreams of the big day since that day in our childhood when we started talking about marriage in the sandbox and, with the short swipe of a City Hall pen, we effectively eliminated their opportunity for sharing what would have been one of the happiest days of *their* lives.

My mother-in-law is the mother of sons only. She was disappointed with our choice.

"I wanted to help you choose a wedding dress. You are my only daughter and my only chance to experience the thrill of buying a bridal gown," she told me later over the telephone.

Okay, 'thrill' is her word to describe dress shopping, not mine, but you see the point. In the meantime, I have been recruiting girlfriends from far and wide with the hope that one will capture the heart of my husband's decidedly bachelor brother, and ultimately go shopping with a mother whose unfulfilled wish in life is to buy her daughter-in-law a bridal gown.

When a tree falls in the forest

Kurt and Andrea undertook the Secret Wedding and had a similar experience.

"Our friends had mixed reactions. There were some jolly congratulations and slaps on the back, but there were also tears, and accusations of breaking a promise we made in 4th grade when we agreed to be each other's bridesmaids," Andrea told me.

"It took years before everyone accepted that we were actually married. I took my husband's surname, but some friends always 'forgot' and addressed me by my maiden name. It was like the tree falling in the forest with no one to hear it. People don't really understand that even if they did not see it or hear it, the wedding still happened," she said resolutely.

Their choice of wedding, or as one girlfriend put it, 'non-wedding' actually hurt the feelings of friends and family, and that made them sad. The day and the method was their choice, but the reaction of friends and family demonstrate that a wedding can be a powerful emotionally packed event for others.

Social customs serve a purpose in society. A wedding ceremony serves the purpose of recognition in transferring the culture and civilization from one generation to the next. Through the ceremony, society recognises a shift in tribal dynamics, which is necessary to understand your own position within the clan structure. Family, friends and other clan members need to know where they stand in relation to you and your tribal connections, whether you wear a big white dress or not.

When the social network does not approve of the bridal choice, the Secret Wedding may only further illustrate how renegade and unworthy the pairing may be.

In summary, the Secret Wedding is a quick and easy alternative to primeval wedding hysteria, and certainly helps facilitate a working permit which for some, I am not ashamed to say, is perhaps a secondary goal. However, be aware that this route may have an emotional price tag. Fortunately for me, when my parents received the postcard I sent them from Venice telling them about the big news, my mom said, "We may have missed the wedding, but we have the best postcard ever." The postcard is still stuck on the fridge door with a gondola magnet.

The New Fangled Wedding

The New Fangled Wedding often results when attempts at the Cultural Merger Wedding have failed and the Double Wedding seems overwhelming in its duplicate form. It is often the chosen route when there is religious strife within the families of the marrying couple or when the couple live in a third country where they have met, usually saving rain forests or helping children. So that they do not have to choose one culture/religion/tradition over the other, the couple chooses a New Fangled Wedding that is void of practices indigenous to either ethnic background. Hence the New Fangled Wedding often takes place on a beach in Hawaii or on a cruise ship or in a country known for its tax advantages. The New Fangled Wedding is a close cousin to the Secret Wedding, which is probably also Hawaiian born. The difference is that the New Fangled Wedding does not integrate any element of either partner's culture – it is a cultural no man's land. It can be spiritual however the focus tends toward uniting global citizens rather than blessing children of God or Allah.

Global citizens unite

The New Fangled Wedding is usually attended by friends – liberals who support the union as a step for world peace – and often not by family, whose internal unrest hampers the spirit of love between the bridal couple, or simply because they all live far, far away. It often includes wind chimes, organic flower bouquets, and other non-materialistic new age themes, which the couple may endorse as part of their lifestyle or simply for the wedding day. Gifts are appreciated in the form of a charitable donation, usually to the rainforest or group of children the couple are working to save. Rather than pastors or priests, a bearded guru wearing white robes and those leather flipflops from the 1970s, presides over the ceremony. The couple may even write their own wedding vows.

The advantage of the New Fangled Wedding is that it is culturally neutral, and therefore strong compromise on the part of the bride or the groom is not necessary. And let's face it, standing barefoot on a sandy beach is a lot more comfortable than those killer sling-back heels in white satin. The couple can focus more on themselves and concentrate on their personal union, rather than fetching Aunt Louise from the airport and preventing Uncle Frank from making Nazi jokes. The friends who attend the New Fangled Wedding are like family, at least for the duration of that particular overseas assignment.

The disadvantage of the New Fangled Wedding can be acceptance and legitimacy. Families often hear news about the New Fangled

Wedding long after the event has taken place, perhaps at an airport when the offspring arrive home from a long absence abroad and it goes something like, "hi Mom, hi Dad, this is Raphael who I met in Congo and..." (See: Secret Wedding, "disappointed, hurt, and possibly even resentful"!). There are sometimes questions about the validity of the marriage in other countries, particularly in the new home of the married couple.

Gemma, a British aid worker on assignment after the Tsunami, met Wolfgang, a German architect working on the same project, in Thailand. Amid the devastation, broken homes, and broken hearts, the two met, fell in love, and married, all within the space of six months. The ceremony was pure New Fangled. They were barefoot, on a beach, with a sunset in the background, and an international guest list of aid workers, many of whom they knew only on a first name basis.

"It was more than just a wedding," gushes Gemma, "we had all been working in this crisis region for months, and this was a celebration of surviving together and helping each other."

"Yes," Wolfgang put it, possibly in more sober terms, "it was unconventional for us perhaps in our old lives in Germany and in the UK, but we became different persons and our marriage expressed the new peoples [sic] we became."

"Only when we were back in England did I notice that our marriage certificate looks more like a university degree, but from a dodgy university," Gemma admitted of her 'made in Thailand' wedding to Wolfgang.

Her father, a lawyer, immediately started asking questions about the document and the institutional stamp in particular.

"I had no answers," Gemma admitted, "maybe I am married according to British laws, maybe not."

"Of course we are married in our hearts," concluded Wolfgang, "and that is all that matters."

Lucky Gemma, I thought.

In summary, the New Fangled Wedding is a highly individualised choice. It is romantic and can be very special, as Gemma and Wolfgang experienced. It will also make a great story for the kids, proving that Mom and Dad were once groovy and cool. However the New Fangled Wedding also breaks a certain societal code and the couple should be ready for at least some recrimination from family members or even immigration officials. To deliberately choose an alternative to existing norms is to reject the *status quo*, and hence quite possibly offend friends and family who adhere to long held traditions.

As with the Secret Wedding, acceptance that the marital union is legitimate within the social network may take longer because the couple has not earned their rite of passage. In the meantime, the New Fangled bride and groom can enjoy the vegetarian buffet and the sound of surf!

Conclusions on the wedding

There is a lot to say about weddings. It indicates perhaps the importance of the wedding as a social ritual or rite of passage in our society, as well as how complexity is added when the couple is multicultural. As at any wedding, the GloLo wedding will bring out the best and worst in people. Remember, *intensely primeval*? Hence the multicultural lovebirds will benefit by maintaining their sense of humour and willingness to compromise.

Now that we have discussed how GloLo couples meet, who they are and how they marry, the next section of the book will look at what happens after the whirlwind of falling in love and jetsetting about in globally appropriate bridal gear. The daily life a multicultural couple will continue its winding path of negotiation and learning, frustrations and triumphs, and little steps toward cultural understanding and world peace.

Top 10 clues that you had a GloLo wedding

1. You cannot read the language of the wedding contract fluently.
2. You wore a traditional wedding gown and your in-laws said how 'unique', 'unconventional' and 'ethnic' your dress was.
3. The menu for the wedding dinner was printed in two languages but your family still poked at the meal suspiciously and asked, "What is this?"
4. The pastor performing the religious services from your religion complained that he "did not get as many lines to say" as the cleric of your spouse.
5. Your think your wedding date was _____ (insert date of wedding ceremony in your culture here) and your spouse thinks the date was ______ (insert date of wedding ceremony in your spouse's culture here).
6. A few of the wedding guests rudely whispered to each other that the wedding was just so that you or your spouse could get a visa to stay in the country.
7. The wedding guests were not entirely wrong.
8. When you said, "I do" in the officiating wedding language, everyone asked, "Huh?" and then your GloLo partner taught you how to pronounce the words correctly.
9. The only person at the wedding who you had met prior to the ceremony was your GloLo spouse.
10. You had a Secret Wedding and sent a postcard to tell your parents that you married a foreigner they had never met. Your father said, "They must have some brave men over there, nobody from here would dare to do it".

Part II
Big Hairy Audacious GloLo Issues

Religion

During the writing of this book, which took a very long time remember, the subject of interfaith marriage received a short-lived burst of media attention. Headlines were all about 'Chelsea and Marc' and their 'interfaith union'. In case that was the week you tried to live without TV and Twitter and every type of media in between, 'Chelsea and Marc' are none other than Chelsea Clinton, the daughter of US Secretary of State Hillary and ex-President Bill Clinton. Marc Mezvinsky is Chelsea's long time friend turned fiancé and now husband and is himself the son of a political family. As if the wedding of Billary's only daughter was not enough to bring out the media and paparazzi in full force, America's 'royal' wedding was made all the more newsworthy because Chelsea is a Methodist and Marc is a Conservative Jew. Chelsea and Marc, this chapter on interfaith relationships is for you.

Despite dedicating this chapter to Chelsea and Marc, I was not invited to the wedding, but neither were the Obamas, so I think the guest list was indeed *very short*. According to some quick Google research, Chelsea and Marc had, by GloLo definition, a Cultural Merger Wedding. A rabbi and a United Methodist pastor performed the ceremony, quite lavish apparently, under a floral *chuppah*. Marc broke a glass, deliberately I mean, and there are reports that President Clinton danced the moonwalk, although I guess the moonwalk is not exactly *religious*.

In any case, the Clinton-Mezvinsky wedding brought interfaith relationships into the limelight. There were reports on the hip new trend toward religiously mixed marriages, interviews with relationship experts about the 'transformation of tradition' in interfaith families, both dire and optimistic statistics about the success rate, meaning *divorce* rate, and 'marital satisfaction levels' of interfaith marriages as well as speculation on whether Chelsea would convert to Judaism. Given the celebrity status of the wedding, the Vera Wang bridal gown, the glutton free wedding cake, and whether the event cost $5 million or just a modest $2 million, it is very telling of today's society that the interfaith aspect generated as much airtime as whether or not Barbra Streisand was on the guest list. So interfaith relationships are making headlines.

In this chapter, therefore, we will look a bit closer at the issues in an interfaith marriage and see if all the fuss is worthy of front page news.

What's the big deal about an interfaith marriage, anyway?

Why was such a big deal made about the interfaith aspect of Chelsea and Marc's relationship, particularly in America, the multicultural melting pot society? Well, firstly, and perhaps most profoundly, religion is culture. Let's look at it this way: religion plays a strong role in defining your sense of identity, and influences opinions and beliefs about core values such as gender roles and family and community relations. In their book *In Love But Worlds Apart*, authors Grete Shelling and Janet Fraser-Smith write that even if people claim they are not religious, they are "influenced by their religious upbringing, by the ethics, principles, and rules that their families in past generations followed, and by the moral and ethical rules that are by-products of the dominant religion(s) in their country." So religion is not just a superficial label you give yourself. It is the ultimate GloLo challenge, even in a multicultural melting pot society.

Secondly, religion is controversial. Let's face it, there is a lot of religious strife going on in the world today. If you compare world religion with football (soccer for Canadian readers), it is like the players all share a common passion for the game, but instead of playing the game, the teams argue about wearing a different colour of jersey. I mean, it's still football (soccer), isn't it? Anyway, when two individuals from differing and even warring belief systems hook up GloLo style, the world watches this microcosm of religious politics in fascination. Let's just say that an interfaith relationship stirs up a complex and even contradictory range of emotions. There is fear, anger, a sense of loss, hope, joy and, you guessed it, a spirit of the globalisation of love.

Thirdly, and perhaps because of this controversial aspect, religion is a kind of taboo topic. In a highly secular society, where saying 'Merry Christmas' has been deemed 'politically incorrect' and 'exclusionary', and Santa Claus was banned from saying 'Ho Ho Ho' in fear that it might 'offend women', a high profile interfaith wedding is an excuse to open the flood gates on this sensitive subject.

In any case, people are often surprised by the challenges within an interfaith relationship. Since we live and work in an 'interfaith environment', which is really 'the secular world', it does not seem like such a big leap of faith so to speak, to assume that living in an interfaith household will be any different. Like many of the GloLo issues discussed in this book, however, going with the dominant cultural flow is fine in your public life, but once behind the doors of your own castle, you tend to want to be your own cultural queen or king. That means determining the household culture, including key elements such as customs and traditions, language *and* religion.

What are the big issues in an interfaith relationship, anyway?

Every couple has their own set of issues, don't they? Interfaith couples, like all GloLo couples, just have a longer list of potential hotspots. Some might suggest as well that the monocultural cap-on-toothpaste style issues pale in comparison to the GloLo interfaith my-deity-is-way-cooler-than-your-deity debate. It really depends on the interfaith constellation of the pair, as some religions will mix and match more easily than others, as well the couple's respective level of religiosity.

What is religiosity?

Religiosity is right up there with exogamy, isn't it? It is not really a term you use in everyday parlance, unless of course you are writing a bestselling book about GloLo interfaith relationships. Religiosity is your degree of 'religiousness' (also a real word by the way), your intellectual and spiritual affiliation with religion and the active role that religion plays in your daily life. So, for example, if you go to the church, chapel, mosque, synagogue, temple, wat, jinja, hof, kingdom hall or basilica several times a month, and you pray or worship several times a day, and you eat or do not eat a long list of simple unleavened or festive fancy foods, and you wear a traditional Muslim veil to cover your hair, a Christian cross around your neck, or you have a Shinto Torii on your T-shirt, an Islamic Rub el Hizb baseball cap, a Hindu Omkar tattoo on your shoulder or a wheel of Dharma bumper sticker on your car, then you are probably high on religiosity. If, on the other hand, the last time you were contemplating your spiritual self was when you were too short to reach the door handle to the house of prayer by yourself, then you probably have a low degree of religiosity.

Now, GloLo partners come from all spectrums on the religiosity scale, however they *tend* to be on the lower end of the scale. This makes perfect sense because remember that GloLo individuals are a bit 'marginalised' and 'culturally unique' and therefore not so tradition-bound. However, GloLo couples can also be extremely devout, and their shared affiliation with different divinities can act as a powerful bond in a culturally colourful marriage or a deep divide. Let's look at these key interfaith issues more closely:

- Conversion
- Worship
- Children
- Death
- Religion and law
- Religious celebrations

Conversion

Conversion sounds pretty dramatic actually. What conversion is really about is what you and your GloLo interfaith partner expect from each other in terms of believing, practising and living with two religions. Some religions, and some people, are exclusionary. They only recognise one way of doing things. Faith is something that is *not negotiable*. Other religions, and other people, believe that everyone has a right to pursue their own spiritual path in life. The religion and belief system can be more individualised let's say. Faith, according to these terms, *is* negotiable. GloLo interfaith couples then, just by virtue of their relationship, find themselves 'negotiating' between differing belief systems.

Mandy, an Irish-born designer who moved to Connecticut with her family when she was 12 was a non-practising Catholic. She and

Stewart, her Jewish husband, were together for several years before they became engaged. Religious conversion was the turning point for them.

"Maybe religion was the thing that divided us," Mandy began, and you could still hear just a trace of the Irish lilt in her speech. "Stewart always brought me to family events and for religious holidays. I guess I kind of grew into it. I wanted to belong to this bigger world. There was never any pressure from Stewart or his family."

"When Mandy told me that she wanted to convert to Judaism, it was amazing," said Stewart, a high school principal who looks like George Clooney playing a high school principal. "It was such a statement and a commitment. I felt really proud. I guess it prompted my proposal."

I asked if he would have proposed without the impetus of Mandy's conversion.

"Yes, we had talked about marriage frequently, but her conversion had this effect on me, like we are one, we are family now," he answered with confidence.

I asked Mandy about her experience with conversion.

"It's all gone really well actually. At first my parents were a bit surprised, you know a Catholic converting to Judaism," she rolled her eyes slightly. "But I told them my reasons and they know Stewart and love him, so they were very supportive. My mum thought it was really nice actually."

In contrast to Mandy's voluntary conversion, some GloLo couples who want to marry *have* to convert, all in the name of love. Some religions do not permit marriage to a person of a different faith. Austrian Lukas, a blond and blue-eyed airline pilot told me that, before he married Souri, he converted to her religion.

"Muslim women are not allowed to marry non-Muslim men," Lukas explained. "Other than religious lessons taught in school, religion was never a theme in my life. When I asked Souri to marry me, it was clear that I had to convert to Islam."

I asked how he felt about his decision.

"Look at me," he laughed gently, "I don't really blend in that well, do I? But I follow tradition at home, including all of the ceremonies. I do not go to prayer however. But Souri is happy with my muslimness."

Lukas was clearly low on religiosity and therefore the conversion was not a big deal for him. I asked Souri how she felt about religious conversion.

"Since we had lived in Austria most of my life," she answered in perfect German, "I knew and my parents knew that maybe I would meet someone from outside of our faith. There was initial resistance to Lukas, but when I knew he would convert and my parents knew, everyone was accepting. It was a sign of good character, I think."

Believing is not belonging

A British man I met on a flight to Toronto had a less successful experience with his own conversion. Somewhere over the Atlantic, when the lights were out and the other passengers were well into their on-flight movie or fast asleep, this young gentleman shared his story.

"Sally told me when we first met that she would only marry a Christian believer," he began. "It didn't surprise me really because I have always been a Christian and I feel the same way. Sally wanted me to join her church and fit into the same framework," he said, drawing a box in the air. "It was only after time that I realised that what we believed as Christians was fundamentally different." After some turbulence, which under the circumstances seemed kind of *ominous*, he continued to talk.

"I wanted to believe like she did, believe me, and I tried. But I felt like a phoney, like I am just doing it for Sally. I broke it off with her," he said, sounding sad in the din of the airplane hum. "I felt like I wasn't good enough for her, although I actually lived a very spiritually guided lifestyle. We were both heart-broken but I couldn't live with someone who did not accept me the way I was. Nor could she for that matter. We were both under family pressure too. Her family would not accept me as a convert, even if I was willing. They said the mountain to climb was too high. We went our separate ways, both spiritually and in our daily lives. The irony is that my new girlfriend thinks that I am the deeply devout one. Now I am the Holy Roller. I have changed roles. Funny, isn't it?" he asked melancholically.

If religion is culture, then conversion really means changing culture, doesn't it? It can therefore pose itself as a conflict between the guiding light of your life and the love of your life. Through a GloLo interfaith relationship, you can learn about your partner's religion but that is not the same as embracing it and believing in it. Like my airplane friend said, "Believing in faith does not mean belonging to faith."

Worship

Once interfaith couples have their religions sorted out, there is the issue of worship. 'Let us pray' can mean a lot of different things to people of different faiths.

Worship comes in many shapes and sizes, from a solitary spiritual moment on top of a mountain peak, such as Brad Pitt in the movie *Nepal*, to a dynamic group activity such as Whoopi Goldberg in *Sister Act*. It may be a formal and ritualistic observance performed several times a day or an *ad hoc* little prayer you say to yourself at bedtime. In any case, how you pray, never mind who you pray to, is a reminder of a fundamental ideological difference between you and your GloLo partner.

Here is a story about one American interfaith couple who learned a bit of groove and harmony in prayer. Kathy, who has a sort of park ranger / Girl Guide flair to her, is a non-denominational Christian. Her husband Scott, a 'Georgia gentleman', is a southern Baptist. Scott broached this subject first.

"I am proud to be from the Bible Belt," he drawled, referring to the south and southwestern region in the United States where church attendance is high. "Religion is an integral part of our lives, and we *enjoy* religion. God is love, God is joy, and we are blessed."

"I am from the midwest," Kathy continued. "Church-going for me was always a serious and sombre affair. When I first went to church with Scott, the pastor said, 'Let us pray'. I bowed my head for a silent private prayer. Suddenly the organist started playing loudly and the congregation started singing and swaying and clapping. I was so shocked. I thought it was a special event but it's like that every week. It is a truly joyous type of worship," she said, and I could imagine her joining the worshippers.

I asked Kathy and Scott if they also visit Kathy's church.

"Yes, when we visit her folks," answered Scott immediately. "And I have learned to enjoy it too. It has a more meditative quality. It is another way to communicate with our Lord."

Kathy and Scott are lucky that they both learned to respect and enjoy different styles of prayer. It is not always easy to be open to different ideas about worship. Heather al-Yousuf and Rosalind Birtwistle put together an interfaith guide as part of the Interfaith Marriage Project. An anonymous GloLo wife tells the story about her interfaith marriage to a Shi'a Muslim.

Part of a commemoration ceremony for the martyrdom of Imam Hussain involves men beating themselves and sometimes cutting themselves with swords. She wrote, "When I found my husband had bruises on his chest from doing the beating part, at first I was really upset, I suddenly felt he was alien to me. Now I've got used to it but I admit I don't want our son to go to those gatherings."

How you and your partner pray and the religious ceremonies that you observe can challenge some fundamental values. Roger Gil, a relationship counsellor and therapist, and host of LuvBuzd.TV says that religion is "like political affiliation, a personal work ethic or preferred ice cream flavour. It must come from within." The way you pray, on the other hand, is an *outward* expression of your personal culture and belief system. It is often where the internal discrepancies become visible.

Children

There is a whole chapter dedicated to GloLo children coming up, including a specific discussion on religion, so this section will be brief. The main point about children in an interfaith family, if we can get back to the football (soccer) analogy, is that their parents usually want their children to be wearing the same colour jersey. However it is not always easy for GloLo parents to transfer their religious values and beliefs to their children. If they are minority members in a dominant monotheist society, for example, there may be conflict between what the children hear and learn at school and amongst friends compared to what they hear and learn at home from their parents and grandparents.

Further, there are certain religious ceremonies and certain rites of passage that a child might experience within one religion that has the potential to alienate them from their friends, particularly if there are visible signs such as special clothing or shaving hair. So GloLo children learn early that a belief system is *a* system and not *the* system, at least not within their own family. Interfaith children therefore have a special role to play in the world. They grow up with an acute awareness that every team has a different colour of jersey, but they all love the game.

Death

Just like taxes, death is unavoidable, and the policies and procedures around death, just like taxes I guess, are different around the world and culturally determined. Death and religion are therefore intrinsically intertwined.

Religion provides the framework for the rituals that are performed before and after death. Beliefs about eternity of the soul and the afterlife are part of religious doctrine. Therefore people 'prepare' for death differently, they have different attitudes toward death, and they have vastly different expectations about what happens when you get there. Roles within the family at a time of death, preparation of the deceased human remains, and the farewell old friend ceremony and service have a strong religious basis too.

Sadly, part of the globalisation of love story includes death. And when you have an interfaith family, you may be exposed to death in a way that contrasts starkly from your own cultural and religious views. If you consider that a funeral is awkward enough on its own too. You have to think of something 'comforting' to say to the bereaved family *without* sounding like a greeting card. You are usually dealing with the selfishly morbid thought, '*I could be next*' as well. At a GloLo related funeral, you have the additional burden of not knowing 'what the h___ is going on up there?' as one friend put it, and it can all be very unsettling indeed.

What is 'standard procedure' in one religion may be disrespectful and even vulgar in another. Gruesome subjects like cremation, embalmment, an open or closed casket or even taking photographs of the deceased can really challenge a GloLo partner's religious position. It may require a certain kind of 'cultural fortitude' to overcome these feelings and, quite frankly, not cringe in horror or faint. Whether the deceased is buried in a simple pine box, housed in an ornate mausoleum with a pile of gold coins to ensure safe passage to the their next life, whether the ashes are sprinkled over the Ganges or prepared in banana soup for family members to eat, as is done by the Yanomami tribe in Venezuela, the rituals following a death fit together with their understanding of the order of the universe and seen through the prism of religious belief.

The death of a loved one often leads to a special bonding amongst the bereaved. In the GloLo case, a couple can learn more about each other by both witnessing and participating in intimate rituals following a death. It is an important learning experience in the lifelong process of the globalisation of love because there will come a day when one of you must bid farewell to the GloLo love of your life. Hopefully, when it is time for you or your partner to 'meet your maker', join loved ones in a heavenly cloud, start 'pushing up daisies', reincarnate, or roast in hell, you will have sufficient understanding and respect for the family religious practices that you accept, if not embrace, the rituals that go along with death.

Despite your shared multicultural journey through life, death is a time when the interfaith aspect of your relationship can be most challenged. It is ironic that this is probably one of the most significantly religious and cultural points in your GloLo life. Essentially, you are returning your GloLo partner to his or her roots and religion. A 'Cultural Merger Funeral' is not easy to orchestrate, and we know from Cultural Merger Weddings, even at happy events, cultural and religious rivalry can be displayed.

When I met Miranda, the first thing that struck me is that she is young and much too young to be a widow.

"I know," she smiled sadly when she saw the surprise that was surely written all over my face, "I am probably not the type of widow you were looking for." She shrugged. "Most of the time, I don't believe it myself."

American Miranda, still soft and round like a little girl, met Egyptian Kafele at a private international university in Vienna where they were both students. In a whirlwind of romance, negative family pressure, expiring student visas and perhaps youthful impulsiveness, they married within a year of their first meeting, which was in an international relations lecture at the university. Miranda shared her story of her marriage to Kafele who died in a traffic accident shortly after their second wedding anniversary. Miranda put on a very brave face to talk about the funeral.

"We were both 24 when we married and 26 when Kafele was killed, so we had never really talked about death or dying. We didn't really talk about religion either. Kafele was born a Sunni Muslim but didn't practise religion. I was born a Protestant and attend, very casually mind you, an international Christian church. After the accident, it was the only place I knew to go."

Kafele's family, rich Egyptian merchants apparently, had instructed Miranda by telephone what she should do to prepare for his funeral service while they were in transit to Austria. According to Sunni custom, the body of the deceased should be buried the day after death. As a foreigner dying on foreign soil, the bureaucracy alone hindered this Muslim custom. Miranda was caught between administrative issues, religious customs, family expectations and a mixture of shock and grief.

"Everything happened so fast. There was no wake. There was no viewing. I never actually saw him dead. And everything was supposed to face east," she remembered, "towards Mecca, you know, but in our church, the altar is to the west. Even the pews are fixed to the floor so we could not change the direction. So we had Kafele facing east while we faced west. His family was disappointed and very critical. They blame me for his death. If he had not met me, he would have returned to Cairo you see, so I guess it is my fault somehow. The name Kafele means something like, 'would die for you'. His mother told me that after the funeral."

After digesting this memory, Miranda continued.

"I never thought of Kafele as 'Egyptian' or 'Muslim'. He was simply Kafele. It was only when his family was here for his funeral that I realised that his cultural and religious background was so different from mine. The funeral was so bizarre. It's like we never said good-bye."

Tentatively, I asked Miranda if, since Kafele's death, she considered returning to her native United States.

"I have considered it, but only briefly," she said, and it was the only time that an edge of grief caught her words. "This is where Kafele and I met and where we lived together. He is buried here. I could not imagine leaving him behind."

Even in death, the globalisation of love never ends.

When your GloLo partner has departed from this earth, their religion may continue to impact you, the bereaved GloLo widow or widower. Read on.

Religion and law

I know, it *sounds* like a weird combination to have religion and law in the same category, but sometimes religion *is* the law. In any case, where religion and law are written in one book, it will determine certain 'administrative aspects' of a GloLo relationship and your rights as an individual partner. Religion determines the rights of the foreign spouse in their country of residence concerning things like property ownership, inheritance rights if we may risk the death theme just once more, and what happens concerning the custody of children following a death. This is where the globalisation of love clashes with legal jurisdiction.

While your deceased GloLo partner is off playing the harp or pursuing other afterlife pleasures, your life may turn into a living hell as you negotiate a religious legal system that may have a different understanding than you have of your role as GloLo widow or widower. Even if the religious law where you live is not recognised as valid in your home country, as a resident, you are subject to its application. Violation of the law, even if you think it is unfair or 'totally nutty', as one friend put it, could still land you a spot news flash on CNN and take your embassy a long time to sort things out. Even if it is *religious* law, it is still the law, and a spot on CNN is not as glamorous as it sounds.

Religious celebrations

After dealing with unsavoury topics like death and law, which are not so far flung from the globalisation of love after all, finally we get to the fun stuff, which are religious ceremonies and festivals. A GloLo interfaith couple have three possibilities to celebrate religious holidays within their family:

- All of the above
- None of the above
- Pick and mix

All of the above

Some interfaith couples superimpose two religious calendars on top of each other and follow all of the annual festivities and ceremonies. In other words, *it's party time*.

Cokie Roberts, an Emmy award winning journalist, and her journalist husband Steve co-authored *Our Haggadah: Uniting Traditions for Interfaith Families*. Cokie is Catholic and Steve is Jewish and they have had have an interfaith marriage for over 45 years, or long before GloLo became a *household phrase*. In a March 9, 2011 MSNBC interview with 'Morning Joe', they talked about their story of maintaining and upholding tradition in an interfaith household.

Cokie and Steve consciously chose to do 'all of the above' by observing annual religious traditions of both Catholicism and Judaism. It meant, Cokie told viewers, "a lot of cooking and a lot of presents for the kids".

Steve told viewers how his first Seder, the Jewish Passover, was actually prepared by his Catholic wife. He had not had Seder before but by choosing 'all of the above', they actually increased their respective participation in observance of religious holidays. What is common in many interfaith households is that because they follow two religious paths simultaneously, they have actually become 'more religious' than they would have been otherwise. In a mutually respectful marriage, and let's face it, Cokie and Steve *literally* wrote a book about it, a GloLo couple can share and thrive in interfaith harmony.

None of the above

By contrast, John and Lajita, the Christian-Hindu couple who had a successful Cultural Merger Wedding, have looked at the list of holidays in their religious calendars and have chosen 'none of the above'.

"I don't know if it is really a religious decision," John said. "It's more like a decision not to participate in commercialised activities. We go to church services with some degree of regularity, but at certain times of year, we tend to back off a bit."

I asked how their children felt about missing out on all the fun bits. It does seem kind of mean, I thought to myself.

"Not to worry," John chortled. "They have plenty of exposure to the events at church and at the temple and even at school. We don't deny them anything. It is only at home that we decided not to bring in religious elements. No decorating the house and so on."

"John is right," Lajita agreed. "There is a certain pragmatism to this decision. We are both working you see, so we try to keep our life at home simple. Essentially, we have outsourced religious holidays to other institutions."

Pick and mix

The third and probably most common interfaith solution to religious ceremonies is to pick and mix from each faith system. Remember 'floozy Susie', the cheer leader bride who flung the garter belt at her Cultural Merger Wedding to Kassim? Susie and Kassim pick and mix between Protestant and Muslim religious holidays.

"We do a lot," Susie began. "With my family, there is Christmas, Easter, Thanksgiving, although I guess that's not really religious, but it's still with family. On Kass's side, there is Eid al-Adha and Muharram, the Islamic New Year. "

"Anything that has a strong family component and everything that is child-friendly is our rule. We try to be practical about it," said Kassim.

Although I am hardly a religious scholar myself, I noticed that neither Susie nor Kassim mentioned Ramadan, which is a month of fasting and a very important Islamic custom.

"Well," Kassim said, looking at Susie with slightly raised eyebrows, "we tried Ramadan. But we both do a lot of sports and need to eat regularly. Susie could not deal with the blood sugar fluctuations," and then he put up his hands like claws and made some tiger-like growling.

I immediately recognised the universal sign that a husband makes when his wife has not had her daily chocolate fix. My husband has described me in the same way even though I have never participated in Ramadan.

GloLo interfaith couples can choose their religious holidays and ceremonies according to their respective levels of religiosity as well as 'pragmatism', as Lajita put it. Unlike death or law, which are inevitable and unavoidable, a GloLo couple can choose when, in their interfaith relationship, it's party time.

GloLo interfaith constellations

What are the possible constellations in a GloLo interfaith relationship? According to religionfacts.com, there are 43 'belief systems' worldwide, and within each belief system there can be many denominations. Like black pumps in a woman's closet, there are many subtle and not so subtle differences between belief systems. Even within each denomination, believers may interpret scriptures and practise liturgy in a different style, just as one woman will prefer a peep-toe sling-back with a little black dress while another will only wear a classic pump. I guess the point is that religion is highly personal and therefore the number of interfaith constellations relate directly to the personal interpretation of a belief system. And much like the preference for sling-backs or pumps, religious association may change over the course of a lifetime. Your 'religiosity' may fluctuate according to life changes and external influences, *such as a GloLo interfaith spouse*, for example. Hence I do not have the answer to my own question. Let's look instead at general possibilities for GloLo interfaith constellations.

Cath-Wics, Hin-Jews, and the Church of Latter Day Rastafarians

To avoid using religiously specific and politically charged terminology such as 'churchgoing' or 'fundamentalist', I will use the term 'into it' to describe a person who is a devout believer of any of the 43 world religions and the term 'not that into it' to describe someone who is not practising and, well, not that into any of the 43 world religions. Being 'into it' could mean that you are a Christian, a Hindu, a Shinto or anything else. Being 'not that into it' could mean that you grew up as a Christian, a Hindu, a Shinto or anything else, but now you are not that into it, or maybe you were never into it. There are three general possibilities for GloLo interfaith constellations:

- 'Into it' + 'into it'
- 'Into it' + 'not that into it'
- 'Not that into it' + 'not that into it'

'Into it' + 'into it'

Probably the most 'radical' form of a GloLo interfaith relationship is between two people who both have strong convictions and adhere *religiously*, pardon the pun, to the rituals, customs and practices of their respective faith. 'Into it' and 'into it' is not a common GloLo mix however. If you are in a GloLo interfaith relationship, you have probably already compromised on religious exclusivity by choosing an interfaith mate. Hence, even if you may be very 'into it', you are also 'open to it' too. GloLo interfaith couples, therefore, tend toward maintaining two religions, a kind of 'his and hers' approach to faith.

Cokie and Steve Roberts, the Catholic-Jewish author couple who, not surprisingly, practise 'all of the above' religious holidays are both 'into it'. Each of them grew up in either a 'very Catholic' or 'very Jewish' neighbourhood. The point they made in their interview, or perhaps the secret to their success, is that because they were both 'into it', they could understand and respect how important the religious value system was to the other partner. They are both 'old-fashioned traditionalists', even if the traditions they grew up with are different. Now they share a 45 year history of celebrating traditions together.

Turn right at the synagogue, left at the mosque

Sometimes a strongly 'into it' couple will mix and match or merge their religious beliefs or even find something completely new. They have a faith-based framework for their relationship and enjoy practising together in prayer. Through the globalisation of love, and some would suggest divine intervention, their spiritual journey through life, which began separately and then led along parallel paths, merges together into one family faith. Heidi and Thomas have such a story.

Heidi and Thomas are a GloLo couple who, despite different cultures, languages and religions, finish each other's sentences. There seems to be a vibrating energy between them. They shared their story with the request that I not reveal their original or current faith. The reference to a synagogue and a mosque are also not reflective of their religions. They are a 'red herring' Thomas told me. Heidi gleefully started the story.

"We were a religiously mixed couple," she began. "As we got to know each other better, we learned more about each other's faith and religious position. There were some points of minor controversy."

"It was more like an examination of our own faith and religious framework," Thomas smoothly interjected.

"Then one day, just before going to our respective places of worship, the car wouldn't start," Heidi explained. "Usually Thomas drove me first to my group and then continued on to his gang, but on that day our car, which was new, wasn't taking us anywhere."

"So we called a cab," continued Thomas. "When we got in the car, we started explaining the best way to drive the route, which is a bit complicated."

"And Thomas kept mixing things up and saying 'Turn right at the synagogue, left at the mosque' and then, 'No, I mean left at the synagogue' and the driver was just looking at us like we were crazy," she laughed merrily. Then Thomas picked up again.

"The driver was getting a bit grouchy and when he stopped at a red light, he turned back to us and said, 'Why don't you join the folks across the street? They all look happy to me.' He pointed to a house of prayer on the next corner. We were running late by all accounts anyway, so we both said, 'Yes, let's do that'," Thomas finished with the clap of a determined man.

"We walked inside and were warmly welcomed by the congregation," Heidi said, with her hands clasped like Thomas. "We found the service meaningful and inspiring. We just looked at each other towards the end and realised that this was the place for us. It spoke to us as a family."

I asked the symbiotic couple if there were any problems with swapping religions.

"Some old friends criticised me," Thomas answered. "They said that it is not up to us to choose values that suit us but to live by the words that were written centuries ago. Fortunately the new persuasion provides us with the support network that helps us to overcome this negativity. It works for us. That's the thing, it has to work for everyone in the family."

"We still wonder who that man in the taxi was because he changed our lives," exclaimed Heidi.

"He sure had an important message for us," concluded Thomas.

'Into it' + 'not that into it'

There is a second GloLo interfaith constellation that can be tricky even if all other ethno-cultural-lingual background issues are identical. It is the interfaith relationship that crosses the great divide between having a faith and having none. Now part of the hullabaloo around interfaith relationships is that people fear a dilution or loss of faith. Here is a story of exactly how that happened, or is it?

Irene and Emmanuel are a young, idealistic GloLo couple. They both work for NGOs, they do not drive a car 'because of the CO_2 emissions, not because we cannot afford it' and they are both vegetarian (do you know the CO_2 footprint of a kilogram of beef?). Emmanuel is European and Atheist. I wanted to write 'not that into it' but he asked me to write Atheist with a capital 'A'. Irene is African, from a community where 'everyone is Catholic, I didn't know there was anything else'.

"When I met Emmanuel," Irene began, "I was not at all interested in him. I knew that he was not a Christian. I didn't need to know more."

Emmanuel, however, had immediate interest.

"I knew I liked her right away," he said. "It was obvious that there would be a religious challenge, but I saw it as an intellectual challenge, not an emotional one. I knew I would never convert to Catholicism or anything else for that matter, but I never expected Irene to convert to anything either. It was more like a drifting process how we came together," he added philosophically.

Irene held her arms open with her palms up in a yoga-like position and explained what happened to her religiosity after spending time with somebody who is 'not that into it'.

"Here we have God," she said, lifting her right hand slightly. "And here we have prayer," and this time she lifted her left hand. "Is there any difference if I say 'universe' here and 'meditation' there?" she asked me, again lifting her hands in turn.

"By spending time with an Atheist, not only was my belief system challenged. It also freed me from the confines of conventional thinking. My mother and our priest are not happy with my religious development but I actually feel more spiritual than ever, and more connected with a god than ever," she emphasised.

"I showed her the path," joked Emmanuel, perhaps in poor taste, "what does that make me?"

What is interesting in the story of Emmanuel and Irene is that there is a similar, if opposite story, within the family. Irene's sister also fell in love with a 'non-believing man' and he eventually became a 'believer'.

"My sister," Irene said, "prayed for his soul every day for seven years. My mother prayed, I prayed, my family all prayed that Denzi would one day accept God and be baptised. And then one day he did. He found God and became Christian. Now he is praying for me."

'Not that into it' + 'not that into it'

Wait a minute here, if both GloLo partners are 'not that into it' and therefore *not religious*, how can religion pose a problem? Well, religion is part of your internal 'personal culture'. A lot of things that you believe in so deeply that you think they are your own ideas, such as ethics and values, like not stealing candy from a baby for example, are actually ideas that are learned. They are part of your culture and education and family background which, you guessed it, has a religious component.

So when two 'not that into it' love birds get together, they often start exploring each other's history and ideas and belief systems. A GloLo interfaith relationship is different than an interfaith or secular work environment and different than having interfaith friends from different religions, even if they are 'not that into it'. In a romantic relationship and in a household, 'not that into it' can be challenged.

Doug and Ruth are a 'Jewish, but not really' and 'Christian, Episcopalian actually, but not practising or anything' couple. Doug is 'west coast Canada' and very laid back and Ruth is 'very Toronto' and slightly more 'control freak' than Doug. We met at The Bloor Street Diner in Toronto. When I asked about their respective religious affiliation, they told me that neither of them had given much thought to religion since grade school.

"Other than weddings and a few funerals," Doug began, "religion was just never a part of my life. I don't know why."

"My parents did not go to church," Ruth joined in, "but my grandmother did. Both my parents did shift work and often slept on Sunday morning, maybe that's why."

I thought that was the end of the conversation on religion but then Doug launched into a story.

"It was only when we moved in together that our 'religious war' erupted," he said with a laugh. "We moved in mid- January, after the Christmas holidays. Everything was fine between us until Easter came along. I came home one day and the apartment was full of coloured eggs and bunnies everywhere."

"He's exaggerating," Ruth said. "It was just a table setting and a few decorations on the window ledge."

You could tell by looking at her that she would decorate tastefully.

"For you, it was just a few decorations," Doug retorted, but not in a mean way. "But I was like, I am Jewish man, I don't want Easter bunnies on my kitchen table. It was like this revelation, I am Jewish! Maybe I am not *that Jewish*, but I am still Jewish. And that's when we starting talking about it."

"Of course my association with Easter bunnies is very different than for Doug," explained Ruth. "It was a fun tradition in our family and even at school. For Doug, it was a point of exclusion. So I 'undecorated' immediately."

"The result of the bunny incident," Doug continued, "is that it opened up a whole new way to talk about our history with each other. We kind of intellectualised it. But then we started going to church together and to the synagogue together. It's like we are visiting each other's history when we go."

"We don't go every week or anything," Ruth cautioned me. "But we wanted to do it together. That was important for us. No exclusion, you know."

"And we learn something new from the service every time we go, so it's like, we're kind of into it actually," Doug finished up.

Although they thought that they were 'not that into it', because their world view was challenged, Doug and Ruth found themselves drifting back to the value system of their childhood. Even if it did not include active religion, it held components of religion. Groovy, I thought.

Let us say...

So, let us say that an interfaith relationship can have any effect on the religiosity of the GloLo couple. We have seen examples of a change in faith, a loss of faith and an increase of faith. Dealing with 'the religion thing' can be a powerful bonding exercise for a GloLo couple. It can lead to an enriched spiritual life and to the creation of blended and new family traditions. It is an opportunity for the extended family of the GloLo couple to learn about a 'foreign' belief system and by learning about it, to respect it too.

So what about Chelsea and Marc? Will they live in interfaith harmony? Will Chelsea be angry about the glass Marc broke at their wedding? Will Marc find Chelsea's glutton-free diet kosher enough? Well, if you look at their background, they have a lot in common, if religion is not among it. They have known each other since high school, so Marc knows that Chelsea's hair is not naturally straight. They went to the same Ivy League university, so probably 'did not inhale' at the same parties. They both have political parents so they understand the politics of politics and they both have working moms, so neither of them expects fresh-baked cookies after school every day. These elements combine with their religious background to create a personal profile that is overlapping in many key areas. Do I think, despite their religious differences, that they will make it as a couple? Of course I think they will make it. Hey, Chelsea and Marc, this chapter was for you, and other GloLo couples like you around the world. Amen and Shalom.

♥

Top 10 clues that you have a GloLo interfaith marriage

1. You are deeply religious and pray for the lost soul of your spouse, even though your spouse tells you, "My soul's not lost, man. I'm at peace with the universe."
2. The house is decorated for a holy season more often than it is not decorated.
3. The house is never decorated for any holy season because 'we are citizens of the world and do not partake in practices that are exclusive and possibly offensive to others'.
4. The negotiations for the christening/*bar mitzvah* of your child make peace in the Middle East look easy.
5. Your spouse does not understand the connection between cute Easter bunny rabbits and Christ being nailed to a cross.
6. The day you consider to be the most significant spiritual holiday of the year, your partner calls Tuesday.
7. When a teacher at school asked your child which religion he is, he held a closed fist to his heart and said, "God is here, it doesn't matter what name you have for Him."
8. Your child, who is 12, is a spokesperson for worldwide religious tolerance.
9. That one year when Ramadan and Christmas fell together on the calendar was the toughest period of your marriage.
10. Your child asks you if it is better to die and go to Heaven or to be reincarnated into a dolphin.

~~Race~~
~~Ethnicity~~
~~Diversity~~
GloLo Colours

"So what's the title of this chapter?" my editor asked me impatiently. I think I may have mentioned that she can be a bit edgy if you reach her at the wrong time of day.

Well, after a lot of reading and interviewing, it became clear that the, um, subject matter of this chapter is very sensitive.

"What's wrong with 'Race'?" she barked.

"Race is divisive," I answered. "It categorises people according to criteria which, in the GloLo context, is largely irrelevant. Underneath our skin, we all look the same."

"Uh huh. And 'Ethnicity'?" she queried, but this time she was less snarly.

"Ethnicity may *possibly* be an indicator of your personal culture however it is in no way a *reliable* indicator," I was on a roll now. "If you are White, you could be a Russian Jew, a Canadian Protestant, or a South African Calvinist. Pretty different culture, right? If you are Black, you could be a Jamaican Rastafarian, a Gabonese Bwiti, or an American Christian (and US President). If you are Asian, you may have never even been to Asia..."

"I get it," she cut me off. "Diversity? Don't tell me, too diverse. Underneath our skin, we all look the same," she mimicked.

"GloLo colours," I ventured. "is culturally sensitive, politically correct and globally appropriate," hoping that would satisfy her.

She mumbled something about 'post-modernist authors' and 'demise of the Queen's English' and I think I heard 'thinks she's the Jane Goodall of love', which was her way of giving approval. So the title of this chapter on the globalisation of colour is just that, *GloLo Colours*.

Paradox

There is kind of a strange paradox too, if you compare this with the previous chapter on religion. Religion is a *conscious* choice that is deep in your heart and soul, and religious affiliation can reveal a great deal about your personal culture, yet, short of the glittery religious icon hanging on a chain around your neck, your 'God Squad' T-shirt, or unrolling your portable carpet and kneeling in prayer five times a day, your religious belief is *invisible*. By contrast, skin colour is *highly visible*.

Skin is the body's largest organ by the way, even if it is just two millimetres thick, but as I have already said, underneath, we all look the same. Despite the 'cultural ambiguity' of, er, race or ethnicity, it is probably the most controversial form of the globalisation of love. As Joel Crohn writes in *Mixed Matches*, mixed race relationships are "the most visible and inescapable." J.C. Davies wrote *I Got the Fever*, a sort of 'how to' guide for women who are seeking to date interracially. Some are calling her book 'racist' because she dared to talk about it.

And to be perfectly honest, it is also the one subject area of this book where I have very little hands-on experience. I mean, I *do* have hands-on experience of course, however as a happily married woman, I cannot put it all down in print for the world, *and my husband*, to read. I mean, not that I have had *that much* hands-on experience. Oh, never mind; let's get back to the book.

Gender and 'machismo'

Karyn Langhorne Folan, author of *Don't Bring Home a White Boy*, interviewed scores of women specifically about GloLo *coloured* relationships. She quotes Mona, a really GloLo gal if there ever was one, who probably sums up the content of this chapter.

"I've dated Austrians, Ghanaians, Sierra Leoneans, White and Black South Africans, Italians, British, French, Dutch, and Mexican guys – which sounds like a lot of men, doesn't it?" Apparently she laughed at this point and then continued. "The conflicts usually come over issues of gender and machismo rather than race."

So if what Mona says is true, GloLo coloured relationships are just like any GloLo relationship. Problems arise due to attitudes toward things like gender roles and the male-female dynamic, which is, you guessed it, culturally determined. My not-reputation-damaging hands-on experience would support Mona's body of research shall we say. The couples I interviewed also confirm what Mona and I are theorising. The colours of a GloLo relationship are only important in terms of culture and personality. Skin colour is just the wrapping around the culture.

Still, GloLo colours get a lot of attention in society. Why? What is the big deal about a GloLo coloured relationship, anyway?

History of interracial relationships

Dear GloLo reader, this may come as a shock. Up until 1967, less than 50 years ago, a GloLo coloured marriage was illegal in many American states. A *law* against love's young dream? The USA is not the only country with a history of GloLo colour segregation on marital matters, however I will use it as an example for the following reason. Given the inherent multicultural nature of the USA, like Canada, a country of immigrants from different cultures *and colours* from all over the world, it does seem rather incongruent that law makers put statutory limits on who gets to marry whom, doesn't it?

Well, in 1958, Mildred Jeter, a Black American Indian woman and Richard Loving, a White man, both residents of Virginia, were having none of it. They could not marry in Virginia due to a law which prohibited marriage between 'Whites' and 'non-Whites' so they crossed the state border and went to the District of Columbia to get married. When they returned to the State of Virginia, they were charged with the felony of 'miscegenation' which means interracial marriage, including, ooh, 'interracial sex'. The Lovings pleaded guilty to their 'crime' and were banned from living in Virginia, but then they appealed the ruling as a violation of the Fourteenth Amendment to the Constitution. (Sorry for dropping this legal stuff on you, but it is significant.) Here is the good bit: The Supreme Court of the United States *overruled* a State of Virginia law that forbade interracial marriage. The landmark case is known of course as Loving *vs*. Virginia. Loving rules!

The following year, 1968, *Star Trek's* Captain Kirk (played by White William Shatner) kissed Lieutenant Uhura (played by Black Nichelle Nichols). *Star Trek*, in case you have the great misfortune of never having been a 'Trekkie', was the *Zeitgeist* of modern society. Captain James T Kirk guided the 'Starship Enterprise' – think of a minimalist interior décor, with the functionality of a Club Med cruise liner, including a really great restaurant – across the galaxy, exploring planets and encountering societies and cultures that deeply challenged our own assumptions about fundamental social rights and wrongs. No matter where Captain Kirk flew the Enterprise, the women were *very sexy*. It was a hotbed for the 'intergalaticisation' of love (my next book perhaps?) and the crew were forever entangled in inter-planetary GloLo romance. And this is what led to the first ever GloLo coloured kiss on American network television. It generated the most *Star Trek* fan mail that Paramount Pictures had received about any episode to that date.

It is very telling then, that even in the American 'cultural melting pot', skin colour was, and many would successfully argue still is, such a big issue. What does it mean, then, for the GloLo coloured couple? In this chapter, we will look closer at what happens out there in the great big GloLo coloured world, what happens between the GloLo-coloured couple, and then finally we will discuss children in GloLo coloured families, as follows:

- Great big GloLo coloured world
- The GloLo coloured couple
- What about the kids?

Great big GloLo coloured world

Remember in *Chapter 4 – Meet the Parents*, there was a long list of unflattering labels such as 'Thief' or 'Lottery Ticket' that parents and friends might have for your partner when you are dating and marrying 'exogamously'? Well, it is more or less the same in a GloLo coloured relationship. There is one difference in that a GloLo *coloured* relationship is more visible. Only family and friends who know about the cultural, linguistic and religious background of you and your partner know about, and may have opinions on, your GloLo status. In a GloLo coloured partnership, *everyone* knows that you are GloLo. What goes on then, when GloLo couples parade their colours? Here are a couple of things to add to the list.

Staring

Remember lively African American Sheida and soft-spoken Romanian Andràs who we met in *Chapter 3 – Profile of a GloLo*? They are multicultural, biracial, interfaith, multilingual and intercontinental, or "just about as GloLo as you can go", Sheida told me during an interview at a Vienna coffee shop. I asked about their experience, specifically as a GloLo coloured couple.

"People stare," Andràs said, matter-of-factly. "I don't know what they are looking at actually, because they don't stare when we are separate."

"Speak for yourself," Sheida said with a smile. "I get a lot of stares, and whistles too," she added with relish.

"That's not what I mean," Andràs said. "I mean they stare at us, you and me, Black and White."

"They do," Sheida agreed playfully. "Maybe it's because they're jealous of you."

András rolled his eyes. I asked if there was a difference between the staring in the US, in Austria and in Romania.

"Definitely," András answered. "In Chicago, biracial couples are common. In Romania and here in Vienna, we are unique, so it's like there is a spotlight on us. I'm not saying people are staring in a racist way or anything, but they do look at us longer than if we were not biracial. We call the people who stare 'starists'. Get it?" he asked pleasantly.

I did get it. I know that since I started writing this book, I have become a bit of a 'starist' myself. Maybe, I suggested to Andràs, that some of the 'starists' are researchers or they are writing a book, a bestseller even, about love stories and globalisation and biracial relationships, or something along those lines. Maybe the researcher/author is thinking, 'Should I approach them? Would they mind? I would love to hear their story. I bet they fit right in with the globalisation of love.'

"No," Sheida stated. "Starists are not researching. They are staring and thinking, 'she's Black, he's White, what the hell is going on?' It's times for people to mind their own business."

It was a commonly shared experience amongst the GloLo coloured couples I interviewed and leads to the next point on stereotyping.

Stereotyping

Slovenian Petra told us that she and Dahnay, her Ethiopian husband, along with their two biracial children, are the only interracial family in the small town where they live in Slovenia. Dahnay, tall, dark, and if Petra does not mind, I would like to add *handsome*, explained.

"We are the only GloLo family in town, you see," Dahnay said, picking up the GloLo parlance immediately, I was pleased to hear.

"It creates a certain kind of pressure for Dahnay and the girls. They must always be on their best behaviour, otherwise there tends to be stereotyping. If Dahnay doesn't shave for one day, then they think, 'Black men don't shave'," Petra explained.

"I've become the Black ambassador to Slovenia," Dahnay laughed. "If I do something differently from the locals, they think that it is the 'Black' way. I try to tell them that there is no such thing as the 'Black' way. We come from all over the world. But they still think, 'oh, Black men don't shave' or 'Black girls can sing'," he said, referring to the girls' recent performance in a school musical that was quite a success apparently.

"It was an impressive show," Petra reminisced with pride. "They certainly didn't get their musical talent from me though," she laughed.

"Nor from me," Dahnay said. "I wish all Black men *could* sing."

"And White women too," Petra continued the joke.

This got me thinking about *GloLo The Musical*, but I cannot sing either.

The meta-identity

Something that is similar to stereotyping is the so-called meta-identity. It is a phenomenon many foreigners experience in a racial minority situation. Continents and skin colour replace nationality as a cultural reference point. For example, everyone from Sweden to France to Greece is clumped together as 'White'. Everyone from Peru, Bolivia, Brazil, and Ecuador become 'Latino'. National characteristics of one nation are transferred and applied to all nationalities in the same group. It does not allow for individual national identity or personality and can be frustrating for the inadvertent 'ambassador' in that role.

'Asian' Lin and 'White' Angus are a Chinese-Scottish couple who live in China. They both work in intercultural communications and training and have been together for five years.

"As the local White guy," Angus told me, "I have to answer for all of Europe. I try to tell Lin's family that I am from Scotland, not even on the continent of Europe, and that the countries of Europe are very different. No one in Lin's family has ever left China," he explained. "So in some ways, I represent all White people, and to a certain degree anyone who is 'not Chinese'. That's about, what, five billion or so."

"In our workshops," Lin continued, "we try to educate people about these different layers of culture. It means different things to be Scottish, or European or even White," Lin explained, drawing upon her expertise as an intercultural coach and interpreter.

"It's interesting," Angus continued. "I even notice that Lin's personality changes according to her workshops. If she is with American clients for a week, she becomes more like them, more assertive."

"However in Scotland," Lin asserted, "I am 'Asian' and I am 'Angus' Asian wife'. Also like an ambassador for the Asian region. They are sometimes surprised that I talk so much. They expect a quiet Asian wife who is submissive. A Geisha girl."

"Yes," Angus chortled, "Lin has broken the mould of the submissive Geisha girl. They now believe that Asian wives are rather chatty indeed."

Lin blushed with pride.

Betrayal

In *Chapter 1 – Global Alliance Strategies*, some of the proof readers for this book were a bit shocked when Diana, a Black African American woman in a Same But Different relationship with Nigerian Omar who is also Black, said that she definitely wanted to marry a Black man and that 'marrying a White man would betray my Black heritage'.

"You can't write that," Reader X said. "It's racist."

Well, firstly, I did not write it. I *quoted* it. Secondly, Diana is not alone in desiring a partner who shares her language, culture, ethnicity, and yes, colour. Let's put it this way, 300 years of Black slavery in America, followed by continued racism, discrimination and unequal economic opportunity, I think it is fair to say that Diana has her reasons for wanting to stick together with her ethnic group. She feels that dating and marrying 'exogenously' would betray her forefathers and foremothers who suffered and died in slavery.

Crossing the so-called colour line, therefore, is really about history and politics, which is all about loyalties and allegiances, isn't it?

Malaysian Laila and Dutch Jelle, who we met in *Meet the Parents* as the 'Traitor' and the 'Thief', as their 'titles' imply, met resistance from both sides of their family who did not accept the Asian-White mix.

"When I started going out with Jelle," Laila told me, "my family was very upset. It was not because he was White, it was because of the history between our two countries. It was post-colonial pride. I was dating a colonialist and it was family betrayal."

"And my parents were also not that thrilled with Laila," Jelle picked up. "It was not about race either. It was about geography. They didn't want me to live so far away. If she was a Malaysian girl from Zwolle," he said, referring to the neighbouring town in the Netherlands where his parents live, "there would not have been an issue."

GloLo 2G

But let's be honest, sometimes it is only about colour and nothing else. Vanita and Julian are a typical GloLo intelligentsia couple. They met during their university studies and have faced a few obstacles in maintaining their relationship over the past few years. Vanita, from India, went to England to study economics at Cambridge and, oops, fell in love with Julian, her tutor. She spoke first.

"In a middle-class Indian family, education means everything," began Vanita, who is sporty in a Sporty Spice-with-gold-bangles kind of way. "It was always clear that I would study abroad, so going to Cambridge was a natural step for me. I had not considered the possibility of actually meeting someone. I expected to return to my family after graduation and they would help me choose a husband."

"I rather botched up that plan, didn't I?" Julian suggested jovially. Julian, who grew up in Chester in an affluent neighbourhood, is second generation GloLo (GloLo 2G). His father is White and his mother is Black.

"I'm biracial actually," he explained. "When people say, 'you don't look biracial', I ask them, 'what does biracial look like?'. And then there is this wonderful silence," he laughed in good humour.

"The sad part of our situation is that my parents are terribly displeased with Julian," Vanita said primly, "although he is well-educated and from a well-to-do family. This is all my family would ever want for me, but they call him a 'dark boy'."

"They have a different upbringing," Julian offered, which I thought was very magnanimous. "They live in a different world. I can forgive them. They are not my parents, but it has been both harrowing and heartbreaking for Vanita."

She has returned to India to see her parents only once since she began her studies in Cambridge six years ago. Her family tried to prevent her from returning to England. In high drama, they took away her passport and airline ticket, without knowing that the confiscated passport had expired and her new valid passport was tucked safely away in a side pocket of her handbag.

"The irony of it is that their argument has one glaring flaw," Vanita continued. "Look at this," she said, holding out her arm, and then Julian held out his arm next to hers.

"In the summer, when I am tanned," Julian interjected politely, "I am a 'dark boy', but in winter, my skin is fairer than Vanita's. My 'dark boy' status is seasonal, so they should accept me for the winter at least." He chuckled.

I asked Julian if his family has any objections to his relationship with Vanita.

"We are culturally a very mixed family. My parents are biracial. I am biracial. My siblings have brought home a diverse range of partners. So Vanita fits right in actually."

I commented that his family sound very GloLo indeed.

"If every member of my family buys a copy of *The Globalisation of Love*, you'll have a bestseller," he assured me.

These economists, they do predict market behaviour, don't they?

Household help is here

Another GloLo phenomenon is the assumption that one partner, usually the one with a darker skin tone, is hired household help.

"When my parents first married in the 1970s," Julian said, "it was frequently assumed that my mother was my father's housekeeper. She loves to tell the story of how a utilities man arrived at our home and asked if he could see the lady of the house. My mother said, 'Yes, I am here,' to which he responded, 'Lovely, would you call her please' and looked over her shoulder." He shook his head at the family memory.

This phenomenon is further exaggerated when there are children involved, particularly if the children look more like one parent, this time more like the lighter toned parent.

"My older brother Gavin is very light skinned. When he first started at The Academy," Julian said, referring to an expensive private school they both attended, "not just the other boys but also the teachers asked my mother which family she worked for, assuming of course that she was Gavin's governess. One mother even commented that Gav seemed to 'love her like his own mother'. But my mother just laughs about it. I guess we have created our own majority opinion within our family. Multiculturalism is the norm. We haven't managed languages though. I guess that should be our next step," he added cheerily.

Julian's alacrity in the face of blatant discrimination is common amongst second generation GloLo children and testimony to the power of the globalisation of love too.

It's-all-about-sex

One final point I would like to include, and not just because I did promise a bit of sex in this book, is the it's-all-about-sex assumption. In a GloLo *coloured* relationship, particularly where one partner, usually the woman, is from a poor country, there is the assumption that she has 'sexed' her way into the man's heart. At the same time, the man is said to have some kind of 'fetish' for a certain type of woman. Well, let's be honest here, what relationship, at least at the beginning, is not all about sex, really? If cultural and religious beliefs do not allow sex before marriage, then it is all about chemistry and flirtatious come-hither glances and the promise that, as soon as the ink on the wedding contract is dry, it *will* be all about sex. Further, anyone who has gone through the process of an international marriage, what with the infuriating bureaucracy and ludicrous waiting periods and the extortionist expenses incurred to translate birth certificates and police records checks will know that there are much easier and deeply more satisfying ways to obtain sex and fulfil 'fetish' fantasies than to start a GloLo coloured relationship.

Sheida and András spoke of some of the proverbial banging on the bedroom door and the 'what's-it-like?' line of questioning.

"We have both been asked by friends, 'what's it like to be with a White guy or a Black girl?'" Sheida said, not hiding her irritation. András nodded his head in agreement.

"It's not racist to be curious and to ask questions, but I tell my friends, it's not like chocolate and vanilla ice cream. Sex is between two people and not between two ethnic groups. At least not the way we do it," she added with her trademark flair and humour.

Laila and Jelle encountered the same attitude.

"As an 'Asian'," Laila began, putting her fingers in bunny ear quotation marks to express emphasis, "many Europeans think that I must have no education and work as a bar girl. Jelle must have saved me and I am his 'sex slave'," she emphasised again.

"You know if I say anything right now, I will end up sleeping on the sofa tonight," Jelle deadpanned.

We changed the subject so Jelle could get a good night's rest.

The GloLo coloured couple

The funny thing about the 'big deal' about a GloLo coloured relationship is that typically, the GloLo coloured couples, at least the ones I interviewed, give little-to-no thought about GloLo colours. Petra explained her experience.

"When I first started dating Dahnay, I thought about the colour issue simply because he was the only Black man I have dated. He is also the only non-European for that matter. But after the first date, it disappeared. He is simply a wonderful person," she ravished.

I asked Dahnay about his thoughts when he started dating a White woman.

"I was completely immersed in a White world, you see. I was one of four foreigners from Africa, all men. If I wanted a wife, it was obvious that it would be a White wife. Colour is not important, you see. What is important is in here," he said, holding his hand to his heart.

As if being handsome wasn't enough. Swoon.

Corporate identity

Yet even if GloLo couples experience little if any 'colour shock' between themselves, the reactions within their social network, as we read in the last section, can influence the dynamic between the couple.

Rajen Persaud, author of *Why Black Men Love White Women*, a pretty scathing social commentary of Black-White relationships in America, writes, "It often creates a tighter bond between the man and the woman. It's them against the world. Life becomes more of a defiant stance against the social order."

It is kind of romantic, isn't it, this 'you and me against the world' theme? It forces couples into a solidarity position and can become a sort of 'corporate identity' for the couple.

Laila and Jelle said how they felt when both sets of parents gave an underwhelming response to the happy news of their engagement.

"Since we didn't get the positive support we had hoped for from our families," Laila began, "we realised that we were on our own. A lot of the wedding planning that I normally would have done together with my mother, I did with Jelle. He has fabulous taste in wedding gowns," she added gleefully.

"We have a lot of international friends and expat friends," Jelle continued, blushing somewhat at this comment on his good sense of bridal fashion. "They were very supportive too. They made it special for us. We didn't intend it to be a post-colonial summit or anything, but somehow it became a Dutch-Indonesian friendship treaty. Both sets of parents grudgingly attended the wedding and were overwhelmed by the international spirit. They later said that they learned from us. I guess you would call it the globalisation of love." He smirked.

Yes Jelle, I would.

Black panther from Bombay

"I've become a Black activist," Vanita said proudly, describing how she has responded to her parents' disapproval of her relationship with Julian. "I had never given racial issues much thought, however since my family was so opposed to Julian, and that based on race alone, it attuned me to racism in general. It forced me to take a stance, which was next to Julian."

"Vanita is probably the most politically active member in our family in this sense," Julian added.

"It's not just my family," admitted Vanita, "We have experienced racism as a couple and even encountered danger."

"That was just bad luck," Julian said, referring to an incident when they were travelling together in another country and a group of young men verbally harassed the couple and made racial slurs.

"It wasn't 'bad luck'," said Vanita indignantly, "it was a 'racist incident'. Julian is so tolerant," she said to me more than to Julian. "He only sees the good in people. I suppose that's why I love him."

What about the kids?!

I do not think it is going out on a limb to say that every GloLo coloured couple at some point hears the 'what about the kids?' question. There are two main queries. On the one side, there are those that cry in distress, 'What about the children?' as though GloLo coloured children, from 'BlAsians' to 'LatIndians' to 'Jewpanese', and any other genetic combination is somehow similar to cracking open an atom in terms of technical complexity and subsequent fallout. It is quite funny when you think that the extent of the big genetic experiment is that GloLo Junior will be a few shades lighter or darker than Mom or Dad. Make no mistake, GloLo children do have identity issues, *just like all children. Chapter 12 – Children* covers the main issues.

On the other side of the 'what about the kids?' spectrum, there are those who cry, in delighted anticipation, 'What about the children? *What will they be*?' They are referring, of course, to GloLo coloured children who are famed for their cuteness and beauty.

"It puts pressure on us to produce super-models," Sheida blurted out. "Friends are always talking about 'chocolate babies' and saying, 'oh, your children will be so beautiful', which they will be of course," she added with a laugh.

Petra and Dahnay's girls, less than ten years old, have a clear explanation for their own White Slovenian-Black Ethiopian gene pool.

"They say, 'Mommy is very white and daddy is very dark and we are half and half, right in the middle,'" Petra said proudly. "It makes us proud as parents when we hear how well they describe themselves. They are proud to be in the middle. It is a safe place for them."

Karyn Langhorne Folan also writes that the birth of a GloLo child can help to rebuild broken relationships between parents and their 'wayward' children who have married outside the clan. In some cases, she writes, "grandparents began to understand more about racism by gauging others' reactions to their grandchildren." One look at a little GloLo coloured baby and most grandparents forget about 'betrayals' and 'meta-identity' and engage in the universal new baby monologue, presented here in English, that goes something like, 'THAT'S MY ANGEL! Who loves Angel? Granny loves Angel. Yes, Granny. How about a kiss? A kiss for Granny?' and so on. GloLo Junior is a most convincing messenger for the globalisation of love.

Conclusion

Race is culture, sometimes. But even when it is not culture, it is still a visible differentiator. Even though it is a visible differentiator, we all look the same underneath, don't we?

Richard Loving died in 1975 and Mildred Loving died in 2008. Fortunately much has changed since their brave steps toward GloLo coloured marriage. There is now even a 'Loving Day', with free beer apparently, that 'fights racial prejudice through education and builds multicultural community'. Mr and Mrs Loving, may you rest in peace, side-by-side as husband and wife, with the knowledge that your love and GloLo courage changed the world for a better place, this chapter has been for you. GloLo Loving rules!

♥

Top 10 GloLo celebrity couples

1. German **Heidi Klum** and English **Seal**
2. Argentinean **Princess Màxima** and Dutch **Crown Prince Willem-Alexander**
3. English **John Lennon** and Japanese **Yoko Ono**
4. South African **Charlene Wittstock** and Monegasque **Prince Albert II**
5. American **Grace Kelly** and Monegasque **Prince Rainier**
6. American **Johnny Depp** and French **Vanessa Paradis**
7. Somali **Iman** and English **David Bowie**
8. Australian **Mary Donaldson** and Danish **Crown Prince Frederik**
9. English **Elton John** and Canadian **David Furnish**
10. Russian **Anna Kournikova** and Spanish **Enrique Iglesias**

Language

Okay, so you are aware on a cognitive level that your partner grew up speaking a different language than you. You have noticed the way he rolls his R's a bit longer than is absolutely necessary or that her R's are absent altogether. Sometimes the accent is charming or cute, and sometimes it is as pleasant as finger nails scratching a chalk board. This audible variance to the language that you speak together is the tip of the intercultural language and communication iceberg, with wonderful, frustrating, funny and even unintentional life altering consequences. Let me explain.

Globalisation of communication

Kissing can solve most big relationship problems, but not all. Tripping and stumbling over a language barrier when talking about important life issues, like the upcoming visit of the in-laws for example, can be aggravating. Finding the right words and expressing feelings and emotions accurately can be taxing in any relationship. In a multilingual marriage, the meaning of words and how we use them to communicate can therefore be an area of enormous challenge.

Any decent advice book on living abroad in general, and multicultural relationships in particular, will write in bold capitals, somewhere very close to the beginning of the book, LEARN YOUR PARTNER'S NATIVE LANGUAGE. Learning the language is toted as one of the key 'survival strategies' for living and loving cross-culturally. What I would add to this sage advice is that there is a lot more to learning the language than just learning the language. In addition to all those tongue spraining words that are too long to say without stopping for an oxygen break, there is a second parallel world of communication that can lead to miscommunication and cultural misunderstanding.

Thanks to the seminal work of Dr John Gray, we already know that men are from Mars and women are from Venus and that there is a communication dichotomy between the two planets. In a GloLo partnership, and with no disrespect to Dr Gray, understanding the language of Mars and Venus is not enough. This is not something for the faint of heart to hear, but on both Mars and Venus, there are hundreds, possibly thousands, of parallel regions that will influence your partner's communication style. As if we don't have enough to worry about already with learning vocabulary and conjugating verbs, multicultural Mars and Venus, with their different styles of communication, need to learn the language within the language.

Here is a personal example from the time when I barely spoke enough German to order a beer at Oktoberfest. When I met my German-speaking *Austrian* husband, thankfully not at Oktoberfest, my German-speaking girlfriends *from Germany*, where I lived at the time, were charmed by his accent. It was Austrian, it was Viennese, it was a 'cute southern dialect from Styria' they exclaimed delightedly. I was a tad flabbergasted. I thought he spoke German, *just like they did*. Each of these elements however, being an Austrian rather than a German, living in Vienna, the capital city, rather than in the country and hailing from the cute southern region of Styria, all influence the way my dearly beloved uses the German language. Confusing, no? Essentially, learning the language requires an understanding of and sensitivity to the cultural background behind the language and how the language is spoken and transmitted.

I realised that I had to learn a lot more than German. I needed to understand the difference between German-German and Austrian-German, the caustic grumpy humour of the Viennese, and the playful joking of the Styrians. It is not something you just memorise overnight by placing a language textbook under your pillow, if you know what I mean. Now it is years later and I hear the difference between German-German and Austrian-German and, wow, it really is different. I recognise the Viennese dialect and the Styrian humour, and perhaps most importantly, like my German girlfriends, I am now charmed by my husband's accent.

So you see, it is vital to understand language and communication within the GloLo context, if only to allow yourself to be charmed.

Pardon me a moment for getting all academic, but it is perhaps easiest to think of the interaction, the real *globalisation of love*, if you may, in two categories. The first category is *language*, a collection of words and grammatical rules that must be expertly combined in order to be used effectively for self-expression. The second category is *communication*, or how we exchange information between ourselves; in other words, how we use and apply the tool. The language, the world of words, is *what* we say and communication is *how* we say it.

The world of words

Language shapes our thoughts. It is the tool that allows us to express our inner selves to the outer world. Every language has its own repertoire of words to describe feelings, emotions, and situations, and this is further determined by culture, but let's not get carried away. The point is, there are words in your language that help you to express yourself and some of these words *do not even exist* in another language. Even if we are completely and utterly fluent in the native language of our partner (perhaps a far stretch for the imagination I know, but bear with me for a moment) we still do not necessarily have the precise tools to express ourselves.

Let's think about the implications of this wordy dilemma. Some words are similar in most languages and therefore translate easily. As I am not a linguist nor do I have the million euro research grant to study the many thousand languages and dialects of the world, I will create a fictitious example.

Chocolate is a word that I hope is truly universal. But if, heaven forbid, chocolate does not exist somewhere, why would they have a word for it? And even if they had a word for it, without having 'experienced' chocolate, and chocoholics will know what I am talking about, what would that word really mean? So if you happen to marry someone from this barren, uninhabitable land where chocolate does not exist, and you say "chocolate makes me happy", inevitably there will be confusion, and possibly even jealous questioning such as, "Who is this Chocolate and what does he give you that I do not?"

To explain that chocolate is compressed roasted cacao beans, an elegant dessert to complement and highlight a fine meal, a source of comfort and salvation after a nasty break-up, or a celebration of food in its finest form does not convey the weight of the word, and the world, of chocolate.

Other words are very, very similar, and translate to maybe 85 per cent accuracy, but are not quite right. My favourite example is the English word 'compassion', defined by Merriam Webster as 'sympathetic consciousness of others' distress together with a desire to alleviate it'. It is more than a word, isn't it? It encompasses a concept, and that concept in its English constellation does not have a German equivalent. *Jawohl*, to all you German speakers, there is sympathy and understanding, and being helpful and nice, but there is no one-stop-shop German word that just means compassion, full stop. Hence, it requires playing around a bit with similar alternatives, and tossing in one or two extra words, in the attempt to convey the meaning and concept of the word compassion. It is just one example of millions.

So when a GloLo couple is chatting away in any language, there may be this built-in restriction for self-expression. For some conversations, finding a very close translation is enough, but there are indeed situations when you really, really want that one word. And *Jiminy Cricket*, it doesn't exist.

Getting lost in translation is just one aspect of the language issue with a GloLo couple. The following is another story about misused words and the peril it may bring.

The adorable Margaret Thatcher

When I first met my husband, I often felt a bit uncomfortable, or maybe raging jealousy is more accurate, when he said that he 'adored' another woman. Well, I thought at the time, Europeans, or French presidents at least, are renowned for their more open approach to relationships. Who was I to judge, right? (Okay, I admit, it was darn close to a deal breaker.)

Fortunately, I noticed that the women he proclaimed to 'adore', Margaret Thatcher among them, were, in my admittedly biased opinion, not actually that adorable. (Sorry Maggie, you have other fine qualities and I respect you deeply.) The word *adorable* also kept popping up in incongruent ways, such as during political discussions or talks about business and captains of industry. The clincher came one day when my husband stated that he 'adored' Bill Gates. In his nerdy I-am-a-billionaire-but-I-don't-care way, I suppose Bill is kind of cute, but not really 'adorable'. Tentatively, and yes hopefully, I asked my husband a question that I hoped would sort out this confusion once and for all.

"Do you mean that you *admire* Bill Gates?"

"Yes," he replied, sounding a bit annoyed. "That's what I just said. I adore him."

Suddenly I adored Bill Gates too, along with Margaret Thatcher, Christiane Amanpour of CNN, Indira Gandhi and the Austrian Minister of Foreign Affairs.

One unintended word can have significant consequences, particularly when neither party realises that the chosen word is not the word of choice. Now when I catch my husband adoring Keira Knightley or other rising starlets and supermodels, I say, "don't you mean that you *admire* her?"

"Yes, dear," he responds without hesitation.

Another language issue is accents, which can work either way in a global love story.

I rove you, but sometimes I ate you

Bradley, a baseball loving Californian, shared his story about an argument he had with his French-Vietnamese girlfriend, Kim Swan. They spoke English together.

"I had been insensitive to her needs," he admitted, "working a lot during the week and playing baseball with the guys on the weekends. She was in tears and her voice was a bit wobbly, so combined with her French-Asian accent, what I heard her say was, 'I rove you, but sometimes I ate you too'. It melted my heart and I asked her to marry me on the spot."

"Lucky for me," Kim Swan interjected, "if I was native English speaker, maybe we would not be married. If a girl wants to marry, maybe she just need right accent [sic]."

"Could be," concluded Bradley, "but probably divorce, even wars, have also started due to the wrong accent."

"We aim for grobal [sic] peace," Kim Swan assured me.

Their lovely story demonstrates the incredible power of the spoken language and how it can influence our feelings, impressions, and emotions, *and* how the influence can be unintentional. Bradley's proposal to Kim Swan was the spontaneous result of the effect her accent had on him. With that, we are one step closer to grobal, er, global peace.

Cave man

Unless you happen to marry into a foreign royal family and therefore *owe it to the people* to speak their native language flawlessly, attention to the details of accent and enunciation can sometimes be less romantic than Bradley's proposal to Kim Swan. In the early days of a GloLo love affair, accents and flawed language add to the drama and flair of a multicultural relationship. Once love's first blush has faded however, the once charming flaws may lose the charm and remain just flaws.

Emily, as London as Big Ben, suffered wilting enchantment with her Czech husband Ivan.

"I am truly British and therefore speak English. Ivan is a global citizen" she explained. "He grew up in the Czech Republic, was educated in Boston, has worked for international organisations in four different countries and he speaks three languages fluently. When we first met I was charmed by his rough accent and his grammar is excellent. After seven years of living with his personal live-in English language coach," she said, pointing to herself, "his accent has not changed and now it drives me crazy," she grimaced. "He sounds like a caveman. I wish he would speak English like a gentleman!"

I also found Ivan's rough accent charming, and although I heard the cave man parallel, I thought he was a remarkably well-educated and sexy cave man.

Somehow an accent acts as an auditory marker in a GloLo relationship. It goes beyond "you say tomAYTAH and I say tomAHTOE" and acts as a daily reminder that our language and cultural frames of reference are different. It matters within a relationship because the use of language and speech pattern reflects, often unintentionally, on your personality. You may sound cute or caveman-like even when you do not want to be cute or caveman-like. The real you is somewhat hidden behind the quirks of accent and other unintentional lingual impulses. And your real partner may not be as cute or as caveman-like as what you perceive. The presence of the accent warps somewhat the getting-to-know-you phase and may even undermine the now-that-I-know-you phase. *Hmm, I vunder vot my huzbant zinks ven I spik Jermin.*

No big words

Independent of which language(s) you and your GloLo partner speak, and all accents aside, another linguistic challenge in multicultural communiqués concerns vocabulary. If you speak your native language with your partner, you will likely have the advantage when playing Scrabble and shine when doing the Sunday crossword puzzle together, but daily verbal exchange requires a filter of sorts. In order to eschew obfuscation, or *avoid confusion*, the global couple can do well to restrain themselves a bit when speaking their mother tongue. The use of gratuitous embellishments and excessively decorative language can make the less fluent partner uncomfortable, and even intimidated.

A considerate GloLo partner needs to speak the language in a way that the non-native and less fluent speaker understands. The translation for this is simple – no big words. Sometimes it is easier said than done.

Editor of a national magazine, eloquent Mary is a true wordsmith in both her professional and private life.

"I captained the high school debating team in upstate New York, and we pummelled every opponent with a voraciousness usually reserved for the sports arena," she boasted.

When it came to Juan, her Argentinean partner, Mary was less ecstatic.

"Sometimes I miss the electric charge of a good debate or discussion. I have reduced my vocabulary to grade three level."

Juan, a journalist in his own right, albeit not in English, concurred.

"I don't want every discussion to be a challenge or learning opportunity," he said. "Sometimes I just want to talk, okay, and mistakes are okay. I think, no English lessons today please," he said putting up his hands.

"Yes," Mary agreed, "but after years of speaking a sanitised version of your mother tongue, you tend to lose familiarity and fluency with big words. And I need those big words – that's my job."

The flip side of the same issue is when you speak your partner's language, and then you probably do not know many big words anyway.

"Mary's Spanish is much better than my English, but she does not sound like an editor-in-chief either," continued Juan.

Mary laughed and continued. "I don't edit a Spanish magazine, I share cooking recipes with your mother. That's a challenge too."

Make good team

The third lingual possibility is if both partners speak a non-native language. In this case, it is often a kind of bond between GloLo partners. Japanese Linda met Indonesian Banyu at an English course.

"She was the best in class," Banyu told me while pouring jasmine tea at We Will Wok You, the restaurant they own together. "I thought, smart girl, be nice and maybe she help me learn English. Now we are married and she still better. We make good team [sic]," he said, gesturing to the restaurant surroundings, a sort of Asian style Hard Rock Cafe.

"We both have areas of specialisation," explained Linda, "I manage the contracts so I specialise more in English. Banyu manages the kitchen so he specialises in food."

It should be noted that the food was delicious, so indeed I agree with Banyu, 'they make good team'.

Banyu's reliance on Linda in the language department does mean that his own language skills are not likely to improve. Penelope and Kimo, by contrast, were both keen to improve their language skills and help each other learn their common language. Penelope, a vivacious Spaniard from the Mediterranean island of Mallorca, explained their game to me.

"I look at the Spanish dictionary and Kimo looks into his Japanese dictionary, and between the two definitions, we try to come up with a word solution in English," she explained.

When I asked the Spanish-Japanese couple if it was sometimes a case of the blind leading the blind, Kimo answered. "We have English-speaking friends and sometimes we call them as a referee. From San Francisco to Tokyo, somebody is always awake," he said, referring to the time zones between the continents.

In summary, whether you speak in your mother tongue, in your partner's native language, in a third language, or a mix of all three, there will exist a sort of *No Big Words Rule*. As each partner learns more about the main language(s) spoken, and we are talking about lifelong learning here, the big words can slowly make their reappearance. That is, if we can still remember any.

Colloquialisms

As with big words, colloquial expressions are also victim to multilingual lovers. Colloquialisms, such as 'quick as a whip' and 'sharp as a tack', do not usually translate well, and can be distracting, confusing and misleading. After years of non-use, these fun little phrases fall out of your personal vocabulary. Personally, I often end up saying things like 'quick as a tack' and 'sharp as a whip'. I confuse my husband, who does not know what a tack is anyway, and embarrass myself. If I had a dime for the many times I have had to explain why I cannot speak my mother tongue with real fluency, well, I would be 'rich as a Rockefeller', 'filthy rich', or even 'one rich beeeeeep'!

It can be great fun trying to decipher foreign colloquialisms that your partner attempts to translate into your common language. The resulting new phrase can mean something slightly different or may have no meaning whatsoever. The blooper is often adopted into common parlance and becomes part of the multilingual repertoire in the relationship. Children of multilingual pairings really do grow up thinking a tack is quick and a whip is sharp.

In a loose translation of a German saying, my (adorable) husband once described a friend as 'a girl you can steal horses with'. What, I thought, she's a thief? Ursula is crafty, but surely not criminal. Maybe she grew up on a farm and has advanced equine knowledge? No, this girl is pure Vienna, as *Sex and the City* heroine Carrie Bradshaw is to New York. 'A girl you can steal horses with' means that she is good fun to be with and ready for new adventures, like stealing horses I guess. Come to think of it, you could steal a horse with Carrie Bradshaw, couldn't you?

She said a four letter word

Another linguistic peculiarity, and one that has the potential to undermine a budding GloLo romantic match, is the use of coarse language. There are certain words in every language, which clearly I am too ladylike to list here, which are generally not accepted in polite society. The words do exist though, so somebody must be using them, right? However, there is no official guide book outlining when and where swearing is or is not appropriate. At the risk of sounding repetitive, it is kind of a cultural thing. The following example of the curse of cursing is from a couple who even speak the same language but still were challenged by a few four letter words.

Remember Canadian Kevin, the diplomat living in London and Carole, his posh English girlfriend? Carole is a bond trader who worked in London's financial district, an industry known for its colourful application of expletives in daily business rapport.

"Here was this beautiful, intelligent, classy woman with a posh accent whose vocabulary would shame a trucker, as we say in Canada. I almost fell out of love," Kevin recalled.

"In the City [London's financial centre]," explained Carole, who really is beautiful and classy, "tough talk and crude language is part of the business culture. We are like verbal pit bull terriers chomping at each other. It is part of survival."

She has learned to censor her language when away from work, and particularly when anywhere near his work, and to be the classy dame on the diplomat's arm.

Carole and Kevin are both native English speakers so they both more or less know the bad words from the good. In their case, swearing really was a cultural thing. For multilingual couples, however, swearing can just be a language thing, and even an *unintentional* language thing.

Partners will typically have a great deal of influence on the development of each others' language. I burst with pride when I hear touches of Canadian in my husband's English, for example. For Sheila, it was a different experience.

"I knew not a word of Dutch when I met Pieter," Irish Sheila told me. "He's a lorry driver and we met in Sicily on vacation. At the time, I was finishing my PhD and by coincidence, was going to Holland for some post-doc research two months later. I know it is not typical that a university professor and a truck driver come together, but he is smart, smarter than me actually. His English is excellent but what I did not know is that his Dutch is sometimes crude or crass. That's the Dutch that I learned to speak in any case. A couple of colleagues at the university are trying to coach it out me, fingers wagging, saying 'that's not ladylike'."

"Well," Pieter picked up, "it's true she's not as smart as me because she married a lowly lorry driver, whereas I married an educated lady with a fancy title on her name. About the language, well, I could try to speak like a gentleman, but I'm not one, so that would be deceiving, wouldn't it? I have to be myself. Sheila will learn which words to censor and find a way of speaking that suits her. She has to be herself too," Pieter concluded.

He sounded kind of Shakespearean, with a Dutch accent of course. I wonder if he has a brother for my friend Sue.

Between editing and omitting big words, colloquial phrases, and other fanciful and foul language, ultimately, what this means for you and your partner is that you speak in a language that you both understand. For those of you reading between the lines, yes, it means finding a common denominator, and, well, no point in denying it, the *lowest* common denominator. It is a small compromise for household peace.

The language of love

In the bid for mutual understanding in a multilingual relationship, your native language tends to deteriorate somewhat, however it is an opportunity to learn or improve a second, or third or even fourth language. Having a personal in-house language coach is a fantastic opportunity to learn. My girlfriend Veronika, obviously not at all her real name, has more or less perfected three languages this way. Let's say she comes from a small Eastern European country. If she only spoke her native language, her choice of a future mate would be 'restrictive', she told me, and there was no chance for the globalisation of Veronika's love. To increase her global love capacity, so to speak, she had to learn new languages.

I must be deliberately vague here, but having learned a really posh-sounding Queen's English from Harry, and an animated and rapid Spanish from Miguel, both with Berlitz-like efficiency, it seems that her current beau, Jean Paul, French – a really difficult language to master – will remain on as her personal language coach and mate for some time to come. The verbs alone have taken her years.

Veronika, remember, *not* her real name, extolled the virtues of a personal language coach. "No course fees to pay or inconvenient lesson times. I *live* the language. We lounge in bed and... *communicate*," she relished.

Well, who can argue against this clearly inspirational pedagogic method?

Some would advise to choose a GloLo partner who speaks a broadly used language such as Spanish or Mandarin rather than, pardon me, a more *obscure* language. Austrian Barbara married Pavel from Prague.

"Yes," she started, "Czech Republic is right next door [to Austria], and I would like to be able to speak with Pavel's family, but where else will I speak Czech? No offence to Pavel, but the input-output of learning the language just does not seem worth it."

"Instead, we have eliminated the German and Czech languages," Pavel added. "My parents are taking an English course. It is better for everyone."

I spent an evening in a beer hall in Czech Republic once, and I admit that after saying *Na zdravia* a few too many times, my tongue sprained from the effort, I also reverted to speaking English.

We speak Jinglish

When any kind of bilingual fluency is achieved, GloLo couples become masters at creating their own language by mixing their native languages or their knowledge of a third language. Even in a monocultural partnership, having a special language is a positive bonding factor. A whole concept can be communicated in a word or two. It's like having a secret handshake which indicates that you belong to a special club.

Multicultural couples have a field day mixing language, vocabulary, and even grammar to communicate with each other. Our household is rife with germanified English and anglicised German. As I write this chapter, my daughter is just learning to walk. She has been talkative her whole life and now, according to my ESL husband, she is also 'walkative'. Walkative is a brilliant addition to the English language, isn't it, and I invite Merriam-Webster to pick it up right here.

So between learning a new language and creating a unique blend of Jinglish or Francish or Gerpanese, the multilingual couple deepen their own bond. A single word can bring a smile and reinforce the long and diverse history of the relationship. That is the power of the world of words, and a good thing too, as there are many more nettling communication issues ahead.

Communication

Remember that words represent just one part of the multilingual communication confusion. The second part of the story is how words and other non-verbal expressions are used to, as Veronika put it, communicate.

In their book *In Love But Worlds Apart*, Grete Shelling and Janet Fraser-Smith make a distinction between direct and indirect communication. *Direct* verbal communication includes the choice of words, the use of names and terms of endearment, flattery and compliments, and even how refusal and disagreements are expressed. *Indirect* communication includes the subtleties of, for example, the use of silence and pauses, and the not so subtle use of hand gestures, facial expressions, eye contact and volume of voice. These indirect communication signals are as much a part of the language as the words themselves. For all you gals out there who have been mistaken for a flirt, or even been asked, "how much?" just because you looked a man in the eye when he asked you what time it is, you know what this means.

The significance of indirect communication in the multicultural love story is described by Joel Crohn in his book *Mixed Matches*. GloLo couples will have "...difficulty separating the *content* of their differences about religion and cultural identity from the process of discussing them." Therefore, in addition to the heated debate about the logistical arrangements for the visiting in-laws, such as master bedroom or pull-out sofa in the den, and home-cooked meal or restaurant, for example, there is the additional complication of *how* you say 'pull-out sofa' and 'restaurant'. Let's take a closer look at the main issues in the globalisation of communication.

Tone and cadence

Every language has its own tone and cadence, so people simply sound different according to the language in use. Linguistically gifted people seem to have different personalities in different languages, and this can be confusing and even irritating for their partner. Danish Dorte and her New Zealand husband Peter met in a third country and speak English together, and Peter had always liked Dorte's 'soft, feminine voice'.

"Dorte has such a gentle way of expressing herself. It is very pleasant to hear her speak English with a Danish accent," explained Peter. "When we went to Denmark for the first time, however, I was shocked. When she speaks Danish, she sounds cold and hard. I don't know who she is – certainly not my lovely wife."

"Poor Peter," said Dorte, "he thinks I am angry and mean whenever I speak Danish, even with my grandmother, but I am just being me."

"Are you ever mean and angry?" Peter asked jokingly.

"When I am, you know it, because then I speak English," she grinned back.

Touché Dorte.

Peter is not the only GloLo husband who feels like he has two wives. My Austrian friend Christian is married to Paula from Brazil.

"In German, Paula sounds relaxed and easy-going, but in Portuguese," Christian explained, "she sounds like she is in panic, like the house is on fire. I find it confusing that she has two different tempos. It's like she has two personalities."

"Well," Paula explained in a relaxed but matter of fact tone, "I have one mother, three sisters and two aunties. If we don't speak quickly, we will be on the telephone all day long."

"But more time on the telephone is not possible," Christian exclaimed. "What do these girls talk about?"

"Learn Portuguese and then you will know," said Paula, very relaxed.

Sometimes the tone and cadence of the mother tongue transfers to the second language.

"He has reinvented Finnish," Minna, from Finland, said of her Italian husband Bruno. "He has taken a linear language and given it Mediterranean flair. I call it Fintalian. I hear it in the kids too. The 'A's and 'O's are everywhere, like an opera. It certainly creates a good mood."

As if on cue, Bruno continued, rapidly I should add, in English.

"Finnish is like Italian, no. It's true, A-oh and O-oh is often. No problem for me. I like Finns, Finnish, Finlando," he added, indeed with Mediterranean flair.

He really did create a good mood too.

Touchy feely

The meaning of physical contact, *particularly between men and women*, is culturally loaded. In so-called 'high involvement' countries like Greece and Brazil, a conversation is not a conversation without at least a hand reaching out to secure the line of communication. In other countries, this same gesture can lead to a public stoning followed by doing time in a no frills penitentiary. When 'touchy' cultures and 'non-touchy' cultures merge in the globalisation of love, the rules of communication are not so straightforward. While landing yourself in jail is more the exception than the rule, there are still many misunderstandings.

Italian Sylvia, from Pisa, went to Heidelberg, Germany as an exchange student, and it was not long before she met Torsten. At first, it was a cultural communication clash.

"The Germans have a reputation in Italy for not being warm," she started to tell me. "With Torsten, it was clear by his eyes that he liked me, but he never touched me, not even after the first date. You know, I had to kiss him first. I felt like a man!" she exclaimed, clearly still shocked by her own behaviour.

Torsten agreed.

"At the beginning, Sylvia was all over me, always touching me on the arm or leg. I felt a bit overwhelmed. She seemed very aggressive for a woman, like she wanted to own me."

"I explain to him," continued Sylvia, "in Italy we touch. That's how we connect. It's not sex or flirting. In Italy, everybody touches everybody," she added with a flourish, reaching for my hand.

Then there was jealousy.

"Sylvia is right, Italians touch everyone. Sylvia touches my friends, the postman, my *Oma*. Sometimes I was jealous when I saw her hand on my friend's arm. He was also thinking, 'hey, Torsten's girl is a flirt'."

"Yes," interjected Sylvia, "at first, many Germans thought I am flirting, but now we are all touching, connecting. Now I feel at home," she smiled, looking sweetly at Torsten.

We were captivated by her happy smile as she managed to hold both my hand and Torsten's. We probably would have stayed connected for a while had our waiter not stopped at the table to clear away the lunch plates.

"You know what I would love," Sylvia asked him, reaching out to put her hand on his forearm, "I would love an espresso."

I looked at Torsten who was grinning.

"I've gotten used to it," he shrugged. "She always gets the best service," he laughed.

Rachida and Gunter, university students in Berlin, fall at the other end of the touchy-feely spectrum. They are a Same Same couple, the new generation of multicultural romance in Germany. Rachida, whose family is from Turkey, was dressed to kill in 'Muslim chic'. In red patent stilettos, the skinniest of skinny jeans, and a full head scarf, she could pass for a cover girl on the Muslim edition of *Vogue*.

"Obviously," she started by flicking a hand, manicured with red nails, toward her head scarf, "I am Muslim. But that doesn't mean I only wear black," she said pointing to her shoes. "I was born in Germany and know the culture here. But I am still Muslim. Women are not to be touched, especially not in public," she said succinctly.

"It was confusing when we met," Gunter told me. "I knew she was Muslim and I knew the rules, but she is so hot looking. She's a German girl with Muslim values. I would just like to hold hands when we go out together," he added innocently.

"But," Rachida continued, "there are also German girls, Catholic girls, who are like me. We can be sexy and we are still in control. We have a lot of power," she added with pride.

He who laughs lasts... or is thought of as frivolous and disrespectful

What is funny about laughter is that some folks do not see it as a laughing matter. It can even be considered rude or arrogant. Both how you laugh and what you laugh about have strong cultural roots. Since humour is big and complex, there is an entire section about it toward the end of this chapter. Let us just look at laughing as a stand alone form of communication and ignore what you laugh about for the moment.

Laughing ranges from a delicate tee-hee-hee with your hand covering your mouth to a loud roaring ha-ha-ha with your mouth open and back molars fully exposed. It is tone and cadence on steroids.

For example, Canadians, and let's include Americans here to emphasise my point, are known for 1) having good teeth and perhaps therefore 2) laughing loud and exposing back molars. We laugh in a full body kind of way, and the more we laugh, well, the more we laugh, because laughing is funny too, right? Well, not for everyone.

Laughing, and here I include smiling, is a way of non-verbally communicating our intention and our mood to those around us. That in itself is fine. Where things can go wrong is that smiling and laughing mean different things to different people, just as the wagging tail of a dog means something rather different than the wagging tail of a cat.

I can say, again from painful personal experience, that the Canadian style big molar show laugh, obviously a *cultural norm* in Canada, is not so positively viewed elsewhere in the world. Rude, disrespectful, and attention-seeking are a few responses I have heard when I ha-ha-ha in public. Do not worry though, I just laughed it off. GloLo couples also have a funny thing about laughing together.

When Swedish Jan and Canadian Jill first met, Jill laughed. Jan did not.

"I thought it was funny," Jill told me, wearing a big smile just ready to burst into laughter. "Jan and Jill, I said to him, like Jack and Jill who went up the hill, we should get married."

Jill laughed again, head back of course, exposing beautiful dentistry, while telling me the story, and I had to laugh with her (remember, I am Canadian too). Jan sat rather stone-faced I must admit.

"I thought she was rude, laughing loudly, attracting attention," Jan explained, if not in a humoured way, at least a bit more relaxed.

"She wanted to marry me instantly, I could not believe it," he said, not at all flattered.

"No, I didn't want to marry you instantly," Jill, still bubbling with laughter, explained.

"I didn't even know your name. I just liked your tie," she continued teasingly.

It turned out that Jan is a bit of a sports celebrity in Sweden and therefore has had many women wanting to marry him instantly.

Despite Jill's joking way, she held up her hand and showed me, I must say, a very modest engagement ring.

"Now I want to marry you," she said, "because I know you and love you, not because you can kick a ball. I am your fiancé, not your fan."

I asked how it was that after a poor first impression, Jan changed his opinion and fell for Jill.

"We met at a formal sports event where I was to receive an award. Jill was a stand-in for a friend whose boyfriend fell ill and could not attend.

She was joking about her potential acceptance speech, thanking her dog and cat for helping her to become a sports legend. I realised that she didn't know who I was – she liked me as me, without the sports title. I had not experienced that in a long time. And okay, I admit it, she made me laugh," he succumbed with a broad, if not molar-exposing, smile.

Remember Emily and Ivan, the British-Czech couple where his accent was an issue? Laughter was not the best medicine for this couple either. This time, it was Ivan who was griping.

"Emily laughs at her own mistakes instead of apologising, like it is funny to make a mistake. We had six guests for dinner last week and she burned the meal. She came out of the kitchen giggling like a school girl. It was not appropriate. I felt ashamed," he said glumly.

"Well, silly, I'm British remember," Emily chided Ivan although her voice tinkled with laughter. "We are not always as serious as you continental Europeans. I cannot un-burn dinner, and I knew that the only thing to do was to enjoy the pizza delivery," she laughed again.

I have to admit that I was with Emily on this matter, however it was plain to see that Ivan was, in the Queen's English, *not amused*.

Crying

The other end of the emotive spectrum is crying. In some cultures, crying big shiny tears is perfectly okay. It is healthy and therapeutic, and it releases the negative energy from within, or something like that. In other cultures, crying, *particularly for men*, is shameful and weak. The quiver of the stiff upper lip is the start of the end of self-control. It reveals too much emotion and is not considered to be socially appropriate. Men are deemed 'unmanly' and women 'hysterical'.

Privately then, what happens when criers and non-criers fall in love? As with so many non-verbal communication issues, there can be misunderstanding and confusion amid the laughter and tears.

Canadian Ron taught English in Tokyo for eight years so it is no surprise that he came home with a Japanese wife. Despite his cultural immersion in Japan, he still struggled with Ikuko's display of emotion.

"Ikuko cries about literally everything," he told me while looking at Ikuko. "She cries if we have a disagreement, even a small one. She cries when she watches love stories on TV. She cries at the shoe store when the shoes she wants are not available in her size. It is hard to know when to take the tears seriously and when to just let her emote."

Since I do know the feeling when you cannot get the shoes you want, I asked Ikuko how she felt about crying.

"Ron make me cry more when we argue [sic]. I cry, and he stands still," she indicated with her arms crossed. "A man should help a crying woman, be a gentleman, show his love," she continued, sounding a bit like a guidebook.

"That's called emotional blackmail," said Ron, through slightly gritted teeth. "It's your responsibility to control your emotions, not mine," he finished.

"Ron also cries," Ikuko continued, sounding both sweet and condescending at the same time. "I dry his tears. One day he learn to dry my tears too [sic]."

Ron rolled his eyes and looked menacingly *at me*. I could not have orchestrated a better segue into the next topic for GloLo couples, that is dealing with disagreements.

International dispute settlement

Even the loveliest couple has the odd argument now and again. With the diverse cultural issues that we discuss in this book, and the tricky language problems covered in this chapter, a GloLo couple has ample opportunity to argue. "Never a dull moment between us," my husband likes to say. (To avoid a potential argument, I have chosen to interpret his statement in a *positive* light.)

How couples express disagreement or anger within the relationship is another PhD thesis on its own. For the sake of finishing this book within my own lifetime, I will try to condense the vast subject onto a few pages.

Given that a disagreement usually indicates a breakdown in communication in the first place, the GloLo couple has the added burden of choosing a language, finding the right words, understanding the weight of the words, translating the words, *pro-nun-ci-a-tion* and so on. A monocultural couple can usually understand what Tina Richardson describes in *Contemporary Issues in Multicultural Counseling* as "the emotions behind the words" and can therefore navigate a route back to peace whereas a multicultural couple have to "...learn new emotional patterns, syntax, the grammar of meaning."

The discussion about the dirty socks on the living room floor, then, is more than just about the dirty socks. It is also about the *syntax* of the dirty socks. Are you still with me?

When it comes to multicultural dispute settlement, the couples I interviewed could basically be divided into two conflict resolution camps, so to speak. One camp is very vocal and emotional during disputes. The focus on the conflict becomes intense. Voices are raised, the subject matter is broadened to include events and transgressions of the past decade, and a life together seems almost unbearable. Tears are optional. It is like a Greek tragedy that can be performed, and forgotten, within the space of ten minutes because nothing meaningful was said. The Greek tragedy can occur several times a day.

The other camp is quiet and more rational. The focus on the issue is also intense, but voices are kept low and the discussion is punctuated by long silences. The subject matter remains the subject matter and words are chosen carefully. A life together seems negotiable as long as both parties are willing to compromise. Tears are not an option. It is performed like a 1920s silent film in black and white. It is also performed, and forgotten, within ten minutes as not much was said anyway.

The combination of the Greek tragedy style of conflict resolution combined with the 1920s silent black and white film can exist in a monocultural relationship as well. In a monocultural context, it is about personality. In a multicultural context, it is personality *plus* culture. Both partners think that their way of discussing/debating/arguing is normal. Once again, it is not just the conflict that needs to be resolved, it is *how* the conflict will be resolved, and neither style is inherently right or wrong.

Let's take a look at a few examples of the Greek tragedy – silent film cultural conflict resolution clash.

The pasta incident

Early in Minna and Bruno's Finnish–Italian relationship, they experienced their first cultural clash conflict in the kitchen. It led to a relationship meltdown which surprised them both because all they were trying to do was cook dinner.

"We were cooking together in the kitchen," Minna began, "and I poured cold water over the cooked pasta, apparently a sin in Italy.

There was this explosion from Bruno, like I was butchering kittens. He was yelling and his arms were waving in the air like a mad man. I was shocked. It was best just to leave the kitchen."

"Yes, can you believe it?" Bruno asked me, astonished. "She ruin the pasta and she walk away from me and no talk to me [sic]. I am so insulted. Little problem for me and for her, the end," he added dramatically, his finger sliced at his throat.

"It seemed like a very big problem to you," Minna defended herself. "So much emotion, *over pasta*, and very disrespectful toward me. It felt like an attack."

When I asked how they resolved the problem, Bruno jumped in.

"Luckily I have a friend, also with a Finnish beauty," he said, the charm back on. "I call him and he explain my mistake. He tell me, 'You are in Finland, be Finnish now'. So I go to Minna and apologise. She ruin pasta and I apologise [sic]," he added with a small laugh and a shrug.

"Since the pasta incident, Bruno does most of the cooking," Minna added, also laughing.

Intercultural communications expert Michael Gates, who is Group Managing Director at Richard Lewis Communications, explained what happened in Minna's kitchen.

"In both love and business transactions, there can be large differences in the degree of emotion or logic people feel when they disagree. What is rational to one culture can be highly irrational to another," explained Mr Gates. "And hanging on to words literally, even when both parties speak the same language, can be dangerous. The gap between what is said and what is understood is often significant, and can lead to misunderstandings that are deal breaking. For instance, an Englishman could say about his American wife's new dress 'I've seen worse'. Americans tend to take this comment negatively, focusing on the word 'worse'. In fact, this is extremely high praise in British English. A rough translation into US English would be 'awesome' or 'phenomenal'. It is all about understatement for the Brits."

So we see that one word, even if unintentional, can add fuel to the fire. Irish Liz was angry with her German boyfriend, Klaus, who had ruined a carpet they bought together in Morocco by leaving it out in the rain, even though Liz had asked him, three times apparently, to bring it indoors before the storm started.

"All I wanted was an apology and to move on," Liz stated. "I'm sorry, how difficult can that be?" she asked, clearly still bristling at the memory.

"Klaus did say 'excuse me, please' several times. He wanted forgiveness and he had not even said sorry!" she blurted out, slightly enraged.

Klaus, obviously the peacekeeper in this household, explained.

"In German, we say '*entschuldigen*' which can mean sorry and excuse me altogether." He sighed. "We are learning."

Literally lost in translation

Lydia, from the US, married to Ton from Holland, said that her language barrier actually helps her to keep the peace at home.

"An argument in Dutch is an excellent tension buster," she confided. "I cannot just blurt out those nasty things I am thinking. I have to translate my words carefully. It tempers my temper, and probably leads to fewer regrets. My anger literally gets lost in translation."

"She does seem feistier in English," Ton admitted, "so I prefer the Dutch-speaking opponent."

Lydia growled something in Dutch and they both laughed.

"Okay," Ton continued, "she is right in any language."

Many couples mentioned switching languages, frequently, during heated discussions. Dorte shared her story.

"Before I blow up in response to something Peter said, I ask him to repeat the sentence in the other language. Then I recognise if he really intended to use the words the way he did. If he says something in Danish, it sounds so cute that I forgive him immediately."

I cannot say this with 100 per cent accuracy, but I am pretty sure at this point that I saw Peter wink.

It is therefore good to have at least a basic knowledge of your partner's mother tongue. It furthers understanding of how they use the language in which you are speaking. Some multilingual GloLo couples recommend taking a time-out for a short language lesson. There is a lot of 'when you say this, do you really mean that?' style of questioning and consulting with dictionaries.

Ukrainian Svetlana and American Bob have not yet concluded a single argument.

"By the time we have sorted out what Svetlana really wants to say, we have forgotten the original source of the problem," he said, shaking his head and laughing.

Svetlana, probably the one to have the last word in any language, took over.

"Original problem is no problem. Always peace," she concluded, holding up two fingers in the 1960s hand signal for peace.

By helping each other and working together on the language and the cultural framework behind the language, the couple reconnects and the big issue of discussion is usually minimised or even forgotten. World peace reigns.

Here is another perspective on the lingual consequences for comedians, clowns and comics.

Three facets of humour

Once again, I must risk a bit of academic indulgence in this section. I have chosen three ways to think about humour; maintaining a sense of humour, understanding humour, and then of course expressing humour. All joking aside, there are funny and infuriating aspects to each application.

1. Maintaining humour

First, and probably most important in the multicultural and multilingual context, is maintaining a sense of humour. Unless you are Keanu Reeves starring in the film *The Matrix*, where it was possible to upload a language or skill such as Kung Fu the same way that a software programme can be uploaded onto a computer, the learning curve on language is long and steep and mistakes will be made.

Yulia, from Russia, recalls her early days in Vienna when she met Austrian Patrick.

"I had a basic knowledge of English, learned primarily by audiotapes sent from London. Sometimes I wanted to tell him things but I did not have words or phrases. I was near to crying," she explained.

Patrick managed to see the humour in it.

"Yulia had basic phrases that she used in all situations, whether or not they were appropriate. Her favourite was, 'it is rather marvellous, isn't it?' She said this about *everything* – food, people, the weather. I loved it that she thought so many things are rather marvellous," he laughed.

"Now I can say that something is spicy, or tasty, or interesting," Yulia, clearly proud of the progress she has made in the meantime, continued. "Not everything is marvellous," she smiled.

"Am I still rather marvellous though?" Patrick turned to asked her.

"Yes, he is rather marvellous, no?" Yulia laughed.

I thought they were both rather marvellous actually.

2. Understanding humour

The second challenge to the intercultural sense of humour is in understanding it. Dealing with humour is symptomatic of any international intercultural experience. The difference between this funny challenge while on vacation or even at work compared to having a multicultural relationship is *exposure*. Not to frighten off anyone new to a GloLo love affair, but this is an issue that does not go away.

Humour is highly culturally specific, so what the locals find uproarious may seem banal or even irritating to the foreign partner. A clown stepping into a can of paint and knocking over a ladder can be perceived as slapstick funny, or just an accident that could lead to personal injury. Tossing a cream pie in the face of a two-timing boyfriend can be perceived as vindictive humour, or a shameful lack of self-control and a waste of good food.

Additionally, there are all of those cultural and historical references, well known, understood and hilarious to the locals but without context and meaning to the foreign partner.

Also, humorous speech and conversation often speeds up the natural tempo, so what you are hearing is a machine gun version of the language. Added to that, the use of irony, a play on words, the deadly double entendre, modern slang and colloquialisms result in the non-native speaker struggling just to keep up.

It can be, and I speak from experience here, intensely isolating, like, 'what's so funny?' Ultimately, it can feel like a language landslide and it can be discouraging, and ironically perhaps, it takes the fun out of learning the language. With time, you can learn to appreciate other types of humour, or at least roll your eyes less, but we never really get it.

Sun, from South Korea, has been in Canada for more than 25 years, since she was a teenager, and therefore knows that collecting comic books is a common part of boyhood that can continue into adulthood.

"When we met, I knew that Rob liked comics. His apartment was overflowing with colourful books. No problem, I thought, a funny guy. But some of the pictures are graphic images of war, airplanes dropping bombs on villages, killing people, and the pilots are laughing. When I first saw these images, I did not understand. Why are they laughing when they are killing innocent people? My people," she added, sounding perplexed.

"I have collected comic books since I was a boy," explained Rob, who is warm and clearly devoted to his wife. "I never thought about the meaning or symbolism of the drawings until I met Sun. To her, these supposedly funny comics are worse than pornography. They are an offence to her heritage. I have changed my collection and only buy fictitious action figures."

"I still think it is silly for a grown man to collect comics," Sun said, "but I guess Rob thinks my Hello Kitty handbag is also childish. We have different tastes."

Rob smiled and rolled his eyes in mock exasperation.

I must admit though, I quite liked Sun's Hello Kitty handbag too.

3. Expressing humour

Then we have the third challenge, which is expressing your sense of humour and being funny in another language. I can almost hear readers screaming in alarm, "Don't Go There". No one I interviewed for this book was willing to share their story of failing to be funny. One friend said, "It was bad enough when it happened, I'd rather not have the reminder printed in black and white and bound in hard cover." Hence, I will have to tell my own cringe-inducing experience as an example.

A few friends were visiting from Canada and I thought it would be great to throw a small party to give the tourists a chance to mix and mingle with real live Austrians. In addition to a lovely selection of Austrian and Canadian wines and cheeses, red and white Canadian flags and red and white Austrian flags decorated the flat.

In my utter dedication to creating an Austro-Canadian cultural evening, I also prepared a 'cultural guide' for each respective nationality. It was meant to be a tongue-in-cheek, or 'funny' for you non-native speakers out there, list of 'Do's and Don'ts' such as, "Do ask a Canadian for a good pancake recipe" and "Don't ask if they live in an igloo". All harmless good fun, right?

After liberal wine tasting, which some of you might recognise as the problem already, the camaraderie amongst the guests was tangible and I suspected a couple of GloLo romances were developing right there in my own living room. In my enthusiasm for the globalisation of love, I took it upon myself to guide the flourishing romances and read aloud the cultural guides I had written for my guests. The Canadians laughed cheerfully at references to themselves as funny Canucks with their passion for hockey and having sex in a canoe. With the success of the Canadian list, I continued to read the cultural guide for dealing with real live Austrians.

Inevitably, the 'Do' list made reference to skiing, ski legends, ski resorts, skis, ski boots and ski poles. I encouraged questions such as, "Do ask an Austrian about the latest ski boot warming technology" and, for diversity, I threw in questions on where to get a *The Sound of Music* DVD. Everyone laughed good-heartedly.

It was only at the 'Don't' list where I sort of, um, ceased to be culturally sensitive, shall we say. "Don't ask an Austrian if there are kangaroos in Austria" was a crowd pleaser, but then, darn, I did a kind of parody of an early 1940s military march and one-armed salutary greeting. It was supposed to be a crafty John-Cleese-Fawlty-Towers-don't-mention-the-war kind of humour. Everyone laughed at that scene, didn't they? Um, no, many did not.

The Austrians in the room fell silent and looked confused. The Canadians cringed, presumably on my behalf. The globalisation of love *evaporated*, and I think the music even screeched to a halt. My not-yet-husband gave me a look that indicated that the marriage was *off* and my immediate deportation from Austria was imminent. Guests were heading for the door like herd animals where my now-ex-boyfriend, desperate to avoid an international incident, tried to divert them with more wine, *Austrian* wine of course. It took *several* more toasts to world peace to get the Austrian and Canadian party guests mixing and mingling once again and we were well in to the last dregs of the Canadian wine before the bonhomie resumed (and the marriage was back on the agenda).

Yes, my humour was crass and, in retrospect, I was standing on Austrian soil, where mention of the, um, *war*, is awkward. Obviously Austria has a different historical perspective than Canada, but here is the really funny part, no pun intended. I thought that my cultural *faux pas* was because 'we' won the war and 'they' lost and it was insensitive to mention 'their' defeat. Wrong again. My culturally tolerant, fortunately forgiving then-ex-boyfriend-now-luckily-husband explained, "It does not matter who won or lost. It was a war and a travesty against mankind. It is our job to ensure that nothing like it ever happens again. We should not make jokes about it because the subject matter is not funny." Now I get it.

It just goes to show how perilous world peace is and how all it takes to start a diplomatic breakdown is a few funny lines gone wrong.

Sometimes if we do not laugh, we will cry, or perhaps worse, become bitter and allow those frightful frown lines to set in. Humour is a challenging element to deal with because it is culturally and linguistically loaded. Hence it is a big deal for anyone who is new to the culture and new to the language, and some days there is just nothing funny about it.

The loss of the comedian in you is not the only personality change you may experience in a multilingual relationship.

The Einstein within

Losing the ability to be funny can be demoralising but losing the ability to express your intellect can be downright depressing. With a limited vocabulary, sweet-sounding or Neanderthal-like accent, and primary school grammar, it is asking a lot for native speakers to see or hear beyond your butchered version of their language and recognise your inner Einstein. Not everyone wants to discuss Kierkegaard on a daily basis, but the ability to thoroughly debate a point is an essential relationship component, even if it is to discuss the upcoming visit of the in-laws.

Remember American Bob and Ukrainian Svetlana who have never finished an argument? Bob is a cancer researcher. Svetlana has a PhD in biology. Her poor English vocabulary and omission of articles such as 'the' and 'an' in her speech gave Bob the feeling that rather than courting a highly intelligent research scholar, he was 'dating a pre-schooler'.

"I have read translated papers in academic journals written by Svetlana so I know what she has in there," he explained pointing to his head. "She is brilliant and well-respected in her field of research, but with me, she sounds like a petulant little girl. It is a real barrier sometimes."

"Why does Bob not learn Russian, Ukrainian, German?" Svetlana charged back at him, while looking at me. "For me, no problem. Then we see who sounds like little girl."

I have to admit Bob, she does have a valid point.

Having a different personality depending on which language is being spoken leads to what some refer to as 'cultural schizophrenia'. This can be distressing because it leads to having a new role in the inter-personal dynamic. A dominant 'Type A' personality is transformed into a shy, quiet wallflower. A chatty Cathy is near silenced into monosyllabic expressions.

"It's like being underwater and having those simple hand signals to communicate while diving," explained Australian Robyn. "Danger is just generic danger, or 'look at the magnificent scaling of the fish' is simplified to 'look'. I feel like I've had a frontal lobotomy when I speak French. I just can't think anymore," she confessed.

Robyn's frontal lobotomy feeling is not atypical of anyone learning a new language, particularly when you are immersed in the country of the new language.

Three steps ahead

Another dimension to the language issue within the GloLo relationship is what happens when one partner is on home turf and the other partner is just learning the local language. Every day activities such as banking or taking the kids to the doctor for their annual vaccination, where the language needs to be understood perfectly, fall into the domain of the more fluent partner. Issues of dependency creep in. While this linguistic domesticity can leave a woman feeling relegated to the role of a 1950s housewife, a man's ego can suffer when he has to learn to accept dependency on his wife's language skills.

Danish Dorte expressed her amusement when Peter, from New Zealand, asked her to check a written business offer he was considering.

"Peter understood the basic points of the contract, like the starting date," she laughed, "but the terms and conditions were beyond him. I have become his translator, his lawyer, his accountant, and that's a lot of things to get right when I have no training. I write children's books!"

"I married a smart woman," added Peter, "even when we speak English together, although it is my native language, she is always one step ahead of me. In Danish, however, she is three steps ahead of me. Language has emasculated me." He sighed dejectedly.

Dorte laughed and jokingly punched him on the arm.

"I'm just good with languages," she admonished. "You are always better than I am at math."

Good wife, Dorte.

Let's also be frank about learning the language, because there seems to be a conspiracy out there concerning the truth of this matter. Let it be known that I am a full advocate of becoming as fluent as possible as fast as possible, wherever you are in the world. But even if it takes only a short time to learn some basic *survival* vocabulary and grammar, such as "Do you have these shoes in a size 8?", it will take years, and possibly even *years and years*, to become proficient to a level that you can negotiate a business contract and present yourself in court if need be (who knows?). In the meantime, "honey, can you just take a quick look at this," is a phrase that will be heard often.

Hence language has an often significant influence on the dynamic between the GloLo couple, determining their roles both within the family and externally. Peter explained this point beautifully.

"My son thinks that banking and contracts is 'women's work'," said Peter. "He said to me once, 'Dad, Mom is doing the boring stuff so we can play football.' I guess right next to the loss of control is an attractive grey zone of freedom."

To summarise the issues on language then, and this just loosely, the typical GloLo couple will converse together in primary school level language that excludes big words and colloquial phrases, and say words that they do not mean with an accent that can charm or annoy their partner, and the things they say will be void of humour, intellect, and any cultural references, in a mix of their mother tongues and random third languages, ultimately making them feel the effect of, or sometimes desirous of, a frontal lobotomy. Kissing, remember, needs no translation.

♥

Top 10 clues that you have a GloLo multilingual marriage

1. You can hardly wait for this book to be translated into _______ (insert name of exotic language of your spouse here) so that he or she can read it too.
2. You think your spouse sounds really sexy when he or she speaks your native language.
3. Your spouse thinks you sound like a pre-schooler when you speak his or her native language.
4. A visit with your in-laws requires professional translators and has as much spontaneity, fun and flair as an EU meeting of ministers.
5. You watch TV 'together' wearing headsets; you watch your TV in your language and your spouse watches his TV in his language.
6. You realised that when GloLo Junior said the 'F-word' for the first time, you could not blame your spouse.
7. The household computer requires two keyboards – one in your language and the other one covered in hieroglyphics.
8. Your name is Stephen and your spouse calls you Stefan, your name is Mary and your spouse calls you Maria.
9. You think a rooster says 'Cock-a-doodle-doo' and your spouse thinks a rooster says 'Kikeriki'.
10. You think *Grey's Anatomy* sounds better in original version; your spouse thinks the dubbed version gives the actors 'more character'.

Some More Cultural Stuff

There are a lot of things that make up 'culture', aren't there? Each of the chapters in *Part II – Big Hairy Audacious GloLo Issues* dealt with an important aspect of culture. Religion is cultural. Race is cultural (sometimes). Language is *very cultural*. These are the cultural things that are *obvious* in a GloLo relationship. You know almost immediately upon meeting someone that there are ethnic differences. You see it or hear it or learn about it quickly by asking a few questions. Before we end *Big Hairy Audacious GloLo Issues* however, it is well worthwhile to discuss some of the not-so-obvious things that make up culture. I am speaking here about the cultural stuff that is not easy to spot and that you may only begin to discover once you are smack dab in the middle of a GloLo relationship.

Throughout the interviews I conducted for this book, there were a few consistent cultural themes that couples repeatedly mentioned as 'tricky', 'irksome' and 'difficult to nail down'. Some of these topics have already come up in previous chapters and anecdotes from GloLo couples, but they are important enough and complex enough that they deserve closer attention and analysis. It is just a list of cultural stuff actually, so I doubt that Harvard will name a building after me, but if you are a GloLo spouse, or thinking about becoming one, this list of GloLo cultural stuff is for you!

Cultural stuff that is important in a GloLo relationship:

- Some stuff about marriage
- Family stuff

- GloLo sex
- Stuff about friends
- Gender issues

Some stuff about marriage

Marriage is cultural. I do not mean the wedding, which you read about in *Chapter 5 – The Wedding*, although that is very cultural too. I mean the marriage itself, you know, the *institution*. Once again, I sound all prudish by referring to the institution of marriage as if it is the holy grail of relationships. Of course, you could also have a highly committed and lifelong relationship without the institution of marriage, but GloLo couples do tend to get married quickly remember, so it is more that I am speaking *within the GloLo context*. Anyway, let's look at this institution called marriage and see what it means for a GloLo couple.

'Smug marrieds'

Marriage does not get its lofty reputation as an institution from nowhere. Let's face it, marriage is a lifelong framework by which most of us live our lives. Children engage in marriage role play from a young age, don't they? The 'bride' wears a tea towel as a veil and practises walking down the aisle while the 'groom' learns that just because he is wearing the pants, it does not mean that he will 'wear the pants' in the relationship. Teenage girls and even some boys dream about marriage, and a 'big white wedding' or cultural equivalent, particularly if said marriage is to include a pop star or teen idol (my dream wedding included John Travolta). Couples in their mid-twenties, fresh out of college and totally broke, will spend the price of a small car celebrating marriage. If the couple marries in their 30s or 40s, then they spend the price of a large luxury car. Once married, couples become 'smug marrieds' (borrowed from Helen Fieldings' brilliant novel *Bridget Jones's Diary*, in case you are not a fan of contemporary literature) and socialise primarily with other 'smug marrieds', taking occasional pity on 'singletons' by including them in random social events where another 'singleton', desperate of course, might be present (another astute sociological observation in *Bridget Jones*). Anyway, once 'smug marrieds' realise that there is nothing in marriage to be smug about, they 'work on it' and if things go wrong in the marriage, they try to 'save it'. They read books about it, talk about it on *Oprah* and the really successful ones celebrate *silver* and *golden* anniversaries. Long married couples are held in high social regard as the hallmark of decency and good citizenship. They become 'role models' and their car insurance premium goes down. With a few exceptions out there (George Clooney, this means you), marriage is culturally desirable. It's very 'in'.

Yet being 'in' does not mean being easy. Even monocultural couples can find the rigours of marriage a bit over or underwhelming at times. What bolsters the challenge for a GloLo relationship is a that things that 'go without saying', things that are 'self-evident' and things that 'need no explanation' in a monocultural marriage actually do not go without saying, are not at all self-evident and need significant explanation in a GloLo marriage.

To simplify this complex phenomenon we call marriage, let's look at it from three different perspectives:

- Lovey-dovey marriage
- Family empires and kingdoms (including GloLo pets!)
- GloLo sex

Lovey-dovey marriage

Firstly, marriage is an *emotional bond* between two people. This is the lovely part of marriage. In Western culture, it starts with the lovey-dovey beginning when you just adore each other and delight in everything about each other, plus you think that your partner is soooooo good looking (it is amazing that he or she is still single!) and you want to be together as much as possible and even round the clock if possible. During the falling in love phase, you become *connected* in a way that you are not connected with anyone else in the world. Over time, the emotional bond changes and matures. Maybe not *everything* your partner does is delightful, you do see each other first thing in the morning after all, but you still have an intimate appreciation of one another.

The emotional bond between a married couple obviously depends on the two individuals involved. Despite the high individuality of emotions, however, culture will likely determine the *expectations* a couple has of one another within the framework of marriage. In many cultures, the husband and wife are like 'best friends forever' in the third grade. They share everything and their loyalty to each other overrides and overrules any other emotional relationship. Other cultures approach marriage more pragmatically. Couples are like good business partners where everyone has a given role or function within the relationship but the emotional connection is less 'lovey-dovey'. Both scenarios can constitute a good marriage. It just depends on the expectations of each partner.

German Claudia and Indian Arvind had different expectations of their lovey-dovey emotional bond.

"It was like a one-way street," explained Claudia, sounding slightly frustrated already. "Arvind is my emotional base camp. I share everything with him. Of course I do, he's my husband, we should not have secrets," she concluded.

"Wait, wait," Arvind said calmly. "It's not about secrets and sharing or not sharing. As a husband, my role is to take care of my wife. If I have a problem, I can talk to my mother about it. That's what mothers are for," he said, as if he was stating the obvious.

"That's exactly the problem," Claudia took over abruptly. "He tells his mother everything. It's not natural."

It was a problem for Claudia that Arvind had a close relationship to his mother because she expected his primary emotional relationship to be with his wife. However, from Arvind's cultural perspective, the relationship he had with his mother was actually to Claudia's benefit.

"I need to be strong for my wife," he explained. "I should not burden her with my problems. I can talk to my mother or my family about these things. When I am at home, I need to take care of her," he said with sincerity and pride.

So even if Arvind's commitment to Claudia was high and his intentions quite pure, he still failed somewhat to meet Claudia's expectations of the emotional connection in marriage. It leads to a second cultural aspect of marriage, which is, music please, *romantic love*.

I will die for you… if my family approves

Romeo and Juliet I-will-die-for-you style love is idealised in Hollywood movies and supported by romance literature and yes, even social critiques like *Bridget Jones*. Yet the idea that romantic love leads to marriage and 'happily ever after' is culturally specific. It is not even a valid reason for marriage in some cultures. Further, it is not infrequent that a GloLo boyfriend or girlfriend gets dumped, despite or even *amidst* protestations of undying love, for a more 'appropriate' monocultural partner. Sometimes a love story is just a pleasant detour along the way toward marriage to a family-approved partner.

Claudia and Arvind were both encouraged to 'be rational' when their GloLo relationship blossomed into a marriage proposal.

"My parents only objected to my relationship with Claudia when they saw that I wanted to marry her," explained Arvind. "My father said, 'Love is nice, but not practical. It is time to find a proper wife.' That I love Claudia did not necessarily qualify her to be a proper wife."

"His parents were very concerned about who would take care of them in their old age," Claudia said. "Since I am a medical doctor, Arvind could present a convincing argument for my skill set as a daughter-in-law," she joked a bit, and relaxed as the topic shifted. "They were still worried that our love would not last and that it would somehow undermine the marriage. My parents thought I was having an 'India phase' that would eventually fade out and his parents thought we were fools in love."

In their case, Arvind's parents also believed that Arvind's choice of wife was a *family* decision rather than a *personal* decision.

"I had to stand up to my family," Arvind continued, "surely that must be considered romantic. I broke the mould by choosing my own wife and bringing her into the family, and in the end, I did it with their approval. The negotiation took months," he sighed in post-negotiation exhaustion.

That brings us neatly to the second aspect of marriage which is the union between families. For those of you who think along the lines of, 'I married the man, not his family', I have a news flash for you: OH, YES YOU DID!

Family empires and kingdoms

Marriage unites two families, doesn't it? Historically, empires and kingdoms were built and maintained through strategic marriages between ruling families. Aristocrats and royalty were the original GloLos remember, however the rise of social democracy, and probably too much inbreeding, has tempered this trend. Marrying a 'commoner', and a foreigner at that, is practically *de rigueur* these days for any crown prince, but that is another book altogether. In any case, even without grandiose ambitions of ruling the world, a marriage still unites the respective families of the bride and groom. But what does 'family' really mean?

Perhaps appropriately, there are several definitions of family in the dictionary such as 'a basic unit in society traditionally consisting of two parents rearing their children' or 'a group of individuals living under one roof'. But probably the easiest way to look at the family issue within the GloLo context is to consider the fundamental difference between 'individualistic' and 'collectivist' societies. Individualistic societies emphasise personal happiness and satisfaction of the individual whereas in collectivist societies, personal satisfaction derives from the well-being of the family. In the first case, the family is very focused on the so-called 'nuclear' family members – the two people in the marriage plus their offspring. Once the offspring grow up and marry, they create their own 'nuclear family'. By contrast, in collectivist societies, the family includes the so-called 'extended' members from outside the nucleus. A collectivist family includes the two people in the marriage and the offspring, the brothers and sisters of the married couple, plus their parents and *their* siblings and possibly cousins, aunts and uncles, grandparents, and so on. When a GloLo couple bring together these two spectrums of family, it can be a bit crowded for those sitting on the bride's side.

Sitting on the bride's side

Angel is Mexican-American, from Texas, and Edward is, in his own words, 'very British'. They are an unlikely pair in many ways. Edward works for an oil company and Angel works for a non-governmental organisation which campaigns for wildlife protection from oil companies, but that is another story. Another difference between them is their family orientation.

"Before Angel would go on a proper date with me, she insisted that I meet her family," Edward began in his Englishman-in-Texas accent. "As a proper English gent, I had no problem meeting her parents. It struck me as a good idea."

At this point, Angel began giggling so I posed my pen for a good story. Edward continued.

"I drove up to her parents' house but could not park nearby. I thought there must be some kind of neighbourhood festival going on," he said dryly. "The cars were parked along the entire block. Even before I entered the house, I heard a terrible raucous going on. I assumed there was trouble inside. Then Angel's brother or cousin or uncle or some such came bursting out the front door. He grabbed me in a crushing bear hug. I thought I was being robbed until he called me *Eduardo*."

Angel could contain herself no longer and continued the story.

"My mother has seven brothers and sisters, all married, all with three or four children. My father has nine brothers and sisters. The family is kind of big, you know," she said, holding her arms wide. "We meet every week. Not everyone of course, but as many as possible. It's kind of loud sometimes. We all like to talk."

Edward leaned slightly forward in his chair to tell me more.

"When we got married, my mother, my brother and my brother's wife came to Texas," he said while counting them on his fingers. "Angel's family asked, 'Where is Eduardo's family? Why didn't they come to the wedding?' But they did come. All of them," he finished, his posh accent disguising his humour.

"The side of the church where my family sat was filling up," Angel continued, "and there were just the three from England sitting on the other side. No one from my family wanted to move over. They thought a bus or plane load of people would come at any minute. I thought the church was going to tip over, everyone was sitting on the bride's side."

Brown nosing

Through a GloLo marriage, you become intimately connected with a family you often know very little about and you may not even speak the same language. On one level then, the family behind the man or woman you marry is an unknown variable, let's say. On another level, there will be cultural expectations of how the families, now connected through marriage, should be united. Arvind told me his story of family union.

"When we married, I made certain assumptions about how our families would work out together. Despite the cultural differences, I thought that we would still follow the 'Indian model'. For example, I took time and effort to get to know Claudia's mother because that is the Indian way. She becomes my mother. At the beginning, she was sceptical and thought I was brown nosing and just looking to have someone sew a button on my shirt. But now she's really taken to me and we spend time together, even without other family members. It's not very German. The neighbours probably think we are having an affair."

I asked Claudia if she followed the 'Indian model' by becoming close to Arvind's mother.

"A good Indian daughter-in-law should be close to her husband's mother, but it doesn't work for me. I already have a mother," Claudia explained pragmatically. "In Germany, mothers-in-law are treated with respect, but not as a friend or second mother. There is even some competition between the mother and daughter-in-law to take care of the married son, particularly who can best cook his favourite food. In our case, long distance also makes it difficult to build a relationship. It's not something you can do over the telephone."

I could not resist the temptation to ask Arvind who best cooked his favourite food.

"Ah," he answered quickly, "this is where it is good to have a multicultural marriage. My mother cooks the best Indian food and Claudia cooks my favourite German food and I am a happy man."

There was a strained silence before Arvind continued.

"Claudia is also very good at cooking Indian food," he said with a wide Stepford-wife smile, "as good as my mother in fact."

Yet there was another family story that also challenged the German-Indian couple.

'Brother cousin'

"As the eldest son," Arvind began the new story, "it is expected that I help my siblings."

"It sounds nice," Claudia interrupted, with little conviction. "Germans help their siblings too, but it's different. It's not at the expense of the married couple."

It seemed that there was a multicultural skeleton in their closet and I was reluctant to open the door when Arvind proceeded.

"It was my brother Gabe who came to stay with us for a while. He was at the engineering university and I agreed to help him get adjusted in Germany. He is my brother and that's what Indian families do."

"What you need to understand," Claudia said to me through slightly gritted teeth, "is that Gabe is not Arvind's brother, he is his cousin. He didn't *stay* with us for a while, he *lived* with us for 16 months. Every night I came home from work and the whole flat smelled of curry."

Arvind cringed at Claudia's outburst but immediately regained his humour.

"In India, a cousin is a brother, a 'brother cousin'. Family lines are not so well defined. We helped Gabe to get himself established in Germany. He's a great guy. He was just trying to help us by cooking dinner every evening. But that was the end of Claudia's 'India phase' that her father had predicted," he laughed and looked at her for approval. "Gabe finally moved out and we ate *Bratwurst* and *Sauerkraut* every night for a month," he said, referring to German hotdogs.

"Tofu Bratwurst?" I asked, assuming that Arvind is vegetarian.

"No," he chuckled. "Claudia was reclaiming our kitchen for Deutschland."

GloLo pets

I wanted to include house pets in the chapter on GloLo children but my editor said I sounded like a *certified* Crazy Cat Lady (italics and upper case hers). Well, as a *proud* Crazy Cat Lady, I think 'family' is an appropriate place to discuss the GloLo relationship to the animal kingdom.

Pets created the very first GloLo families when you think about it. Dogs, cats, hamsters, birds, bunnies and all other 'domesticated' animals that live together with humans speak a different language, have a different value system, eat different foods and have different table manners. It is all about 'culture' really.

I try to explain this to my cat when she brings home yet another decapitated mouse which she proudly places on my bedroom pillow.

"Thank you for thinking of me," I say while trying to remain calm and remove the headless rodent from my 1200 thread count Egyptian cotton bed sheets. "Please take no offence. I don't eat mice and in my culture, bloody dead animals, particularly when still warm, are not aesthetically pleasing. It's a cultural thing."

She looks at me in that funny wordless way that communicates her thoughts. 'A lovely fresh field mouse, *still warm*, and she tosses it in the bin? How rude. What a weird culture,' and she slinks off insulted.

Man's best friend

The point of this section is that my cat is not the only one who thinks my culture is weird. The very concept of house pets is culturally specific. Even though cats and dogs have long accompanied man through history, it has not been a universal love for 'man's best friend'. In *Swaying*, Le Layslip writes, "In Vietnam, a dog was a guardian first, then a pet, and sometimes dinner." A dog, according to her cultural value system, should feed itself by foraging for leftovers and not expect to be catered to at the family's expense. Layslip explains the 'cultural meaning' of a dog and how ridiculous the love of pets, dogs in particular, seems through her cultural lens. She writes that the soul of a dog is actually considered "a transient spirit (usually a greedy person who had to earn a new human body by suffering a dog's life – most of it guarding someone else's wealth…". It does seem to mock the efforts many of us take to keep our furry friends happy, from the tins of organic cat food to doggie massages and Burberry rain coats.

When Kim Swan, also from Vietnam, met Bradley and his 'dirty dog' Ben, she was disgusted to learn that Ben slept in Bradley's bedroom.

"He was not allowed in the bed," Bradley said a bit defensively, "we are two guys after all. But he always slept near the door, like a guardian. It was very reassuring," he smiled wistfully.

Kim Swan could not understand how Bradley, who appeared clean and orderly in a white baseball jersey (no stains or spots), would allow a 'hairy beast' into his home. It was a difficult message to understand because Bradley had always had a dog as a pet.

"I grew up with dogs and cats," Bradley said, "and they were always considered family members. They even came on vacation with us. We could not leave them at home alone."

However, seeing that the situation was heading toward a 'me or the dog' type ultimatum, and under the guise of a change in working hours and less opportunity to properly care for and exercise Ben, Bradley gave the dog to his mother who has a big house and garden in the suburbs.

"I did try everything," Bradley said, perhaps recognising that I was on Ben's side, "and I mean everything. I bought Ben dog shoes. I thought if he wore shoes outdoors and we took them off before he came in the house, Kim Swan would not complain about dirt."

"It's crazy, isn't it?" Kim Swan asked critically, looking at me. "Children go hungry, children go barefoot and he buys his dog shoes? What next? A rain coat?"

I did my very best I-am-a-professional 'mm-hmm' and forced myself to nod my head in neutral understanding, all the while wondering if I could get shoes for my cat. Just for rainy days of course.

When Kim Swan was out of earshot, I asked Bradley if he missed the dog. He blushed immediately.

"I used to visit my mother once every week or two, now I go twice a week. Who do you think I am really visiting?" he asked, arching an eyebrow.

His answer begged a second question: did Kim Swan notice his continued devotion to his dog?

"She places a high value on family relations. She thinks I am being a good son by visiting my mother," he said, and smiled like the Cheshire Cat.

GloLo sex

Sex was a 'Frequently Asked Question' from many interested readers during the writing of this book. 'Is it all about SEX?' some would ask, with a kind of *hunger* in their eyes. They wanted to read about exotic nights of pleasure and passion in bedrooms around the world. I did not want *The Globalisation of Love* to end up in the wrong section of the book store, however, so this section on sex is tucked away here under marriage.

So let's talk about 'multicultural sex'. How complicated can it be, right? Well, here is the interesting part actually; sex is *culturally loaded*.

Please remember, dear reader (and even more, dear husband), that this book, and this section of the book in particular, is not all about me. However I would be negligent in my duty *as a journalist*, let's say, if I did not have a sound basic knowledge of and even, ahem, *international experience* in the subject matter. I mean, it was a long time ago, *I hardly remember*, but I do remember that the bits and pieces and the general mechanics of the whole operation are kind of 'standard'. There was nothing, you know, *out of this world*. As a happily married woman, however, the possibility of further, ah, field research, was not possible, *nor desirable* for that matter. And talking with the GloLo interview couples also did not advance my scientific understanding of the GloLo 'sexperience'. When I asked them about multicultural sex, either the GloLo couple froze in horror, retracted the plate of cookies lying between us and shuffled me out their front door like I was some kind of deviant pervert and not a *professional journalist* simply doing whatever it takes to get to the heart of a story or, even worse I must admit, the interview pair mistook my questions about sex as a suggestion for 'embedding' myself in their GloLo boudoir, in which case I was the one grabbing a few of those cookies and hightailing it out of there. GloLo sex research, it would seem, is not my area of competitive advantage. Hence I needed to call in a professional.

No, not *that* type of professional. I mean a trained specialist, an expert on multicultural sex. Does such an expert even exist? Enter Dr Faizal Sahukhan, a real life 'intercultural sex expert' and author of *Dating the Ethnic Man*. Dr Sahukhan is a highly respected clinical sexologist and counsellor who specialises in multicultural relationship challenges. He works with GloLo couples, particularly those who find the globalisation of loving a bit awkward. He spoke to me from his office in Vancouver, Canada.

"The guiding rules for intimacy in romantic partnerships vary across cultures," Dr Sahukhan told me in his calm Canadian voice. "In Western cultures, sex is a vital part of a healthy, loving relationship that creates a special bond between the partners. In Eastern cultures, the role of husband and wife is more hierarchical and one partner serves the needs of the other partner. Sexually, they are not equals."

Additionally, there are different attitudes toward things like pre-marital intimacy, 'rules' for the initiation of sex, the purpose of sex, a kind of 'fun versus functional' dichotomy, and public displays of affection. The universal language of love is perhaps not so universal after all.

"In a multicultural relationship, there may be confusion and even contradiction about what is considered desirable and pleasurable for each partner. Without understanding this fundamental difference between cultures, multicultural couples may become sexually frustrated and confused, and that can impact the basis for their relationship," Dr Sahukhan explained further.

Sex, and the role of each partner while rolling around in the multicultural hay, is culturally determined, or at least once you get past the pure animal lust part, culturally influenced. If you want to learn more about GloLo sex, I highly recommend reading *Dating the Ethnic Man*. Dr Sahukhan gives you the feeling you are talking to a close friend, and there are lots of juicy stories too.

Stuff about friends

Every couple has their own web of friendships, don't they? There are 'his friends', 'her friends', 'our friends' – often the most disputed point in a divorce settlement, after who gets the cat that is – 'work friends' and even 'family friends'. And if my girlfriends are in any way representative of the world's married population, the friends issue does seem to be one of the peskier 'til death do us part challenges. Dugan Romano, author of *Intercultural Marriage Promises and Pitfalls* writes that "finding and maintaining friends often presents 'unique problems for intercultural couples'." Why?

Well friends are, as odd as it sounds, kind of a luxury item. You are *born* into your family, but with friends you are allowed to pick and choose. And while you can accept or at least learn to accept your spouse's quirky/imposing/meddling/chaotic/loud family *because they are family*, you and your partner are less likely to choose and accept the same group of quirky/imposing/meddling/chaotic/loud friends. If you add a bit of the GloLo component to the quirky friends, the whole network is heading toward multicultural circuit overload. Why? Let's look at the key issues.

Firstly, in a GloLo relationship, at least in the early days, one of you probably has no friends. It is not that you do not have any friends anywhere in the world, it is just that you do not have any friends where you are in the world, which is with the GloLo love of your life. Despite the thrill and excitement of your new found love therefore, you may actually feel achingly lonely.

Remember Carla and Andrei who met in a remote Russian town where Andrei was the only one who spoke English? They eventually moved back to Chicago where Carla lived before her brief Russian exchange. Andrei was by her side.

"We have reversed our roles," explained Carla. "I was alone in Russia without a single friend and Andrei was my island. When I came back to Chicago, it was Andrei who was friendless, and lonely too."

"Carla is very popular," Andrei started. "She has girl friends, guy friends too, young friends, some old friends. It's nice to have many friends like this. But when I came to America, I had only Carla. Her friends were friendly but they are *her* friends. I like to have my own friends," he declared.

I asked if that meant Russian friends.

"No. Yes. Maybe European, like me," he stumbled a bit over his words. "Russian language would be easier."

"When we first came back to Chicago," Carla picked up, "Andrei's English was not that good in group situations. We had always been alone together in Socci. It was awkward when we were with my friends. So we stayed at home a lot. We became really fuddy-duddy for a while, at home watching TV every evening."

Andrei spoke with a strong, let's say 'manly' accent, but otherwise his English seemed excellent. I asked if anything had changed.

"One thing is I learned more English," Andrei answered. "We watched so much TV and one day I looked at Carla and said, 'I understand everything'. I couldn't believe it," he said and they laughed together at the memory of this moment.

"We went out with friends to celebrate," Carla continued. "But I think equally as important is that Andrei found his own friends."

Andrei is a talented ballroom dancer apparently. He first joined a dancing club in Chicago and then even started to give lessons.

"I agree. I could move out of Carla's world. We met other couples like us too. Very nice people. GloLo people," he said with a smile, "six people, four nationalities. Lots of English mistakes," he laughed heartily.

The two GloLo couples with whom Carla and Andrei spend a lot of their free time have risen the ranks of friendship within a relatively short time span, which brings us to the second point.

GloLos love GloLos

"Many couples find that they get along best with other intercultural couples," Romano writes, "not only because they share some of the same experiences and problems, but because they are better able to empathise with the delicate and difficult balance these couples have managed to achieve in their marriages." It is not that monocultural friends are not nice. I heard many wonderful stories about friends welcoming the new GloLo partner into the social circle, it is only that often 'they just don't get it', as one GloLo couple said. Carla provided a painful example.

"Is it true," she asked me philosophically, "that multicultural couples think more about things like family and friends? Does it take more effort to find the right balance?"

I do not know the answer but I agreed that it might be the case.

"Andrei's younger brother developed an aggressive cancer which was discovered at a late stage," she said with sadness. "Andrei could not go home to Russia to see him. It was impossible financially and Andrei had just started a new job. All we could do was call every day. With the time change, that meant calling before we left for work. We got up every day at 5:00 am to call Russia."

"It was a sad way to start the day," Andrei said.

"We were out with some friends," Carla took over again. "One woman had an ailing parent who she was very worried about. She went home every second weekend to see her mother and she told everyone at the dinner table how difficult it was to be 'so far away', just four hours in a car."

"She has a right to be sad too," Andrei said.

"Yes, but your situation was much worse," Carla broke out and tears pricked at the corners of her eyes. "Andrei could not go even once to say goodbye to his only brother. He could not go to the funeral. He could not be there for his family to support them. Couldn't she see that?"

Even if Carla's hurt and anger might seem irrational, I understand her. GloLo friends, I will dare to generalise, would have understood the situation intuitively. GloLo couples experience many of life's biggest and most painful milestones 'remotely'. The separation from family and friends is kind of a constant companion of sorrow, if that is not being too dramatic. A death in the family, or a birth as I recently experienced myself, serves to amplify the distance. GloLo couples understand that and are sensitive to it; *they get it*.

"It sounds weird," Andrei said with a bit of hesitation, "but I was jealous of our friend. She could visit her mother every two weeks. I just wanted to see my little brother one last time, that's all."

What is interesting is that while Andrei did feel sadness and even jealousy, it was Carla who was angry. A GloLo spouse may feel particularly protective of their foreign partner and have expectations, sometimes even unrealistic expectations, of their old friends. Sometimes monocultural friends 'just don't get it' and that can create an unintended rift between friendships.

Pigeon holing

In *Chapter 7 – GloLo Colours*, we discussed stereotyping and the so-called 'meta-identity'. It's a colour thing, a race thing, and some might say a racism thing. A close cousin to the meta-identity, but based on nationality rather than race, is what Eliz Martinez, a British woman married to an Argentinean, calls 'pigeon holing'. It is the tendency of family and friends in the host environment to try to label and 'pigeon hole' the behaviour of a GloLo spouse as part of their national character. In her essay 'A Nice English Girl' in *Swaying* Martinez writes, "Nobody in Argentina wanted to know who I really was. They wanted me to be the archetypal English daughter-in-law." Rather than seeing her as she saw herself at the time, 'a teenage misfit dreaming of escape', they saw her as 'a nice English girl'.

Admittedly, pigeon holing can be annoying. I feel tremendous responsibility to the 30 million Canadians who actually live in Canada, not to misrepresent them. Every time I do something or express an opinion that deviates from that of my Austrian family, they will jollily point out to other visitors or even to themselves, *'she's Canadian'*, as though that offers explanation for everything I do. As a result, there is a certain social network in Austria that believes 1) Canadians drink peppermint tea instead of real tea (sorry tea-drinking British heritage and British grandmother who called me her 'Tea Ginny'), 2) Canadians cut open the toothpaste tube with scissors and scrape out the last bits of paste and 3) the one of which I am truly quite proud, Canadians are passionate skiers. Granted the excellent performance of the Canadian national ski team in recent years bolstered this generalisation, however I like to think that my talent on the alpine slopes confirmed this belief.

The Frankenstein effect

A further confusion about pigeon holing, if you recall from *Chapter 3 – Profile of a GloLo*, is that typically GloLo spouses are *atypical* in character from their home culture. I am not 'typically Canadian' just by virtue of the fact that I have not lived there for the last third of my life. I am no longer up-to-date on current social trends and the *Zeitgeist* of modern Canada. I do not know who the greatest hockey player is (remember my confession about football), much to my father's great shame. My daily cultural existence is not Canadian, but something more like a GloLo Canadian in Austria. I think of myself as a cultural Frankenstein, where the nuts, bolts and miscellaneous limbs of my personal culture are welded together by daily cultural influences of life in Vienna, the years of living abroad in Europe and the emotional whirls and twirls of a GloLo marriage. This Frankenstein effect happens to both partners by the way.

GloLo culture

You know how couples who have been married for 50 years start to look alike? They mirror each other and take on each other's facial expressions and mimic. GloLo couples do the same with culture. Little bits and pieces of your culture get scrambled up with bits and pieces of your partner's culture and over the years, presto, you have your own unique 'GloLo culture'. "Intercultural couples tend to form a unique bond – a special identity together that is quite unique from the identity of each individual," writes Marla Alupoaicei in *Your Intercultural Marriage*. The equation for your GloLo culture is rather simple actually, if mathematicians around the world will forgive this qualitative calculation: you and your culture plus your partner and his or her culture all divided by the location where you live.

My husband and I have been together for almost 15 years, or 'decades' as he likes to say. As much as I have become a cultural Frankenstein, or just 'Frankenstein' as he likes to say, my husband is also in a constant process of changing cultural identity. Having a resident Canadian around the house for all these years does not go without notice. His reference point for 'a cold winter day', for example, has dropped dramatically from a mere minus five degrees Celsius, a frosty Vienna day by any measure, to a proper Canadian-style don't-lick-a-metal-pipe minus 20 degrees. He has developed a thing for 'Canadian fashion' too and loves to wear clothing with a maple leaf splashed across the chest (it is a very Canadian thing to wear 'Maple Leaf fashion' in case neither you nor your spouse are Canadian). Further, he has developed a passion for barbecuing that would impress even the most hardcore Canadian grill enthusiast. He has transformed, some might say *evolved*, from a barbecue-is-a-fun-summer-meal-

every-once-in-a-while to a barbecue-is-a-superior-cooking-technique-*year-round* kind of guy. He has special barbecue 'tongs' that we bought in Canada and I am not allowed to put them in the dishwasher and, get this, he has a grill 'bible', a cookbook dedicated to barbecuing. His family and friends are slightly amused by his Canadian gourmet passion.

My GloLo husband has not become Canadian, despite my attempts he might add, but he has been influenced by Canada, by Canadians, and by me and my barbecue-crazed family in particular. His 'world view' has changed, let's say. And when your world view changes due to a GloLo marriage, your friends may struggle to accept or even recognise the new multicultural you. My husband's friends debate with him about the definition of 'a cold winter day' and eye him suspiciously when he wears his 'Maple Leaf fashion', thinking 'must be a gift from the wife' or 'why is there a maple leaf in the middle of the Austrian flag on his shirt?'. With the barbecue, well, there was initially some scepticism about the legitimacy of the grill as a gourmet instrument, until they tasted one of his steaks that is, and then they were begging to become a little bit Canadian too.

There are other salient GloLo friendship issues that will be covered in *Chapter 10 – Location, Location, Location* (not a misprint) which is about how GloLo couples choose a place to live. The point of this section is simply to understand that friendships are cultural and culture affects friendships.

Gender issues

Gender issues and gender roles could have gone into the marriage section because it deals with the roles of the husband and wife team, but I thought it was so important that it deserves its own section, like house pets I guess. And again, I use the word 'husband and wife', but it is not meant to be exclusive. If you are British Elton John and Canadian David Furnish, husband and husband, or American Ellen De Generes and Australian Portia de Rossi, wife and wife, you will still experience 'gender issues'. The label each partner has is not as important as the role play and the dynamic between the partners.

Gender issues are not in the exclusive domain of GloLo couples. Gender issues are globally ubiquitous, let's say, and plague most romantic relationships if the widespread and enduring popularity of John Gray's *Men are from Mars, Women are from Venus* is any indicator. Still, like many of the issues in a monocultural relationship, I will again poster that gender is *further* complicated by culture.

Cultural attitudes toward gender may determine two things. Firstly, GloLo couples will have expectations about the role each partner has within the functional framework of the marriage and family. Things like who will cook and care for the children and who will earn the household income can be culturally influenced and even as a modern GloLo globe trotter, you may sometimes be surprised by the expectations of your GloLo spouse. Remember, culture and gender issues pop up *even during sex*, as if there was nothing better to think about during the globalisation of love. Secondly, gender play will determine the emotional roles within the relationship. Things like who is openly loving and warm and who gets to cry have a strong cultural basis. Sometimes GloLo couples and their families are a bit surprised when their partner reverts to their cultural gender framework.

Che Guevara in the kitchen

Anita and Bernd are a young Mexican-German couple who met at an international computer company near Stuttgart where they both work. Anita had already been living in Germany for two years when Bernd asked her on a date. It was gender role confusion from the word go.

"Bernd was my first date in Germany," Anita explained. "I didn't find German men that attractive actually. They are physically attractive but they act confused with women. Equal sometimes, but sometimes sexist. It's confusing. Mexican men are known for being *machismo*," she continued thoughtfully, "but at least you know what to expect from them."

"Ha," Bernd interrupted, opening his eyes widely, "you can expect them to open doors, big deal, but that's it," he made a cutting gesture with his hand.

Apparently on their first date, Bernd picked up Anita from her home and opened the car door for her to get inside. So far so good, right? They then drove to the restaurant and Bernd parked the car. Anita remained in the car waiting for Bernd to open the door again so she could get out. She and he waited for two minutes before he knocked on the window to ask if everything was okay.

"Here is this well-educated, modern, independent woman, an engineer who travelled the world, sitting in the car like a *prima Donna*," he said teasingly, "waiting for me to open the door. It was so strange," he laughed. "How did she get from Mexico to Germany, I wondered, without ever opening a door?"

Anita laughed about the incident too.

"Men in Mexico always open the door," she explained. "In Germany, you never know what to expect. But I also did not know that German men can cook. That was a nice surprise," Anita exclaimed.

"In Mexico, real men don't cook. It's not manly," Bernd said with playful exaggeration. "Well, I love to cook so when we were with Anita's parents, I decided to cook them a German dinner."

"I think he wanted to score points with them," Anita added.

It all went terribly wrong apparently.

"Anita's dad kept quiet at least," Bernd started, "but her brothers were mocking me, and basically told me I have no, uh, *manlihood*, because I cook like a woman."

"The worst part," Anita continued, "is that the women, my mom in particular, said to my dad, 'if Bernd can cook, so can you.' She's demanding a meal once a week now."

"The uproar continues to this day," Bernd continued. "Her dad hates me and thinks I'm a pansy and her mom thinks I'm some revolutionary houseman. A lot of German men can cook and a lot can't, but she doesn't see that. She thinks I am Che Guevara of the kitchen."

To the factory

The important thing, writes Romano, is not how roles are divided but that both partners are in agreement with the roles. In *Chapter 3 – Profile of a GloLo*, Bea, a Danish woman, surprised her friends and even disappointed her mother, on this very point. She liked the clear and distinct gender role split between herself and her Spanish husband. Bea gave up a well-paid job in Copenhagen to become an 'old fashioned' and 'traditional' homemaker in Barcelona.

"Enrique grew up with a stay-at-home mother who did all the cooking and cleaning," Bea explained. "She was proud of it too. Enrique wanted the same kind of wife and mother for his children. My mother always worked, and she worked a lot too, so my dad cooked as many meals as she did."

"Her dad is 80 years old and tells me I am too old-fashioned," Enrique said. "He tells me that modern women work. Strange, huh? I provide everything for my wife so she doesn't have to work and her own father wants to send her to the factory."

"It's not just a gender issue," Bea explained. "Both of my parents are workaholics. I wanted something different. I am really happy with Enrique even if they scorn my role as homemaker."

"She's a princess," Enrique said. "I like to take care of my princess."

Even if I did not want to become a 'princess' like Bea, I recognise some of her cultural adaptation in myself. Sit down for this dear reader, as I have a confession to make. I do *all* of the laundry in my GloLo home.

'OMG,' I hear my younger feminist self exclaim, 'Have you no self-respect? You have sold your own soul washing a man's boxers'. How do I live with myself? It does seem really *sexist*, doesn't it, like I am a domestic servant and not a modern, well-educated woman of the world, not to mention bestselling author? But let's look at the whole case before determining a guilty-as-charged and blasphemy-to-Gloria-Steinem verdict.

Well, it is true that I never thought I would be in a marriage where I do *all* of the laundry, including the time-consuming sorting of the socks. However, I also never thought I would be in a partnership where I *never* have to take out the garbage, shovel snow off my car or clean out the cat's litter box. My husband thinks that these jobs fall exclusively in his domain. Who am I to make a culturally imperialist judgement about gender roles? I have to be culturally flexible in my GloLo marriage after all. And I think my younger feminist self, and probably even Gloria, would agree that it is not such a bad deal.

Funny little feminist anecdote

One man I interviewed said something about culture and gender that, to me at least, was very reassuring.

"It doesn't matter what culture she is from," he stated with full confidence, "women everywhere remember everything."

Conclusion on cultural stuff

When you think about this cultural stuff, like marriage, family, sex, friends, and gender, you realise that each GloLo partner brings their own set of cultural expectations into the relationship. And even though GloLo couples are aware of the differences and are therefore ready for surprises, the GloLo cultural stuff can sometimes lead to a surprise within the surprise, so to speak.

"The more surprises we have in our marriage," Arvind said happily, "the better. Every surprise leads to cultural learning and discovery about each other and about ourselves, even if the process is challenging."

"Sometimes the neighbours learn about our surprises too," Claudia said.

"Many people learn and benefit from a multicultural relationship," Arvind continued, "starting with our children and our families. Even the neighbours in Germany know that a brother cousin is just like a brother too," he chuckled.

♥

Top 10 cultural issues in a GloLo romance

1. The last time your partner invited 'just the family' for dinner, a small village arrived.
2. Your partner's idea of a 'family dinner' is so restrictive that you actually feel lonely.
3. You think your GloLo partner is 'traditional' and has 'old-fashioned values' but your friends say things like 'retrograde' and 'chauvinist' and present you with modern feminist literature.
4. Your GloLo partner ruined a would-be romantic proposal of marriage by saying, "You are the love of my life... and I've already discussed it with my family and they all agree that you would make an acceptable wife".
5. You have been married for 12 years and have three children with your GloLo partner and your parents still ask when your 'ethnic phase' will end.
6. You feel like such an outsider when you are with your hometown friends and you realise how much you and your GloLo partner have influenced each other.
7. You feel like such an outsider when you are with your GloLo partner's friends and you realise how much you are still the same person as ever.
8. Just to be on the safe side, you named your new pet bunny 'Do Not Eat Me'.
9. When your partner is feeling randy and you are just not in the mood, you whisper sweetly, "it's a cultural thing".
10. When you are feeling randy and your partner 'has a headache', you whisper sweetly, "but it's a cultural tradition".

Part III
Life and Times of a GloLo Marriage

10

Location, Location, Location

As any property manager will tell you, the three most important factors in the real estate business are location, location and location. GloLo relationships are like real estate in this sense, and the location of the relationship may well determine whether it is a sunny home filled with love and laughter or a stormy battle field filled with acrimony and tears. Why?

Firstly, no man is an island, right, unless you are Tom Hanks in the movie *Castaway*, where even he started talking to a volleyball just to keep himself company. We are social animals, you see. And therefore no relationship is an island either. You can escape to one of those posh, secluded honeymoon resorts for some 'island living', but the exorbitant prices usually limit your stay to a week or two. The GloLo reality is that the location *where* you live influences *how* you live. In *Cross-Cultural Marriage*, Rosemary Breger and Rosanna Hill write "where a mixed couple lives seems to play a significant role in the flexibility they have in negotiating around their different cultural expectations and escaping many negative effects of public and private ethnic stereotyping." Depending on who you are, what you look like, where you are and the current socio-political climate on multicultural relationships in that society, a GloLo couple may experience, in random order, curiosity, criticism, encouragement, hostility, warmth, rejection, love, discrimination and understanding. It can be a lot of attention just for being GloLo.

Secondly, as part of a multicultural couple, at least one of you is likely to be living outside your country of origin. And let's face it, some countries are more open and friendly toward foreigners. Some cultures and combinations of cultures are easier to navigate. The location may change over time if the GloLo couple moves around, and the couple's needs, desires and feelings about the location may change during different phases of their life. Yet location is something that can have a make or break impact on your GloLo love story.

There are many ways to deal with 'living abroad', and there are many books and blogs about it with all kinds of advice on how to do it best and how to 'master it' so it is not the intention here to repeat existing wisdom. In this chapter, we will look at location and 'living abroad' issues *from the GloLo perspective*. The first part of the chapter discusses the main issues that GloLo couples face when choosing a country to call home, and then we will look at the role each GloLo partner plays according to the location where they live. The two sections are:

- GloLo location checklist
- GloLo on location

GloLo location checklist

Let us assume for the moment that you have choices. You have met the GloLo girl/guy of your dreams, you have had a splash wedding, perhaps two weddings, and you are ready to settle down together into the humdrum of daily GloLo existence. But where? One of you will probably have to move to a new country where the other one of you lives and works. Let's begin by discussing some issues that GloLo couples consider when they are browsing around for a location to live in GloLo love.

By no means is this list of location issues definitive, but within each of these topics, you can determine much about how your daily GloLo life will look. Here we have:

- Social cake and friendly frosting
- Money matters
- Immigration
- Citizenship
- Clothes

Social cake and friendly frosting

Like a nice chocolate cake, there are two layers to consider in the 'social framework' of a potential country. The first layer and main ingredients of the cake is 'society at large'. Society at large refers to the kind of country or region it is and the kind of people who live there, if you will pardon these broad generalisations for a moment. A diverse, multicultural society, for example, with lots of foreigners, with good jobs I mean, not just polishing the toilets, minority groups, 'outsiders', multicultural families and perhaps a United Nations office in the centre of town will create a different atmosphere for living than a homogeneous society where everyone looks the same, eats the same, prays the same, speaks the same language and is related to half of the town forefathers lying in the local cemetery. Obviously you and your GloLo partner will blend in with a heterogeneous society. On the other hand, if, like Madonna, you revel in the centre of attention, then living in a homogeneous society will give you celebrity-like fame.

The second or top layer of the social framework cake, the *frosting*, which some call *icing*, is your own social network, including family, friends and other organised groups such as the Vienna Babies Club, the International Women's Career Network or the Expat Drinking Club, to name just a few. Each group can offer support to the GloLo couple during their integration process. Some sociologists might turn the cake analogy upside down and put this group as the foundation layer, which is fine with me. The point is that there are two distinct layers to this GloLo location cake and both the cake and the frosting can influence the quality and taste of the couple's experience in a given location.

Fame and infamy

In *Chapter 7 – GloLo Colours*, Slovenian Petra told us that she and Dahnay, her Ethiopian husband, along with their two girls, are the only multicultural family in town. They explained what it felt like to be a 'celebrity' and living with fame.

"It's not a negative type of attention," Dahnay began. "It's more like I'm a celebrity. Everyone knows who I am and who the girls are," he said, referring to their two daughters.

"It is a curious type of racism," Petra continued. "My parents, for example, are very proud of Dahnay as their son-in-law. We are a novelty family in the town."

Not all cultures are welcoming and 'curious' about multicultural families however, and it can be painful for the foreign partner and even shameful for the host partner when society shows its ugly side.

Maria is from Mexico and her rich, black curls and sparkling eyes belie her age and experience in life. She has lived in Switzerland, in a small town near Zurich, on and off for more than 40 years. Her husband Gunter, a sculpture artist, described their experience as a multicultural couple.

"Even today," Gunter began almost angrily, "after 42 years, I hear about Gunter's 'exotic' wife. 'She's not from here,' they say. 'Why did you not choose a local girl?' they ask. I tell them," he pointed vigorously into the air with his clay encrusted index finger, "because Maria is the most beautiful, that's why."

Gunter's Mexican wife, Maria, said how lonely it was for her when she first moved to Switzerland all those years ago.

"It was the 1970s when I came here," she began. "Switzerland was still very traditional and quite provincial really. It was long before the internet and European integration. Back then, a national border meant a lot more than today. Ideas and thoughts did not flow so easily in society."

"I looked different than the Swiss girls," she laughed, looking 20 years younger than her age. "My clothes were different, I wore my hair loose and it was like I invaded their world. No, they were not friendly. I think they feared change."

"They were jealous," Gunter burst out. "You were more beautiful than all of them put together, and so lively and vivacious. You are still the most beautiful," he finished softly.

Maria blushed like a school girl and I had to agree with Gunter, she really is 'the most beautiful'.

Money matters

Money makes the world go round, doesn't it? It may sound crass, but money is the theoretical fuel for globalisation, and even the globalisation of love. Local economic conditions will determine how a GloLo couple can live and maintain a livelihood. Yet there are a lot of trade-offs within the economic framework, particularly when careers and kids are involved. So the choice between 'my country or yours?' is not always a 'no brainer' as one GloLo interviewee described it. GloLo partners may have to weigh the relative pros and cons of each country.

Remember Austrian Tanja and Gambian Lamin? They explained their checklist for living when deciding between their respective countries in Europe and Africa.

"Gambia is a poor country and our family income would be lower than here in Austria," Lamin began. "However we would still have enough money for a middle class life style."

"Yes," Tanja agreed. "I liked the idea of having a housekeeper and maybe even a cook, but basic amenities, like water and electricity, are not always available. I just could not imagine living without this basic infrastructure."

"So we live in Austria," Lamin concluded. "And I have learned to ski," he said with a proud smile. Our conversation then took an entirely different direction.

School leaving certificate

Related to the development of the local skiing, er, I mean economy, is the education factor, which is critical for GloLo couples who have or are planning to have children. The availability of good, affordable schooling is a top priority for many GloLo families. Further, GloLo parents often want their children to have an 'international education' or at least the type of education and schooling that is internationally recognised.

"My son should have the option of attending university in Sweden if he wants to," a Swedish father explained. He and his Syrian wife have an export business.

"We chose Egypt for business reasons," explained the exporter, "and for his education, we send him to the American International School in Cairo. His school leaving certificate will be recognised and accepted anywhere in the world."

Economic rationale, however, is not always the basis for a final decision.

"For us it was a no brainer," explained Dirk. "South Africa has 350 days a year of sunshine whereas the Czech Republic has 75 days a year of *frost*."

It has nothing to do with economics but it is a compelling argument.

Immigration

Another potentially frustrating issue in the GloLo location decision is the immigration factor. Just as some hotels are really swift, efficient and friendly with their guest check-in system, and are very happy to welcome lovey-dovey guests, some countries have more open and liberal immigration policies than others. Depending on the two countries of your particular GloLo mix, it may be that it is simply easier for one of you to migrate in one direction over the other, particularly when you just cannot wait another day to be together.

Immigration officials apply their discretion in processing applications. Breger writes "the personal stereotypes and prejudices of individual civil servants can influence the ease with which a couple starts a life together." Since immigrating is usually a harrowing ordeal for anyone, I put together a simple list of the seven secrets you absolutely need to know.

♥

Seven secrets for dealing with immigration officials

1. Immigration officials cannot pronounce your name and do not want to learn, so do not waste your time and the taxpayer's money trying. So, for example, if your name is Wendy Williams, and the person in charge of your visa application and therefore future in the country asks if you are Venn-dee Vil-eee-emz, you smile and nod in agreement and say, 'yes', 'ja', 'oui' or appropriate language.
2. Nobody cares if your great, great, great grandfather's middle name stems from the country where you want to live. You are not from there, so get over it and submit your application.
3. Just when you think you have all the paper work completed, there will be an old/new law that requires an amendment to the original/completely new form that must be signed at the embassy in your country of origin, if you are already in your new country, or in the new country, if you have just returned to your home country to wait for the papers.
4. While you may think that bringing a box of chocolates to the immigration official is a friendly gesture, others may consider it an act of bribery, as in illegal, and punishable by immediate

deportation, *bye-bye love*, or even arrest, *hello loneliness*, and time in jail, *I think I'm going to cry...*

5. Tips on how to 'improve the system' and make it more 'foreigner friendly', particularly in your butchered version of the local language, are not welcome.
6. References to your former colonial power in the country you would like to live in and righteous indignation about a fallen empire are unwelcome.
7. Do NOT submit your visa application the day after your national football team beat the crap out of the country team where you want to live.

Assuming that you do immigrate successfully, a related issue is citizenship.

Citizenship and René Descartes

Citizenship in the country where you live is like being a card carrying member of an exclusive club. It is legal proof that you are a member and that you are *accepted*. It provides you with a sense of continuity at least. Not to dwell on the sordid or the morbid, but sometimes even GloLo relationships do not last forever. GloLo spouses die and, gasp, sometimes divorce. Having citizenship in the country of residence provides the GloLo partner with the assurance that when everything else in life is out of control and falling to pieces, at least remaining in the country is still an option. Further, citizenship usually gives you the right to vote in local elections. Now this book is not about civic duties and exercising your political voice, but the right to vote is actually a very good indicator of your status in society.

"If I cannot vote in the society where I live, then I do not exist in that society. If I do not exist, then what am I?" Bernard, a French-born Canadian citizen who can vote in Canadian elections told me, following a René Descartes line of reasoning.

He did sound very convincing actually. I jotted another agenda item on my 'to do' list. Right after 'finish book' is 'seek right to vote, to exist'. But wait, citizenship to a country is not like going through the drive-thru' of a burger restaurant. Obtaining citizenship requires extended periods of residence, piles of paper work, 'official' (i.e. *expensive*) translations of obscure documents you have not seen since grade school, and sometimes even forfeiting citizenship in your own country. What?!

Even though I married an Austrian, gave birth to an Austrian, pay Austrian taxes – nothing to sneeze at, believe me – and at the risk of mentioning this once too often, I really, really *loooooove* to ski, I am only allowed to become an Austrian citizen if I forfeit my Canadian citizenship, which is obviously *absolutely and utterly unthinkable*. And how chaste really, that I must forsake all other nationalities to become Austrian, like it is some kind of secret boys' club with daring and dangerous initiation requirements. What if I want to go back to live in Canada? What if I *need* to go back? And what if my GloLo family wants to come with me?

Not having Austrian citizenship is not enough to make me flee the country, however it does act as a nagging reminder that I am a foreigner and always will be a foreigner, despite my top performance on the ski slopes. Well, sniff, once this book is an international bestseller, written by a 'resident' of Austria, the authorities may wish to reconsider my application.

Clothes

Clothes? I know, it makes you wonder who is editing this book. Bear with me for a moment. The freedom to dress in your own personal style says a lot about the social and religious politics of a culture. Let's start with the obvious. There are places in the world where women cannot publicly express their fashion flair and individuality with anything other than the number of sequins you can sew on the head scarf of your floor length *burka*. Admittedly, that *burka* can cleverly hide a bad hair day and is very forgiving around the waist line when you have skipped your Pilates class, however you may not be in the mood for it *every day... for the rest of your life*.

It sounds superficial however it is a fundamental indicator of the type of life you will live. No little black party dress means no party, or at least not the kind of party you are used to attending. No power suits for women means no women in power. No micro-bikini... well, you get the picture.

On the other side of the clothes line, certain styles of dress that are part of your religious or cultural heritage are simply not suitable, or even illegal, in other countries. Your turban, your shaved head, your body piercings, your *Lederhosen* (you know, cute leather knee length shorts worn with suspenders and woolly knee socks, as seen in *The Sound of Music*) make a statement about your identity, and it simultaneously brands you as an outsider. It will limit social and professional opportunities as well as general integration if wearing these clothes is important to you and your belief system. Hence there is a delicate line between expressing your own unique individuality and being true to yourself on the one hand, and being culturally sensitive and adapting to your new culture on the other hand.

You may want to consult with your GloLo partner on the clothing issue in general, regardless of where you live. Certain styles of clothing are inappropriate and may lose their sex appeal, let's say, when worn out of context, where 'out of context' may mean *within* a GloLo marriage. Now I cannot publicly humiliate my GloLo husband by going into the lurid, graphic details of the story, but suffice it to say that I have seen him in his Austrian *Lederhosen*. Just the once.

GloLo on location

GloLo couples essentially have five possible roles regarding location. For those of you who are quick with math, five does seem a high factor when there are only two GloLo variables involved, doesn't it? Allow me to explain. Assuming once again that there is freedom and choice involved in choosing a country where to live, there are five different constellations for a GloLo couple and each constellation determines the role they play in the multicultural relationship. The GloLo roles are:

- GloLo Host
- Imported GloLo
- Double Expatriates
- Swingers
- Commuters

GloLo Host

The role of the GloLo Host is very simple. When someone just moved half way around the world to be with you, having left behind their family, friends, culture, career and cat, it places a great onus on you, the host partner, to get things right. If there was objection or criticism from either side of the family, it only ups the *ante* to prove them wrong. The GloLo Host maintains the basic framework of life, so things like social network, job, language, prayer, and baseball with the guys remains pretty much unchanged. It is in stark contrast to the foreign partner who has to recreate and even redefine most aspects of their daily life.

Remember French-Vietnamese Kim Swan and American Bradley who we met in the chapters on *Language* and *Cultural Stuff*? She said "I rove you, but sometimes I ate you" and Bradley fell to his knees with a marriage proposal. It was not only wedding bells and romance for them, and I am not even referring to the exile of Bradley's dog Ben. Bradley came clean with this confession.

"It sounds dumb, but it took me a couple of months to figure out that I had to help Kim Swan more. Basic things like shopping and banking are done differently. I didn't understand how much she was missing her girlfriends when I went to play baseball. She wanted to join me all the time. The guys said I was being hen pecked, but she was just really lonely. I felt like such a jerk when I realised what she was going through. I had to reprioritise and put Kim Swan first and foremost. I am lucky she stayed with me," he said, still sounding relieved.

I asked Kim Swan how she had experienced the transition.

"I never thought to leave," she answered quickly, perhaps wanting to placate Bradley who was looking a bit pale. "I knew I had to hen peck," she joked a bit. "It was sad time for me. Now it is better. Now I have lots of girlfriends, lots of hens," she laughed and Bradley laughed with her.

Fortunately Bradley, the GloLo Host, was sensitive to Kim Swan and gave her the support she needed to adjust to her new country. Kim Swan, the Imported GloLo found her own way in California too. Let's look at her role in more detail.

Imported GloLo

The Imported GloLo is the 'foreign spouse', like Kim Swan in the story above. In contrast to the GloLo Host, the Imported GloLo has to deal with a new love interest *plus* a new country, culture, possibly language and religion, food, job change, social structure, climate, *and* find a new hair salon that has all the fun gossip magazines. It is a big adjustment.

Small things, like buying loo roll at the grocery store, become big things when you only find loo roll at the *paper* store. Big things like signing a legal contract in a foreign country and in a foreign language become even bigger as you flip through the bilingual legal dictionary that conjugates all the verbs for you. Oh right, that dictionary doesn't exist yet. Even Wikipedia, *even YouTube* cannot help.

Hence, as an Imported GloLo, you may grow dependent on your GloLo Host partner to deal with basic life skills such as finding the loo roll and translating legal documents. It can be a self-confidence killer and both you and your partner may be surprised, nay, *burdened* by your new clingy role. (Darling, remember how I once donated generously to an animal rights activist organisation and did not realise that the donation contract I signed was not a one-off payment as I thought but a *monthly* obligation? And then you had to call them and explain my mistake and they were not friendly but we agreed in the end that as long as it helped the animals, it was an okay mistake but it should not happen again?)

No matter how lovely and supportive your spouse is during this transition period, which may easily last up to 20 years or more, when daily mundanities and frustrations creep into life, it is hard not to look at him or her and think or, oops, even say, 'This. Is. All. Your. Fault."

Further, by complaining about the host country, and the new challenges it may pose, as an Imported GloLo, you are reinforcing your position as a foreigner and outsider. And few GloLo Hosts will not take offence.

Remember American Lydia and Dutch Ton who we met in *Chapter 8 – Language*?

"I felt like every criticism of Holland was a criticism of me," Ton explained. "I felt responsible for eight million Dutch. I cannot control everyone I told her, even if I were King."

"He took everything personally," Lydia said. "I just wanted to vent my frustrations but it was clear that I had to change my coping strategy. Being faced with cultural differences as well as spending a lot more time on my own than I was used to was a gift actually," Lydia explained. "I felt like I could redesign my life. It was and still is challenging though. Sometimes I still want to run away, but I am more reflective about my feeling of the superiority of my own culture, beliefs and ways of doing things. I guess being here (in Holland) is more difficult but also more exciting. Every day is different."

Since Lydia had a really nice hair style, a layered bob with a lot of swing, I just had to ask where she had her hair done.

"Just down the street from where we live. I can get an appointment the same day I call," she added enthusiastically, patting her hair in satisfaction. "They have great coffee and all the gossip magazines too!"

"At least Holland got her hair right," Ton added, with a smirk.

Double Expatriates

The term 'Double Expatriates' refers to the situation where both of you are foreigners in the country where you live. It therefore erases the roles of GloLo Host and Imported GloLo because both spouses are 'imports' and are therefore living in a cultural no man's land. *Intercultural Marriage Promises and Pitfalls* author Dugan Romano writes that there are "many couples who maintain that living in a third country is the only (or ideal) way for an intercultural marriage to succeed." It levels the playing field to some extent and the struggles of understanding culture and language are more equally shared.

The Double Expat couples with whom I spoke certainly confirmed this hypothesis. Olivia, who described herself as a 'Canadian army brat' spent her youth in four different countries as her military father worked in different postings as part of the United Nations peace-keeping mission. After graduating from university in Canada, she moved to Denmark for an internship and quickly fell for the charms of Danish Kai, an international trade lawyer. After ten years in Copenhagen, Kai's firm asked him to develop the Spanish division of their practice, so Olivia and Kai have moved to Madrid with their three children. Olivia spoke first.

"Firstly, as a child I saw how my parents dealt with postings in Egypt, Germany, England and Greece. We stuck together more as a family when we lived abroad. In Canada, we could afford to be selfish, but when we were on a posting, we needed each other more and spent more time together. In Denmark, I was the 'minority' member in my Danish family. Shortly after we moved to Madrid, my middle son said, 'Mom, we are all like you now. We don't belong here but it's still nice.' It has also given Kai a greater appreciation of what it means to be a foreigner on a daily basis. It can be exhausting sometimes."

"I have a better understanding of what it's like to be dealing with a different language all the time and a different pace of life," Kai said. "In Madrid, Olivia is free to complain without offending me. If she says something about Denmark, then I feel compelled to defend my culture. Now I understand that she's just frustrated. It's not about me," he said in a beautiful Mars and Venus kind of moment.

"I hope he remembers that when we return to Denmark," Olivia laughed.

Ideal solution

There are, however, also some risks in choosing to live in a culturally neutral third country. At the beginning at least, there is a lack of support network to help you adjust to the new situation. When both partners are finding the adjustment difficult, there is no source of positive energy.

When Australian Robyn and Austrian Harold moved from Austria, where they had met and where they had been living for four years, to France, they thought it was a turning point in their relationship. However, it turned out to be a much more harrowing turn than either partner had anticipated.

"I was tired of living in Harold's world and I wanted a place that was 'ours'," explained Australian Robyn, the frustration already rising in her voice. "France seemed like an ideal solution. We both speak a bit of French, Harold had an interesting work opportunity, I was home with Henry, who was just nine months old at the time, and the climate is sunnier. I missed the sunshine."

The 'ideal solution', however, had a few GloLo glitches. Harold found working with his French colleagues difficult. His basic French language skills were fine for socialising and talking about the football match, however in hard core business negotiations, he knew he was missing out although he was in a management position.

"Between the language barrier, the office politics and the national rivalries, it was like being the new boy at school. It was alienating and I knew that my job was suffering for it," explained Harold. "At the end of the work day, I would come home feeling defeated and even depressed. But Robyn could not support me. She was having her own struggles."

"Yes," Robyn continued, "I was home alone with Henry and I felt trapped. Maybe that is typical of any mother who stays home with a young child, but I had no support network, and no girlfriends to talk to and have a laugh with. It was difficult to meet French moms in the same situation. Harold would come home grumpy and I was getting depressed. It was critical for a while. I really wondered what we had done to ourselves."

I could see that the memory of this time was painful for both of them.

"There we were, two sinking ships, and neither of us had the energy to help out the other one," Harold said. "I think even Henry knew that we were not happy. It was not fair to our child. We had to do something."

Harold talked to his employer about the language issue. Fortunately, they understood his situation and provided him with a language coach. Within a few months, his mastery of the language improved considerably.

"Now I can 'negotiate' in French," explained Harold. "That is different than just 'speaking' French."

Once Harold was happier at work, it gave him more energy to look at the situation with Robyn and think of solutions.

"We lived in a small village close to the company, which we thought was ideal for us. It had a lot of what we were looking for on the weekend, tranquillity and the seaside, but it wasn't what I needed during the week," explained Robyn. "I was lonely and bored."

With very little research, Robyn found that there was a thriving expat community in Marseilles, just 40 km away. It did not take much to convince Harold to move to the city and become a commuter.

"Of course, it means commuting fifty minutes each way to work. But it is better to do that and see my wife happy than to cycle to work and see her miserable. I think we found a balance that works for everyone," he said putting his hand gently on hers.

"Yes," Robyn agreed, "now I have friends in Marseilles and I go with Henry on play dates. We are busy and happy during the week, not just the weekend. We found our place as a family."

Swingers

Some GloLo couples just cannot make up their minds about where to live and they swing back and forth between their two countries of origin. To be a successful Swinger, you need to have either 1) a *very flexible* career path, such as international rock star, where you live in hotels rooms anyway, or 2) *no career path* such as happy houseman or poet, where your workplace and home are the same, or preferably 3) a huge trust fund that enables multiple homes around the world just waiting for the *Architecture Today* photo shoot. Jetsetters *invented* swinging after all.

Swingers are rare though. During my research for this book, I did hear a story about an Indian American couple, both medical doctors apparently, who effortlessly moved back and forth between Detroit and the Indian sub-continent every four of five years. There was also a Canadian family who travelled between Hong Kong and Vancouver, on the west coast of Canada, the way some families travel between home and their local supermarket. There was mention of a private jet *including full-time pilot* so I would guess they are capital J Jetsetters.

And swingers sound so groovy, don't they, as they swing back and forth between countries and continents with their Dallas-today-Dar Es Salaam-tomorrow-devil-may-care attitude. But it is neither as easy nor as effortless as it sounds, and often the basis for moving back and forth, at the risk of sounding ominous, is the search for something missing. Maria 'the most beautiful' and Gunter have 'swung' between Mexico and Switzerland for 40 years.

"Basically it's like this," Gunter explained, again pointing his finger in the air, "we live in Switzerland because the air is clean and it is a safe place to be and life is beautiful. Then we get tired of the orderliness, the formality, the bureaucracy," he said dramatically. "So we go to Mexico where people are friendly, the climate is warm, and life is beautiful. Then we get tired of the *mañana* mentality, the corruption, the broken car that cannot be fixed. So we move back to the Swiss mountains."

"We have also moved to help our parents," added Maria.

"Oh yes," Gunter picked up. "First Maria's mother, then my mother and father, then Raul," he said, referring to Maria's father. "If we move close to you," he pointed to me, "it's bad news. You are probably going to die soon."

Reverse culture shock and the time-warp of life

What is interesting about Swingers is that they both may experience culture shock when moving between cultures. The Imported GloLo deals with the usual issues of 'standard' culture shock, a nasty anxiety caused by the differences between the old and new cultures. The GloLo Host also experiences 'reverse' culture shock. Once you have become accustomed to the foreign place of living, the new place, which is actually your original old place, if you can follow me, seems foreign and strange. Ultimately, you and your GloLo partner both feel like strangers in a strange land. The usual role play of GloLo Host or

Imported GloLo is dysfunctional, since both partners are struggling with the new environment and feeling a bit lost, if for entirely different reasons.

Remember 'it's Brazil, baby' Ryan from *Chapter 5 – Meet the Parents*? Ryan is Canadian and his young wife Alexandra is Brazilian. They met at university in Canada and moved to Brazil after graduation. Ryan did some work for his father-in-law, who owns a small grocery store, however he and Alexandra spent much of their time travelling around Central and South America together. Shortly after Ryan's 30th birthday, he decided it was time to go back to Canada to 'get on with life' as he put it.

Ryan returned to Canada with Alexandra and felt even more out of place in his native land than when he was traipsing around the Amazon jungle. With very little relevant work experience, Ryan found a junior position in the food retail sector.

"There I was with long hair, unshaven, and skinny," he began with his storytelling enthusiasm, "and all my friends from university were clean cut and had put on a few," he chuckled, referring to some weight gain. "They had cruised along in their careers too. I had more stamps in my passport and probably had a more *interesting* life," he emphasised, "but it was hard not to think about their big, expensive watches and big, expensive cars. We were living in a rental place. I guess I was jealous. It has been a tough adjustment," he exhaled slowly.

Alexandra, a registered nurse, quickly found work and enjoys her position in a children's hospital. She told me how she experienced the move.

"I guess I did not have any expectations when we came back to Canada because I had nothing here. But Ryan left as a student just after graduation. Now everyone is older and more serious. He has culture shock and also the shock of the passing of time."

"Yah, it took a year before I felt like I was home again," he agreed. "Even though I love Canada, I think about South America a lot too. Like a mistress."

I asked Ryan if, after years of watching football (soccer) in South America, he still loved hockey.

"Are you kidding me?" he scoffed. "I'm Canadian, man, I love hockey. I said I had culture shock. I didn't die. Go Leafs go!" he pumped his fist in the air, referring to the Toronto hockey team.

Commuters

For the very modern and independent GloLo couple, there is the final option of 'his and hers' countries, which are not necessarily their countries of origin. Hence a commuter marriage can have up to four cultures for the Commuters to deal with on a regular basis.

Over the course of my research, I did meet, for example, a French man living in the USA, married to a Belgium woman living in The Netherlands. I had the pleasure of meeting, and even skiing with, a Finnish man living in Poland married to a German woman living in Holland.

Usually Commuters are very international by the time they meet, so living in two countries is 'no big deal' and having a multicultural marriage is 'no big deal'. Only when airlines are grounded, such as what happened after the 2010 volcano in Iceland spread enough ash across European air paths to effectively ground all flights for almost a week, do they become flustered by the inconvenience of a geographically dispersed marriage.

"Our marriage is highly dependent on modern technology and on low-cost airlines," Anna admitted. "We use the computer to talk every morning and every evening. We book our flights weeks and months in advance."

"It requires a lot of travel and it is expensive," Henrik added. "We have two of everything. Two apartments. Two cars. Two sofas. Two beds. Everything we buy is double – one for Anna's place and one for my place. It requires a lot of organisation."

I asked if they would ever, pardon the expression, 'settle down' in one place.

"We are settled," Anna answered swiftly. "We have a very ordinary routine life. We work and we visit and we travel. It's our life. It's wonderful."

"You are making an assumption," Henrik said, "that we don't want this life. We like it very much. We are global citizens. We are at home wherever we are. That is true freedom."

Conclusion

Home is where the heart is, isn't it? One GloLo husband said that you could 'drive yourself nuts' thinking about such a fundamental question of where to put the heart, that is the problem. GloLo couples tend to deal with a diverse and changing set of decision-making choices when looking for a place to call home. Maybe the weather does not change, but things like political climate, xenophobia, economic possibilities, immigration laws and *burka* regulations do change. And as you and your GloLo spouse monitor these respective changes in your homelands and/or where you live, you may consider relocation and a new place to put your heart.

I think though that Gunter wrote the conclusion on location for me.

"This is my home," he said, drawing a circle in the air which enclosed Maria with him. "Whether we are in Switzerland or in Mexico, it doesn't matter, we are together. Our marriage is our home."

Top 10 location issues in a GloLo romance

1. When you met your spouse and he or she asked, "Your place or mine?", you had no idea that you would need a passport to get there.
2. You have one full wardrobe of clothes that are appropriate for the climate/social norms/religious laws in your culture and a second full wardrobe of clothes that are appropriate for the climate/social norms/religious laws of your spouse's culture.
3. When you go 'home' to visit your parents, after a couple of weeks you feel 'homesick' for the place where you now live with your GloLo spouse, until you return 'home' to that place and then you feel nostalgic for 'home'. Got it?
4. You are neither a financial trader nor a drug dealer but you always have a stash of foreign currency at home and you take a great interest in the exchange rate.
5. It costs the price of a small car to get you, your GloLo spouse and the GloLo children over to see your spouse's family, so you don't have to go often.
6. Your spouse's family spend the price of a small car coming to visit, so they will be staying for a while...
7. Whenever a national disaster or political conflict happens *anywhere* on the *continent* where you live, your mother calls and asks, "Does this mean you and _____ (insert name of your GloLo spouse here) will be moving home to safety now?"
8. You live in a place that was considered a 'vacation paradise' where you grew up.
9. You did not know that there is no Starbucks in that 'vacation paradise'.
10. When your GloLo partner said, "Come live with me in Paris" and, in a burst of romanticism, you readily agreed, you really wish you had known that there is also a Paris in Texas.

Food

Preach not to others what they should eat,
but eat as becomes you, and be silent.
Epictetus, Roman (Greek-born) slave and Stoic philosopher (55 AD - 135 AD)

Well said, Epictetus. I wonder if he had a GloLo girlfriend. There are probably as many opinions about food and what constitutes good food – *Fresh! Aged! Oven-baked! Raw! Organic! Ready in 5 minutes! Extra Cheesy!* – as there are countries and cultures of cooks the world over. Food is highly cultural and strongly influenced by history and heritage, religion and geography, as well as taste and aesthetic preferences.

The good news is that everyone eats. There is no potential GloLo partner out there who has never heard of food and does not eat on a regular basis (except Victoria Beckham, perhaps, and she is monoculturally married to David). Hence you have a fantastic starting point and common denominator with your partner – from the Occident to the Orient, from the North Pole to the South Pole, and all those sweet and salty places in between, everyone loves food! Unfortunately, that is where the commonality, and some would say rationality, ends. Food and eating is *emotional*. Remember the *Perogie*-ban my (Canadian-born) Ukrainian mother faced when she married into a (Canadian) British family? Food is culturally loaded with tradition and family customs and even international politics. On a daily basis, the multicultural meal opens up a whole new range of cultural culinary questions just waiting to be jabbed at with a fork or chopstick held in the wrong hand.

In this chapter, we will look at various issues of the multicultural meal and the foods that pose the greatest threat to the multicultural kitchen, the ins and outs of multicultural wining and dining and finally, entertaining GloLo style. Here are the sections:

- Food glorious food
- GloLo wining and dining
- Guess who's coming to dinner?

Food glorious food

Food is a medium of love and culture. In the 2009 movie *New York, I Love You*, Natalie Portman plays the role of Rifka, a Hasidic Jew who is in the 47th Street Diamond Exchange in New York City where she conducts business with Irrfan Khan, who plays a Jain diamond merchant. Jain is an ancient religion from India. Despite their very different cultural backgrounds, there is a flirtatious chemistry between them, including fantasy visions of their own GloLo wedding (it was definitely a Cultural Merger Wedding). Over diamonds, a highly romantic context if you ask me, they discuss food and their respective religious restrictions on the foods they are not allowed to eat. He says "No meat or fish, onion, garlic, potato, no roots, nothing too spicy because it excites the passion". She says "No pig, shrimp, no milk and meat together, and nothing that hasn't been blessed". Imagine the daily dilemma of cooking dinner in their GloLo household? It would just be easier to order a pizza, wouldn't it? Is pizza the ultimate globalisation of love food? Hmm, let's look a bit closer at the main cultural issues concerning food.

Meat

Probably the most fundamental issue in the GloLo kitchen is the carnivore/herbivore polarisation. Many monocultural couples face the same issue, of course, if one partner has chosen a meat-free diet. The difference in the GloLo context is that the vegetarian partner is not practising a food or lifestyle 'preference' by foregoing meat in their diet. Vegetarianism is not only a personal attitude toward eating meat, it is also a fundamental religious, philosophical and even environmental issue. Ritu and Cole have been grappling with the vegetarian issue since their Indian-Scottish Double Wedding. Cole began the discussion.

"Ritu has never knowingly eaten any kind of meat her entire life. How can I argue with that? It's not that I want *her* to eat meat but that *I* want to eat meat, and I want it every day," Cole stressed. "So cooking dinner is a big production at our place. No matter who cooks or what is being cooked, I will add the meat somehow!" he said with conviction.

"Cole tried to become vegetarian," Ritu added. "It lasted for four months. He was grumpy all the time," she laughed.

"Anything for love," he laughed too. "I would eat a pound of tofu and still wake up at 3 am hungry and dreaming of a big T-bone steak. I just gave up. If I can eat meat at lunch time at work, then I will get my fill then. But if I've just had a sandwich, by dinner time I am ready to dig into something bloody."

I asked Ritu how she felt about seeing meat at the table.

"I don't mind so much when the meat is cooked, covered in a sauce and hidden between the vegetables on Cole's plate," she answered. "What bothers me is the raw meat in the fridge. We have an extensive Tupperware collection dedicated to meat only, as well as a strict No Haggis policy. Yuk," she shuddered and crinkled her nose, referring to the traditional Scottish meal of sheep's heart and liver.

"I admit," Cole concluded, "considering how Ritu grew up, she is pretty tolerant. I admire that about her."

"Love has its challenges," Ritu said with a smile.

I asked Cole if he missed eating haggis.

"Uh, do you know what haggis is?" he asked me sceptically and then described the ingredients and preparation of the meal in greater detail. I tried my best not to shudder and crinkle my nose and, like Ritu, say 'Yuk'.

Spices

As with vegetarianism, a spicy palate can simply be a personal preference. It can be learned and therefore may have nothing to do with culture. In a GloLo couple, however, the 'benchmark' for spiciness tends to be different. If you grew up eating curry, then 'spicing things up a little' means something entirely different than if you grew up on mashed potatoes and lamb chops.

Anne and Gregor were quite polarised in the kitchen regarding the role of spices. Anne, from England, refers to salt and pepper as 'spice' whereas Gregor, from Georgia (the Caucasus country, not the southern American state), where food has Turkish and Asian influences, refers to salt and pepper as a good starting point for spicing up a meal.

"The spice rack is like another woman in our marriage," Anne joked. "I like simple foods with a bit of salt and maybe pepper. Is that really British or is it just my taste? I don't want adventure at meal time."

"That is exactly the problem," Gregor said, pointing into the air like Edison upon the brink of a genius discovery. "Food *is* an adventure. Food should be enjoyed. Don't you agree," he asked me expectantly.

Oh, I hate it when that happens in an interview. Fortunately Anne was feeling chatty and continued to explain.

"I like to taste the food whereas Gregor likes to taste the spices. It's just a personal preference I guess although it can be rather dramatic in the kitchen. Gregor sneaks spices into the meal when I am not looking. I cannot leave a pot unwatched!" she exclaimed. "Even if we are having traditional pot roast, by the time Gregor is finished with his handiwork, it is a spicy Georgian dish," she laughed again.

There was something naggingly familiar about this story. I made a mental note to myself to ask my husband to keep his hands visible at all times when I am preparing our next dinner.

Sweets

Dutch Jelle and Malaysian Laila who we met in *Chapter 4 – Meet the Parents* and *Chapter 7 – GloLo Colours* have lovely dinners together but cannot agree on what should be on the breakfast table. After stating her preference for rice-based breakfasts, Laila, described her first morning meal with Jelle.

"He had a little box of chocolate sprinkles which he put on his bread and a bit on his cereal. When I first saw this, it reminded me of a little boy who would make his own breakfast if his mother wasn't home. I thought he was being naughty," she giggled, "but he eats it every day with a big glass of milk too. It seems to be a Dutch thing."

I rather like the idea of chocolate for breakfast and made a mental note to myself to further explore this 'Dutch thing'.

"During the week, breakfast is very individual," Jelle interrupted my chocolate fantasy. "Usually we have lunch at work. By dinner time though, we can usually agree on something we both like."

I asked if they ate an Asian or Dutch dinner.

"We eat both," Laila answered. "The Dutch food makes us fat," she said, patting her (very flat) tummy. "Asian food is healthier."

"That's right," Jelle agreed. "Laila keeps me slim." He patted his tummy too but I will reserve further comment. It does bring up the next point concerning food which is what I call The GloLo Diet.

The GloLo Diet

The GloLo Diet is not well documented as far as I know and this may well be the first printed reference to the phenomenon. I can imagine that it will revolutionise the whole diet industry or at least make you think about your next GloLo relationship.

The GloLo Diet refers to the five kilograms – yes, that is one full dress size – that mysteriously disappears, just by starting a multicultural relationship. (If I really wanted a bestseller, perhaps I should have put this message on the title page.) It sounds hocus-pocus but it works like this: Core foods around the world are simply different. Not to get too nutritionist on you, but the caloric and fat intake of pasta versus couscous versus rice or a sandwich versus a falafel versus a fajita, is simply not the same. When you have relocated for love, five kilos will come or go depending on the direction of your migration. So for example, if pasta replaces couscous, add five kilos. If rice cakes replace sandwiches, lose five kilograms.

I have heard from many North American friends who moved to Europe that with no effort whatsoever and, most importantly, never going to bed hungry, five kilograms *simply vanished*. Europeans who move to Asia experience the same. A life without cheese also means a life without the fat in cheese. I must admit that I would have to be *deliriously* in love to imagine a life with limited cheese. Fortunately Austria has a thriving dairy product industry so I was not torn between my great love of cheese and my great love.

North American bound love birds suffer the 'dark side' of the GloLo Diet, the mysterious *appearance* of an extra five kilograms. The 'super-sizing' and 'bottomless cup' mentality in the USA and I am sorry to include Canada too, sort of lead to a super-sizing of bottoms, if you know what I mean. A change in lifestyle can offset a fattening change in daily diet, however it may take you a while to find the right Hot Yoga studio or spinning class, at least longer than it takes to say 'yes, when asked, 'would you like fries with that?'.

Between the meats, the spices and the sweets, there are countless ways to eat and eat well. Along the GloLo path to a culturally harmonised kitchen, I hereby declare pizza as the official GloLo dinner.

In the next section, we will look at cultural differences in *how* and *when* we eat what we eat.

GloLo wining and dining

Many GloLo couples, jetsetters in particular, have experience with international travel and 'foreign' cuisine. They can eat bagels for breakfast, latkes for lunch, dim sum for dinner and doughnuts for dessert without having a second thought about taste, nutrition or digestion. Where the GloLo couple might split on their universal enthusiasm for fusion food is not *what* they are eating but *how* and *when* they eat it.

Firstly, and probably the biggest fundamental difference in attitude toward food and eating is the *significance* of mealtime. Some cultures are kind of holy about meal time, aren't they? All of the family members are seated together at a table covered in a crisp, clean table cloth, decked with *matching* dishes, cloth napkins and those funny little ledges on which to rest the butter knife. There may be a little prayer or a word of thanks prior to the meal, there is a hierarchy of serving order, appropriate hot and cold beverages are served, and the meal is savoured. Happy chatter and laughter sweeten the experience. A cultural variation to this same meal time ritual is to slurp a bowl of ChocoPuffs cereal while standing at the kitchen sink. It is hardly fair to call both of these meals 'breakfast', is it?

Remember Katharina and Mark, the 'Noble Cause' German-American medical couple who met in Africa and then settled in California? Their repatriation and relocation issues start every day with breakfast. Katharina, sounding a bit perplexed, began.

"We met in a group context in the Sudan and had only spent time alone in hotels where the breakfast is served in a restaurant," Katharina began. "When we first arrived in California, we had very little furniture but at least we had a table and chairs, and proper plates and cutlery. We had just settled into the new flat and I remember seeing Mark standing in the kitchen eating a bowl of cold cereal for breakfast. I assumed he was in a rush but then he went to the sofa and sat down to read the newspaper. His idea of breakfast is just to consume enough food and calories to carry him through the day. He seems to graze through the day and only really sits down to eat at dinner time."

"Hey, I am a busy guy," Mark said with humour. "Breakfast is just to kick-start the day. Katharina wants cloth napkins and five types of jam and seven kinds of cheese. I think it's a waste of time. I want to get on with my day. We can dine when it's dinner time. Then we have time to relax."

"You can relax at any time of day," Katharina said pragmatically. "It's a proper way to start the day," she said, referring to the more Germanic way of sitting at the breakfast table together.

"Well, I can try it," Mark offered congenially. "But I am not ready to cook and clean three times a day. Are you?" he asked with brows raised.

I have to admit, this scene sounded familiar to me. It is another Anglo-Germanic mix that I recognise in my own marriage. My Austrian husband is just so darn *proper* about meal time. He prepares a three-course meal (fruit starter, whole grain carbohydrate middle, and slightly sweet finish, plus juice, tea *and* coffee), which is timed to coincide with the news (*on the radio, NEVER the TV*), and, worst of all, expects me to sit there with him and... relax. If only he would understand that when I am standing over the kitchen sink slurping down my cold cereal, I *am* relaxed.

The irony of the situation is that the whole process reverses itself at dinner or supper. After a morning and afternoon of a sandwich here, a muffin there, dinner time represents the first real chance to sit and enjoy a hot meal. By contrast, my husband, and I suspect Katharina as well, who have had a 'King's breakfast', and a 'Duke's lunch', think that dinner is just the time to sit with pauper-like bread and cheese, perhaps a tomato slice, for a quick meal. My husband says that he is tired after all, and does not want to make a big fuss about dinner. Here is the really funny part – he wants to 'relax'.

Variety is the spice of life... or not

Another funny cultural thing about how food is eaten concerns variety, at dinner time in particular. In some cultures, meat and potatoes, for example, literally mean meat and potatoes, with perhaps a sprig of parsley added for vitamins and colour. By contrast, some cultures like more variety in not just *what* is served but also how it is *prepared* and *served*. There may be, for example, two duck dishes served at the same meal, but after frying, baking, slicing, dicing, spicing and combining with other ingredients, be completely different in taste and appearance.

When GloLo food fashionistas come from opposite extremes of the variety spectrum, it can be pretty challenging to cook a nice dinner that both parties consider to be 'a nice dinner'. The visiting parents-in-law can intensify this difference, as we will see in the next story.

The Great Canadian Barbecue

Ning, from Taiwan, and Danny, from Canada, both in their early 30s, had been dating for three years before Ning's parents came to visit them in Toronto.

"At first our relationship was a big secret," Ning told me. "I thought they would disapprove. It was very romantic actually, but then my aunt found out and she told my parents. They said, 'No big deal. In Canada you find Canadian men.' All the secrecy was for no reason." She laughed.

"We went to Taipei together once to meet Ning's parents, so they already knew me, which was fortunate given how our meeting in Canada went," Danny said shaking his head.

When Ning's parents came to Toronto from Taipei, Danny offered to cook them dinner. As a fellow Canadian, I recognise that his gesture was very stalwart. He thought it would be something special to offer his future parents-in-law a home-cooked meal. He wanted to demonstrate his prowess in the kitchen and show Ning's parents that he would be a good husband. Danny and Ning were going to tell her parents that they were engaged to marry.

Danny took great efforts to prepare a nice meal. He drove across Toronto to buy steaks at a specialty butcher. I knew the one he meant – my husband, encouraged by my steak connoisseur brother, practically lives there whenever we visit Toronto, but let's get back to Danny. He splurged on the best steaks that money can buy. Since I know the shop and prices, believe me, buying the best steaks takes a lot of money. Danny really wanted to give his future in-laws a fine meal, which he did… by Canadian standards.

"I was so focused on the barbecue, I was in 'The Zone'," he told me enthusiastically, referring to the highly concentrated mental state Olympic athletes experience just before they win a gold medal. "I had the veggies cooked to golden perfection, just a bit crunchy in the centre. The baked potatoes were soft and sweet and the steaks, oh the steaks literally melted in your mouth," he swooned. "It was the perfect meal."

I understood his passion. I am Canadian after all.

"But that was all," Ning broke Danny's reverie. "Just those simple foods. No preparation. Just throw it on the grill like feeding chickens. I know Danny loves his barbecue. But in Taiwan, a proper meal, a meal for future parents-in-law, is not three things cooked outdoors," she explained patiently to the Canadians.

"My Great Canadian Barbecue was a total flop," Danny agreed. "A proper Chinese meal has, like, at least 15 different dishes on the table. Everything is chopped and cooked and fried and sliced and covered in sauce and everything. It requires loads of preparation time. To be honest, it all looks the same to me, but they like that," Danny said of Ning's parents and I suppose Taiwan in general.

"How Danny eats is how poor people eat. One piece of meat. One vegetable," Ning said pointing to imaginary pieces of food on the table. "Good food takes time, skill, love. Eating a big steak, cooked only for a few minutes, it's not proper," she concluded in disappointment.

"Can you believe it?" Danny asked me, still astonished. "They thought my 20 dollar steak is what poor people eat!"

I asked if they could explain the cultural culinary confusion to Ning's parents.

"Oh yeah," Danny guffawed in jest. "Ning's dad understood and suggested that the steak would be good for breakfast because it was fast to cook and full of protein. Can you believe it?" he asked again. "A 20 dollar steak for breakfast? I give up," he said half-heartedly.

I asked how Ning's parents responded to the engagement news.

"Very well," Ning answered. "They like Danny very much. They think he is a little bit untamed because he likes to cook outdoors, like Jack London, my dad said. They think all Canadians like to cook outdoors," she laughed.

Oh, we do like to cook outdoors Ning, we really do.

Brains, muffies and rabbit food

There are countless stories of good intentions gone wrong in the cultural translation of food. There is Kiran, the Hindu *vegetarian* fiancé who went to Georgia (again, the country, not the state) and was given the pig's brain, a delicacy and 'special meal for special guest'.

"The pig, which had been roasted on a spit, was stretched out on a long dining table with an apple in its mouth," Kiran shuddered at the memory. "My fiancé's father cracked open the pig's head with a small hammer and dug out the brain and presented it to me like a precious gift. I thought I was in a horror movie."

Less gruesome is the first time I baked muffins for my in-laws. They had never seen a muffin prior to my Canadian cultural invasion into their family kitchen.

"A muffie?" they asked in neither English nor German. "A miniature cake? But not as sweet? But not bread either? *How fascinating*!"

They put the muffie, er, muffin, blueberry bran, my sort of *trademark* if you will, on a plate and happily ate it *with a knife and fork*. My muffins have never been shown such honour.

Then there was the Gambian mother-in-law who asked her Austrian daughter-in-law why the rabbit food, *also known as salad*, was on the dinner table.

"The whole family finds it terribly amusing that I eat fresh salad and raw vegetables. They call me Bunny," she said with amusement.

Leftovers

The English dictionary definition of leftover tells this story best. 'Leftover' is defined as something that remains unused or not consumed, particularly referring to food. Hence we can keep the food from dinner that is 'not consumed' in a plastic container in the refrigerator and warm it up to eat another time, right? Before you hear the ready 'Ping!' of the microwave oven however, consider the second definition of leftover: an anachronistic survival. *Anachronistic*, as in, it is from another time, it is not supposed to be here, and it certainly is not something that is meant to be eaten for dinner.

If you will pardon a generalisation once again, North Americans love leftovers. The leftover is practically its own food group and, in many households, is part of the weekly meal plan. There are even entire cookbooks dedicated to the preparation of leftovers. Yes, cooking excessive volumes of food is actually *deliberate*. Leftovers can be reheated and enjoyed a second or even third day in a row in a kind of hierarchy of decreasing food fanciness. Think of that gallant Christmas turkey, the one my mother always refers to as 'The Bird', which, following the gluttonous days of Christmas, eventually transcends first into a lesser version of its original splendour, reheated with mashed potatoes and served on the daily plates (the good China set and real silver long polished and returned to storage until the next great feast), then turkey pie and downward we go into sandwiches and salads as the excesses of the holiday season turn to regret and tight trousers.

These anachronistic meals are often eaten with more pleasure than the somewhat frenzied day it was cooked in the first place. Opinions on the exquisiteness of this meal, however, tend to differ amongst cultures.

Julia, an American from Seattle, Washington who now lives in Washington, D.C. told me this story before she even knew I was writing a book on multicultural relationships. We were at a particularly impressive conference buffet when I mentioned how I would love to pack some leftovers to take home for lunch the next day. Julia laughed and said that leftovers had 'nearly ruined her life'. With a comment like that, I was a keen audience. The story goes like this…

Julia and Samson had only been dating for four months when she invited him home to Seattle for the Christmas holidays. Samson had just moved to Washington, D.C. for work, she told me, and she knew, even if he did not know, that he was 'The One'. Samson is an economics professor from Chad. She was hoping that the trip would be a forward step in their blossoming GloLo relationship. Julia was certain that he would be impressed by her American family and their warm American hospitality.

"Samson was new to the States," she told me while we waited in line by the salads. "I thought he would enjoy the experience of an American Christmas. I was also hoping to ramp things up a little bit," she said with a wink and we laughed conspiratorially about women and our cunning ways.

"He was on a sabbatical for 18 months," Julia explained. "I knew I had to act fast."

So Julia and Samson flew to Seattle for Christmas with her family.

And her family was very welcoming. Christmas dinner was impressive, and Julia's mother outdid herself preparing a huge bronzed turkey that dominated the table. Before carving the big bird, Julia's father thanked Samson for visiting at this special time of year. Samson indeed felt embraced by the warmth of Julia's family and that the meal was worthy of kings.

However, the Boxing Day dinner, Samson later reported, was like a poor cousin to the spread of the prior evening. He felt uncomfortable and secretly wondered why this comfortably middle-class family could not afford a more appropriate meal, particularly after the lavish feast of the prior evening. The day after Boxing Day was a turning point in their relationship where Samson became, according to Julia, cold and withdrawn. Samson would later tell her that he was insulted by her family and felt rejected. Here is what happened...

Julia's mother once again brought a turkey dinner to the table, proudly proclaiming that she could stretch a Christmas turkey into a week's worth of meals. Samson was not amused. The message to him was clear: you are not welcome here. He thought that her family did not approve of him because they had nothing but leftovers for him. He flew home early.

In Chad, as in many parts of Africa, social status is largely displayed by food and drink. Leftovers represent food for peasants or farm animals. Amongst the poor, women and children might eat leftovers, but not the men. Guests who are welcomed into the home are given the best food the family can afford, and that best food, no matter how poor the family, is never from the category of leftovers. Samson explained later with humour how his family gives all leftover food to the neighbours who feed it to their goats. The repeated visits of the Christmas turkey were insulting to Samson. His family shops for fresh food at an open market daily. It did not occur to him that Julia's mother, who works full-time outside the home, was being an extraordinary hostess, at least according to American standards.

"How did you get back together?" I asked breathlessly. (I could not write a book about this kind of stuff if I did not find it riveting, right?)

It took weeks of separation, silence, then tears, apologies and phone calls home, before Samson and Julia discovered the one-day-to-be-laughed-about Christmas Bird that temporarily tore apart the Love Birds.

"Three months were wasted due to that darn turkey," Julia said. "We were both back in D.C. and I knew it was a race against time to get back together before the end of his sabbatical." Samson is some kind of economics genius apparently and teaches at universities around the world.

"We had mutual friends who had invited us both to dinner, not knowing that there had been a relationship, and not knowing that there had been a communication breakdown," Julia explained. "During dinner, Samson complimented the hostess on her cooking and then a miracle happened. Gary, her husband, said how the meal would taste *even better* the next day and he would have the meat in a sandwich when he went to work on Monday. All five people at the table agreed about the virtues of the leftover. Samson was looking at me, shaking his head and he said, 'You crazy Americans'. I knew I had been saved and we have been together ever since that evening," she glowed.

I asked if Samson likes leftovers now.

"Are you kidding?" she asked me with a smile. "He loves leftovers. When I am cooking, he always says, 'Make extra please so I can have some for lunch tomorrow'."

That, dear reader, is the globalisation of leftovers.

Alcohol

"It's very telling," my editor warned me "that you put alcohol in the food section. It's not a food group you know." Well, I am the proud inventor of the GloLoTini after all, and it was inspired by the GloLo way to eat, drink and be merry, wasn't it?

Different cultures and religions, and even gender values, prescribe the social standard and acceptance of alcohol. It 'helps the meal to digest' some say, it is 'the drink of the gods' say others, 'tis medicinal in its properties' some claim, it is the 'devil in a bottle' claim others.

I have alread mentioned my failed attempts to make GloLo interview couples more relaxed (okay, I admit loose lipped was my real goal) by offering (okay, *encouraging*) them to drink a few more GloLoTinis. I will share another story with you that exemplifies the GloLo divide on spirits and libations.

Schnapps culture

To put it into context, my father-in-law produces *Schnapps*, you know, that firey-burny drink one associates with ski chalets and open fires. It is served in a doll-sized wine glass and is said to warm the blood and soothe the muscles after a rigorous day on the ski slopes. At least that is the Austrian version.

In Canada, by contrast, *Schnapps*, or 'schnapps' actually, is the drink of choice for, let's say, rogues and vagabonds who chug it straight from the bottle which is oh-so-clever-I-never-would-have-guessed disguised in a brown paper bag. A bottle of *Schnapps*/schnapps was therefore a surprising gift for my parents to receive from my husband upon their first meeting.

"It's from my father," my GloLo husband proudly said, displaying the *Schnapps*/schnapps bottle like a waiter presenting a fine wine. "He makes it himself and my mother makes the labels," he added with relish, proud of his family's cottage industry.

I watched as my parents processed this information. The drink of derelicts, not even produced according to government regulated safety standards but concocted in a musty basement far away in Europe where a great war was fought, and then smuggled across the Canadian border into their low-to-no-alcohol home by none other than their new son-in-law. My mother's eyebrows were just one notch away from their maximum arch when she managed her best fake 'How lovely' before taking the bottle at the neck as you would a poisonous snake or other biting reptile, and putting it safely in a dark cupboard.

The *Schnapps* of my father-in-law is coveted within our social circle and is highly appreciated as a birthday or housewarming gift. My husband therefore did not understand my parents' lack of enthusiasm for his father's moonshine.

The story exemplifies the meaning of alcohol-based drinks in society. Unfortunately in this case, it was a clash of the 'digestive night-cap' mentality versus the 'devil in a bottle'. During my last visit to my parents' home, I saw the *Schnapps*/schnapps bottle, untouched of course, under the kitchen sink, perhaps waiting its inevitable future as drain cleaner.

This reference to Canada and Austria is an isolated event of course, and in no way do I suggest that all Austrians are imbibing *Schnapps* with wild abandon, nor that all Canadians use alcohol and schnapps only as drain cleaner. However the story demonstrates *general attitudes* toward alcohol. The next story further emphasises this point.

Hindu hiccups

Clara and Jai are a Same But Different English couple who live in London. Clara, from Brighton, seemed a bit shy, which makes the story all the more interesting. Jai, who is very cosmopolitan, grew up in London in an Indian immigrant family. They met at university and had not really noticed cultural differences in their relationship. There was, however, what they refer to as the 'Hindu hiccups incident'.

"Clara is a party girl," Jai stated. "I knew it when I met her and not a lot has changed over the years. British girls like to party and drink too much. I am Hindu and Hindus generally don't drink, even though I will have a bit of wine or beer myself on occasion."

"Oh gosh," Clara exclaimed, hands on her reddening cheeks. "Please don't tell her that story." Naturally it was much too late and the story had to be told.

Clara and Jai had taken time off between graduation from university and the start of work to travel India. They backpacked around and stayed for weeks at a time with different relatives of Jai.

"We were quite immersed in India, weren't we Jai?" Clara said, looking at Jai for confirmation. "We lived just like the families we stayed with. Things were going fine until Rebecca showed up."

Rebecca is Clara's best friend and Jai calls them 'the silly sisters' apparently. She brought with her two bottles of wine which she had picked up at the Duty Free on her way over from London to Delhi.

"Well, I had not had any wine or anything to drink in at least three months," Clara explained, "but it tasted *so lovely*. One thing led to another and suddenly Bex and I had finished a whole bottle. Then Bhuvan, Jai's cousin came home and wanted to try some wine so we opened the second bottle. Then, well, things got a little bit out of control. We were singing and laughing and dancing with Bhuvan. We woke everyone up. It was all kind of inappropriate and unladylike," Clara admitted sheepishly.

"Bhuvan had the hiccups," Jai added to the scandal, "and Rebecca called it the Hindu hiccups."

Both Clara and I stifled our own laughter. (I know it was unprofessional, but I just could not help it.) Apparently Bhuvan, not accustomed to alcohol, felt the giddy effects rather quickly and had made his desires for Rebecca known. Clara saw them 'snogging' at some point, she said. Jai tried to smooth things over.

"My aunt asked me, 'why do those girls drink such poison?' She had never seen anything like it," Jai said. "Poor Bhuvan too. He was rather unwell the following day. His passion for Rebecca had also vanished."

Well, I was disappointed to hear that the globalisation of love had not succeeded in this debaucherous evening.

"The real consequences were only realised when we returned to England a month later," Clara continued. "Jai's mother was livid. She said I was disgraceful and that Rebecca should marry Bhuvan. It was a bit of a family scandal actually, wasn't it Jai?" Clara said, turning to him once again.

"Ah, we're English now," Jai consoled her. "It wasn't that bad. It was just a cultural misunderstanding."

They happen all the time, don't they?

Up in smoke

"It's very telling," my editor warned me once again "that you put smoking in the food section. Cigarettes do not provide sustenance you know."

I know. I am not particularly fond of smoking to be honest, but that should not prevent me from writing about it. I am a professional after all. And to be perfectly honest, I do not have any really good 'pass the bong, please' GloLo stories either, however it is a subject worthy of mention.

As with alcohol, general social attitudes toward smoking are very much influenced by national cultural attitudes *and laws* on smoking. In many parts of the world, smoking cigarettes is considered 'cancerous' and maybe a bit 'socially deviant'. By contrast, in other parts of the world, smoking, particularly for men, is considered to be part of a good meal. Attitudes *and laws* are changing all the time however. Where smoking becomes a GloLo issue is exposure to and mixing of cultural attitudes *and laws*.

Apparently one mother-in-law from a puff-happy country was stopped by the police in an anti-smoking country because she had her grandchildren in the car with her and she was smoking while driving. Many countries and states have made it illegal to smoke in a car where children are passengers, you see, so she was actually *breaking the law*. The story is all hearsay but it is fun to imagine the daughter-in-law bailing her husband's mother out of jail for her crimes.

Well, that concludes the section on wining and dining and how and when we eat what we eat. The next section concerns how GloLo couples entertain and who they invite to dinner.

Guess who's coming to dinner?

This last section on food is not really about food itself and more about the GloLo social situations that surround food. First and foremost is a dinner invitation.

Movie night Down Under

Do you remember Robyn and Harold, the Australian-Austrian couple who moved to France? Harold had quite a surprise about the rules of entertaining and being invited to dinner 'Down Under'.

"That was a bit ridiculous," Harold shook his head at the memory. "Friends of Robyn had invited us over for dinner. I had never met them and Robyn had not seen them in three years so I thought it was going to be a special evening."

Robyn looked ready to burst out in laughter and I made a mental note to myself to introduce her to Clara. I think the two would get along.

"Between France and Austria, we cannot get home to Australia often," she added, attempting to be serious. "I really miss my friends but we Skype a lot and email so we are usually up-to-date on current events with each other."

"Right," agreed Harold, "but it was still a bit ridiculous. We flew over 24 hours to get there, then we drove across Brisbane in scorching heat. We arrived at their place and within 20 minutes, we were watching a movie and eating nachos," he cried in exasperation.

"Harold does not believe that finger food is food," explained Robyn, clearly wanting to redirect this conversation. "Australians just love to sit back and watch a movie together. It's very social and makes for a relaxing evening."

"I can stay at home and watch a movie," Harold said, his exasperation still evident. "I don't need to put on a jacket and fly to the ends of the earth."

"I told you the jacket was too formal," Robyn retorted.

Suspecting that Robyn and I might share a bit of Commonwealth culture, I asked her what she thinks of invitations to dinner in Austria.

"Well, it's very nice," she answered. "When we are invited out, the hostess makes a big effort. It's like going to a restaurant. The food is prepared beforehand, the table is set, and you don't have to do the washing up. The hostess does everything. Guests just sit at the table and are served. I like to be a guest but when I have friends over, everyone pitches in a bit," she laughed.

Robyn and Harold's story includes several of the key GloLo issues of entertaining and receiving invitations. Guests and hosts may have different expectations of the role they play in an evening together as well as of the food to be served and the activities and entertainment.

Pat O'Luck

My husband was once very surprised to see me cooking in the kitchen shortly before we were leaving to visit friends. I mean, he was not surprised to see me in the kitchen, because I am there all the time of course, but he was surprised that I was cooking just before heading out for the evening. The hostess had requested that I bring a potato gratin, which I do rather well I must admit. (Perhaps there is a GloLo cookbook in the future however I do not want to create too much excitement.) I told my husband that it was a potluck dinner and I was bringing the potato gratin.

"Who is Pat O'Luck?" he asked me, sounding puzzled. "I thought Sandra and Martin invited us over for dinner."

"A potluck," I explained patiently, as an experienced GloLo spouse does, "is a meal where everyone brings food to share. The hostess co-ordinates the meal and serves the drinks."

"Oh. We bring our own food? Are they having financial trouble?" my husband asked again, clearly unfamiliar with the concept, but I thought it was nice of him to consider the situation from their side.

"No, it's a potluck. Pot. Luck. Everyone pitches in," I thought of Robyn's claim. "Everyone brings food so the hosts don't have to do all the work."

"Then why do they invite us? Why not just go to a restaurant?" my husband asked, and I had to admit they were good questions. I made a mental note to myself to further explore the possibility for the 'globalisation of potlucks'.

On that note, it is lunch time for the author. I have some leftover turkey in the fridge from a potluck barbecue dinner we attended on the weekend. There were at least two varieties of duck, seven kinds of cheese for sure, and at least 15 different dishes in total. Some were *spicy* and some were *not spicy enough*. Not everyone ate the salad and the pet rabbit looked particularly happy. There were sweet deserts and I think I saw the Dutch guest with chocolate on his dinner plate. We drank wine and *Schnapps*/schnapps and sang and danced and the unhappy smokers were quarantined in a shady corner of the garden. We did not watch a movie but the radio played a narrative in the background (the guests were too loud to hear in which language). Everyone brought in their plates, knives and forks from the garden to the kitchen, but we still left a mess for the hosts to clean up. There was some jostling at the buffet when the hostess announced that there were leftovers and everyone should take something home. It was a wonderful evening, I think, because I agree with Epictetus.

Eat as becomes you, and be silent or even better, chat and laugh a bit too. If you want, drink and even smoke as becomes you, and be silent, or chat and laugh a bit too, for food, and the GloLo chatter and laughter it brings, is an undeniable medium for the globalisation of love.

Top 10 clues that you have a GloLo kitchen

1. There are two sections in the refrigerator, divided by bright red tape with colour-coded plastic storage boxes clearly marked Vegetarian/Kosher/Holy and Non-vegetarian/Not Kosher/Heathen.
2. Your partner refuses to kiss you after you have eaten your favourite national dish until you have brushed your teeth… and gargled.
3. When you buy staple foods of your home country, you have to go to the local 'specialty food shop'.
4. When family visit from your home country, you send them a *very long* shopping list of your favourite foods to import.
5. You ration the food, hide it from your spouse, and immediately book a flight home when supplies are getting low.
6. When you prepared your favourite childhood food for your GloLo toddler, your spouse looked frightened and threatened to call the authorities.
7. Instead of asking 'what are we having for dinner tonight, darling?' you and your GloLo spouse ask each other, 'what are *you* having for dinner tonight, darling?'
8. The difference between your idea and your spouse's idea of 'a quick dinner' is about an hour and a half.
9. What you call a 'house pet', your spouse calls 'dinner'.
10. You thought making tea required a tea bag and a mug of hot water; your spouse is painstakingly teaching you the correct seven step process and the meaning of a 'proper' tea set.

Wendy Williams

Children

For much of the time when I have been writing this book, there has been a multicultural baby and now toddler somewhere very nearby or perhaps underfoot or even pounding on the keyboard, usually the 'Delete' button, which I am sure is a pure coincidence. Children they say, in all cultures actually, change your life. So far what I have noticed the most is how they change a stylish living room, if I do say so myself, into a colourful explosion of plastic debris just waiting to be tripped over by the next adult carrying a hot cup of coffee. All children worldwide have this affect on living rooms. Children of multicultural parents, I would dare to poster, have even more interior decoration potential encoded in their multicultural DNA.

What is so special about GloLo Junior, you might ask? Basically, each and every multicultural issue that is discussed in this book, from chapter headings to tiny sub-titles, is magnified once a child is involved. Children are the ingredient that transform nice, savvy, culturally unique, strong sense of self, chummy loving, GloLo genetically enhanced people into 'parents'. If you always thought that your multicultural marriage was 'no big deal', the arrival of a little bundle of GloLo joy can put your relationship on the multicultural pressure cooker. Joel Crohn writes that the "biggest challenge most cross-cultural couples face is in raising children." Note that he did not mince his words, or attempt any diplomatic, politically correct or soft delivery approaches. Let's look further into multicultural parents and the globalisation of children. This chapter includes:

- Best for baby
- Going forth to multiply
- Pregnancy
- GloLo Junior
- Education and discipline
- Language
- Religion
- Who am I?

Best for baby

You want what is best for your children, just like your partner, but who decides what is 'best for the baby'? Attitudes towards babies, children, parenting and child care are highly culturally specific, most of which may not be apparent to a GloLo couple until *after* a little three kilogram dictator in diapers arrives on the scene. Where you once rejoiced in your multicultural marriage and admired the cultural quirks of your GloLo partner, the arrival of a baby may change the dynamic and impact of those cultural idiosyncrasies. Judith P Siegel, author of *What Children Learn From Their Parents' Marriage: It May Be Your Marriage, but It's Your Child's Blueprint for Intimacy* writes "Two people may be attracted to each other because they found their differences to be a source of pleasure, yet bringing up children differently from the way they grew up raises an awareness of otherness which can create tension, anxiety, and even fear of difference." Once again, the language is direct. GloLo parents may eye each other with suspicion and distrust, like double-agents in a spy film, in love but with divided loyalties. So why does a baby turn a happy GloLo relationship into an international spy thriller?

Firstly, caring for a newborn is a high intensity job. There are a lot of management decisions to be made, starting with the frequent feedings, when, what, where and from who, the necessity of 'special pants', cloth, disposable or *au naturel*, and then that wobbly little head that threatens to disengage itself from the main baby body at any moment if not held securely in place. And that is just the first day. How to deal with each of these issues and who should be dealing with the issues is determined by family, history, geography and climate, socio-economics, education, and so on. Most of us believe that how our mothers / fathers / grannies / aunts / uncles / nannies / wet nurses did it was *the way* to do it. Of course, no two mothers / fathers / grannies / aunts / uncles / nannies / wet nurses are alike, particularly if they live continents apart. *The way*, as it all turns out, is only *one* way of a million possibilities, except for the wobbly head part which is universally protected by loving hands of mothers / fathers / grannies / aunts / uncles / nannies / wet nurses around the world.

Secondly, having children will rock your GloLo world because they lead to an increase in social contact with the family. There will likely be more frequent visits with family and friends and an increased *intensity* of the familial bond as everyone chips in to welcome the new family member. Even if the social contact is broken and you are not on speaking terms with your family, a child will change and reinforce awareness of the situation. Your child is not just *your child* after all. The little darling is also somebody's grandchild, somebody's niece or nephew, somebody's cousin and so on, and each family member will have their own idea of the relationship they should have with the baby.

Thirdly, children increase social contact and exposure to the outer world around you. So even if you have been living in your own self-declared Culture Free Zone, and you have pizza or sushi delivered every night for dinner and shop online for your favourite brands from home and Skype with your favourite friends from back home and have no contact with the non-virtual world around you, having a child forces you as a parent to go beyond your own established cultural comfort zone. There is the extended family I mentioned above, and also walking the baby in the pram (it helps them sleep better), taking the tots to baby swimming, which is much more vigorous than it sounds by the way, going to the doctor for those nasty immunisations, play dates, Baby Sing, Mommy Tot Yoga which is admittedly more about mommy but still social, birthday parties, and a trip to the zoo are just a few of the core components of baby's life. *You* are allowed to closet yourself in your Culture Free Zone, but kids will push you out over the edge and suddenly you are in the country and culture where you reside, whether or not this is to your liking.

Essentially, baby's arrival changes the dynamic between you and your GloLo partner and exposes you to your extended family and in-laws as well as the culture where you live. By comparison, a few toys strewn about the living room is child's play. But before we talk about GloLo tots and toddlers and the effect they have on a GloLo couple, let's look at the effect of family expansion even before the stork makes a delivery.

Going forth to multiply

Call it the survival instinct, call it the birds and the bees, or call it genetic narcissism, every species in the ecosystem has the need for continuity which is satisfied by producing offspring. When Mother Nature, or other *divine creator*, devised this cycle of life, college tuition fees were nowhere near what they are today, so the go forth and multiply model probably seemed more reasonable at the time. Anyway, there is a primal need that drives us to procreate and secure the future survival of the species. In addition to 'surviving', 'thriving' is an additional desire for mankind. On a broad spectrum, thriving can mean anything from having ten children who all make it into adulthood by living from the land in a remote jungle, eating nuts and berries, to having one child who makes it into Harvard and graduates at the top of the class, and there are countless variations in between. How societies have developed and the different norms and values they have, therefore, strongly influence our idea of 'surviving' and 'thriving' and going forth to multiply. Hence the social and cultural significance of having a child may vary within the GloLo couple.

Duty to family

Even monocultural couples are frequently pressured or even pestered by family members, friends and even strangers to *breed*. In some families and cultures, the pressure and pestering or 'hopeful enquiry' is only meant to encourage the personal decision of the potential parents. But in some cultures, producing children is a duty which is *owed* to the family.

A lifetime of Woody Allen movies has taught cinema going fans that Jewish mothers have a strong desire for grandchildren and they voice their desires openly. Remember Irish-born Mandy who converted to Judaism in *Chapter 6 – Religion*? Her mother-in-law was no exception.

"My wedding to Stewart was really part two of our integration process," the designer, who moved to Connecticut with her family when she was 12, started the conversation.

"I was a non-practising Catholic when I met Stewart. Then I chose to become Jewish. It was an intense process and I enjoyed it very much. But then we had to plan the wedding, so it was a busy time. We were married for two minutes when Joan, his mother said loudly, 'now when will you finally give me grandchildren?' Everyone laughed of course, but I thought it was intrusive and demanding, like I was just a baby maker."

Stewart, on the other hand, noticed the *absence* of pressure from Mandy's family.

"Mandy's family have never enquired about our plans for children. Don't they want to know? Isn't it important to them that we have children? Their grandchildren?" Stewart asked.

"It's not that they don't care," Mandy answered, "it's just that having children is our choice, something we do for ourselves, not for other people."

"That is a fundamental difference between us," Stewart said turning to me. "It would disappoint my family. They gave me life, I should give life back."

I asked if they thought the difference in attitude was cultural or personal.

"It is family culture I guess," Stewart answered after some thought. "Family culture is both historical and religious. I am not the end of the line for my family. They survived a lot and will continue to survive."

Why can't you?

Wanda and Thomas are both from Kenya but from different tribes. Wanda is Meru and Thomas is Luo, a tribe that practises polygamy. They live in Nairobi. Married for seven years, the pair has endured repeated pressure from family members on both sides who felt that they had failed in their 'duty' to have children.

"My family encouraged me to find another wife," Thomas explained. "I promised Wanda at our marriage that there would not be another wife, but my family believes if Wanda cannot create children, another wife should do it."

Wanda continued with her family's reaction.

"My family, my father in particular, encouraged divorce. He said, look, if you are not going to have children together, you should divorce him. Maybe other issues played a role with my father," she explained, referring to intense ethnic strife in Kenya between the Meru and Luo tribes, "but he wanted me to have children. If I didn't have children with Thomas, then I should divorce him."

"So we both face tremendous pressure from within the family," Thomas said. "Wanda's sister, who is younger, is now pregnant. This has reduced the pressure somewhat," Thomas indicated with his hands pushing downward.

"Your mother said something like, if she can have a baby, why can't you?" Wanda exclaimed.

"Yes, it is very difficult," Thomas repeated.

I asked if their families were typical in Kenya, or typical of the Luo and Meru tribes.

"Oh yes, having children is a duty to your parents," Thomas answered. "I think it is the same everywhere, isn't it?"

I remembered the tears of joy when my husband and I told our parents that after ten years of marriage, we were 'expecting'. Maybe our parents were just relieved that after ten years of marriage, we were not 'expecting to divorce' that they wept joyous tears. And maybe Thomas is right too.

Duty to God

French Joelle and French Canadian Philippe, who we met in *Chapter 1* as a Same But Different couple, also recognised some external pressure on their family planning.

"We are both spiritual," Joelle began. "We are Catholic. Only when we were talking about starting a family did it become clear that we have different ideas about family. I wanted a family whereas Philippe thought it was our duty to God to have children. It was pressure for me and still is. We have two young children. I think that is enough. Philippe thinks it is just the beginning."

"I have six brothers and sisters," explained Philippe, "and I always assumed that I would also have a large family. It's not so much about a duty. It's just the way life was meant to be."

"Where would we put more children?" Joelle asked, waving around their apartment which was very cute, but admittedly a bit crowded. That leads us to a very different perspective on having children.

Luxury goods

If you flip through the pages of any celebrity gossip magazine, it will not take long to conclude that for any 40plus Hollywood actress, having a child is absolutely *de rigueur*. The newest must-have accessory is a sort of life style option, comparable with the decision to live in the city or country, considering how it fits together with careers, travel plans and membership to the gym or yacht club. Children, therefore, have become a sort of luxury good that couples 'indulge in' once they have reached other life 'goals' such as buying a house or winning an Oscar.

Russian Julia and Austrian Patrick, both on the cusp of 30, approached the 'life style question' on children very differently. Patrick was the first to broach this subject.

"In Austria, having children follows a sequence of events. University, maybe travelling, finding a good job, buying a house, and then when we are ready, having children."

"This I do not understand," interjected Julia. "I want babies now when I am young. Babies don't need a big house. Patrick thinks babies are a luxury, hopefully we can afford one day. I think babies are part of our life, not a luxury, a necessity."

I asked how they resolved this issue.

"First step is to marry this summer. Then babies, babies, babies," said Julia affirmatively.

I looked at Patrick for confirmation.

"It's not how I had planned things, but it's okay. We'll manage," he sighed.

"Yes!" squeaked Julia, "very good," and she patted Patrick's hand.

She seemed so happy, it was hard for me not to want more babies, babies, babies too.

Commodity trading

Who a child belongs to and the, uh, shall we say 'economic value' of a child adds another dimension in multicultural parenting. Austrian Tanja had been married to Gambian Lamin without having borne children for several years and it became a family discussion during their last trip to Gambia.

"I am the eldest son," Lamin said, "and we have no children. My family sees this as a great sorrow. By offering us the son of my sister, they would ease our sorrow, strengthen the bond within our family, and give Kebba (the Gambian boy) an opportunity to be educated in Europe."

"At first I wanted to take the boy only because I felt sorry for a child whose parents would be willing to give him away and send him so far away from home. It seemed strange," Tanja continued. "They treat him like a commodity. I did not understand the sense of family and community. Children in Gambia are raised by the family, the whole family, so giving away a child is not really giving it away. It's more like sharing the child."

In the end, Tanja and Lamin did not take Kebba back to Austria.

"Kebba has extended family in Africa. Here in Austria we are alone, without sisters and brothers, aunts and uncles. God will bless us with our own children," finished Lamin.

Adoption

Remember Angel and Edward, the environmentalist-oil man couple we met in *Chapter 9 – Some More Cultural Stuff*? In addition to their different ideas about 'family', they discovered that their cultural attitudes toward adoption are also very different.

"The beginning of our family was very near the end of our marriage," Edward began. "Angel had what I considered to be strange ideas about having children. She wanted us to have our own children and to adopt other people's children and to create a real commune," he said dryly.

"Eddie did not like the idea of adoption at first. In England, it's all about bloodlines and heirs and so on. In our Mexicano community, children were adopted by families as a way of helping each other. Family lines are not so impermeable."

I knew from our mutual contact that Edward and Angel have six young children.

"We cut a deal," Edward continued, and I could not tell if he was joking. "Angel is always negotiating. We had three of our own and we adopted three. There are so many. I can't tell you which ones were born to us and which ones were adopted. My kingdom is complete in any case."

"Never mind his manner. Do you see that cat in the garden?" Angel asked, pointing to a well fed looking tabby. "Tough Eddie 'adopted' him. He saw Tony (the cat, named after Tony Blair) injured on the road side while driving to work one day. Eddie took the morning off to drive Tony to the veterinarian. They worship each other," she added, smiling at 'Eddie' who had the decency to blush every so slightly.

So even if the attitude toward starting a family is personal, culture acts as a kind of reference point in family planning. If everyone in your cultural circle is having or *not* having children, it is challenging not to think you should be doing the same, even if you live somewhere else. Family, religion, culture and *instinct* all play a role in this very personal decision to 'survive'. I almost forgot to mention that babies are cute too.

Pregnancy

Another culturally loaded issue along the family expansion path that might surprise GloLo couples is the different cultural attitudes toward pregnancy. As mentioned earlier in this chapter, the need to 'procreate' and to 'survive' is an instinct in all species. What 'procreate' and 'survive' really mean, when taken out of the purely biological context, is sex. There are some folks who consider the natural way to get pregnant, you know the birds and the bees kind of thing, as a kind of a *private affair*. Then there are folks who think that getting pregnant is more of a *family affair*.

This is not a situation that is reserved for multicultural couples of course. Any couple trying to conceive a child inadvertently opens up their bedroom door for general viewing by family and friends. Questions like, "Have you tried...?" with a detailed description of a kinky contortionist position from Aunt Martha, where she got the advice we do not want to know, and coaching from Uncle Bill on what to eat to "get the boys ready to swim" become common conversations at family gatherings.

Remember John and Lajita who had a successful Cultural Merger Wedding? It seems that everyone in Minnesota is cheering them on for a successful pregnancy.

"Every member of John's family knows my menstrual cycle," bemoaned Lajita. "They make suggestions such as a weekend at home or a weekend away. I had to travel for business and three people mentioned that the timing was not very good. In India, we just don't talk about these things with the entire family. It makes me squirm."

"I know it is hard for Lajita," John said, taking her hand. "Getting pregnant has become a family project with too many project managers. They all mean well, but it is pretty awkward for us."

Once the pregnancy is well under way, and sometimes even before, biracial parents may face questions about what the baby will look like. My friend Michaela, from Czech Republic has very, very fair skin. She is married to Dirk from South Africa, who has very, very dark skin.

"Will the baby be Black or White was the main question we heard, even from strangers," Michaela told me. "Having a biracial baby is not like baking a cake. We had to explain the role of genetics to a lot of people," she said, still sounding amused.

Action!

Even though pregnancy is a natural biological process, there are differences in what is considered 'natural' during this nine month period. It might come as a surprise to a GloLo mother-to-be how society treats her pregnancy. In some parts of the world, pregnancy is treated almost like an illness, with regular doctor visits and vitamins and bed rest whereas elsewhere it is considered a good time to harvest the fields when your centre of gravity is low anyway.

In Canada, for example, there is a more or less nationwide zero tolerance toward pregnant mothers consuming any type of alcohol, not even those tiny chocolate liquors which no one really likes anyway, and a pregnant woman who orders a glass of wine in a restaurant will be refused service. Only bad, reckless, irresponsible, selfish, unmotherly mothers drink wine during pregnancy after all. You can imagine my surprise when I was hugely pregnant and miserable in my whale-like stature and the Austrian doctor encouraged, *yes encouraged*, me to have a glass of red wine. He said something about 'blood circulation' and 'relaxing' and 'feet up', all of which sounded terribly appealing. I was *huge* remember. The Canadian in me, however, doubted the doctor's orders, so I polled a few girlfriends, both Austrian and foreign women, and there was 100% consensus that Austrian doctors and midwives promote red wine, *in very small doses mind you*, during pregnancy.

I will not tell you what I did with this bit of Austrian medical wisdom. I expect that many, probably millions of Canadians will be reading this book. Suffice it to say that our daughter was born with excellent blood circulation, looking quite relaxed actually, and with her feet up.

Another one of my favourite cultural observations on pregnancy and childbirth concerns the video of the baby's delivery. Many North American pregnancy books include a paragraph or two about the 'birth video', you know the filming of GloLo Junior's arrival, with sage advice such as "be sure to have extra batteries for the camera so you don't miss recording this precious moment!" When these books are translated for the German market, the editors need not bother translating this section.

The birth of a child is a once-in-a-lifetime experience, even if you have many, and therefore some families want to capture it all on film so that they can relive the once-in-a-lifetime moment over and over again, as well as share the video with friends and family members who could not attend the original performance, or had back row seats in the delivery room and missed all the good bits. Let it be known that this is not a universally practised birthing ritual.

Filming a woman with her legs up in stirrups, with as much blood and gore as a slasher movie, sweating and grunting, and the poor dear without a splash of makeup on is just not done in some parts of the world. When an American friend asked my husband, Austrian remember, if he would be filming the birth of his first child, my husband said no, he had other things to do, like trying not to faint.

To snip or not to snip

Another area of hot cultural debate within a GloLo family is the circumcision of little boys. Ken, an American father really wanted his newborn to be circumcised although it is not common practice in Austria.

"It is not even a religious issue, it is simply healthier for the boy and it is better to have the procedure done immediately," Ken told me.

His Austrian wife Gabi was less convinced.

"I'm not so sure about circumcision. The doctors here said they would perform the procedure even though they admit to having very little experience. When I handed baby Josh to the nurse to be taken for the operation, it was hard to let go," she said.

"I guess it was the first time we had any sort of cultural discussion. I suppose when Josh is older, there will be more discussions like this one," Ken predicted.

I think Ken is right. I will have to tell him about the bestselling book about multicultural relationships called *The Globalisation of Love*.

More on adoption

The adoption process is much like a pregnancy, with nervous parents binging on chocolate and suffering sleepless nights with anticipation of the new family member, except that adoption usually takes *even longer* than nine months and requires way more paperwork, as Edward and Angel can tell you. Yet GloLo couples are uniquely positioned to become adoptive parents. They have already created a filial bond with someone from 'outside of the clan' so to speak. It follows that since GloLo parents do not belong to the same clan, there is less of an 'outsider status' for the adopted child. When you think about it, it is a very natural process for GloLo families to adopt.

GloLo parents do face a few extra decisions following the initial decision to adopt. For starters, where do they find the little tyke? GloLo parents have three, or possibly four, options. They may adopt in Mom's country, Dad's country, a third country where they live or choose international adoption, which is usually from a poor country far away.

Each of these options will be affected by national adoption laws and international regulations. Further, biracial couples might consider adopting a child who is Mom's colour, Dad's colour, a mix of both or something entirely different. If GloLo parents are adopting older children who can already speak, then language will also be a consideration.

Lily and Emmanuel are a French multicultural who adopted three children from three different countries. Lily, White, was born in France and Emmanuel, Black, was born in the Ivory Coast and now has French citizenship.

"Inclusiveness in our family is achieved through variety," Lily began. "We are all different, that is what makes us a family. Colour, language, religion, everyone brings in something special. When we travel together internationally to visit their birthplaces, passport control is a nightmare. It is assumed that we are smuggling the children, but we all have the same last name and we are all French citizens. Only Angelina has more variety," she joked, referring to Angeline Jolie who pledged to adopt 'one from every continent', which she seemed well on her way of achieving until getting bogged down by twins. When *does* she sleep I wonder?

GloLo Junior

Once GloLo Junior has finally arrived in the multicultural family, then what? Well, first he or she needs a name. What's in a name, you might ask? Well, everything.

What's in a name?

Let's be honest here, every parent tries to secretly, silently, stealthily stake their claim on their child by choosing his or her name. There is polite discourse about including poetic names of beloved ancestors from both sides of the family, choosing a name to 'suit the baby, we'll know when she's born' or, my personal favourite, 'we want her to have an international name'. What happens once the baby is born, however, below the thrill and fanfare of baby's arrival is a fierce cultural battle to brand mark the child and a flurry of helpful family members who offer to 'deal with paperwork' by filling out the child's birth certificate.

What happens in the GloLo baby name game is that the range of potential names is broadened beyond the scope of any one language. What is a common or traditional name in one culture and language can be a tongue twister just across the border. Grandparents, in particular, claim they cannot spell or even pronounce 'foreign' names. Even pronounceable names might not be accepted.

"Mark?" they ask in astonishment. "Ah, Markus, a good name" or "Maaah-Reee-Ah? Don't you mean Mary?" is frequently heard amidst claims of how beautiful the child is and how he surely gets his thick hair from our side of the family. Even using a 'C' instead of a 'K' in Carl, or Karl, can raise eyebrows. One baby name was considered 'not very patriotic' due to tense political relations between the counties of the parents. GloLo babies often end up with compromise first names followed by a long list of multicultural names to satisfy the wishes of family.

"Whether in Korea or Canada," a Korean-Canadian friend told me, "people think my name is a series of typos. Like my parents thought people wouldn't know I am mixed culture just by looking at me. Well, I hope all my dead ancestors are happy."

Some GloLo parents solve the name game by using different nicknames for the baby. It sounds confusing, but when the parents speak to the child in a different language anyway, having multiple names is reasonable. One parent made the humorous prediction that his daughter would surely become a pop star because of the overwhelming use of pet names in two languages.

"She's called Precious, Sweet Pea, and Honey Girl by different family members. Growing up as Honey Girl is bound to imbed itself in her psyche," he joked.

Hmm, that is a good point. I made a mental note to myself to stop calling our toddler 'Mouse'.

Mosquitoes and marshmallows

Once the little bundle of GloLo joy moves into the family home, what do you do with her? Like monocultural parents, GloLo parents will bring in their cultural and family experiences, customs, styles, methods, role definition and filial patterns to parenting. Like all parents, GloLo parents will face the challenge of integrating two sets of parenting values into one set of parents.

The GloLo parents I met with frequently said that they wanted their children to have the same things they had while they were growing up, like roasting marshmallows over an open fire under a starry sky on a summer night and being attacked by swarms of mosquitoes, for example. Roasted marshmallows are *very tasty* by the way. However, when you are from way, way over there and now have children with someone from way, way over here, you have very different childhood experiences. How can you recreate undeniable childhood experiences and rites of passage from two different cultures and create a new type of GloLo childhood experience? Most parents recognise that their children might even have something better. I recognise that roasting marshmallows over an open fire under a starry sky on a summer night and *not* being attacked by swarms of mosquitoes is actually not a bad compromise.

And baby makes three...

The role and involvement of the family and caretakers is another source of potential surprise and conflict for GloLo parents. Perhaps I should amend that sentence to 'the role and involvement of the extended family is another source of potential surprise and conflict for *all parents all over the world*'. Yes, that sounds more accurate, doesn't it? Everybody has expectations and ideas that usually follow culturally prescribed norms.

In individualist societies, where extended families live separately from the nuclear family, the mother and father of the child are at the top of the hierarchy of potential caretakers, which might include babysitters and other 'outsourcing' arrangements. Grandparents may 'visit' and 'babysit' GloLo Junior once or twice a week, assuming that everyone even lives in the same country.

By contrast, in collectivist societies, where the extended family and two or three generations live together under one roof, GloLo Junior will have a whole in-house management team of caregivers. Aunties and grandmothers will be intimately involved in the daily life of GloLo Junior and play a significant role in decision-making and managing what is best for baby.

GloLo couples from each of these worlds will experience some degree of distress over child-raising, ranging from "I'm the mother, I'll make the decisions" to "You're paying a *stranger* 10 bucks an hour to watch GloLo Junior *sleep*?!" Sometimes it is just about seemingly mundane things too. The decision to leave the window open in the baby's room at night, the old fresh-air-is-good-for-her versus she'll-catch-her-death-in-the-breeze debate, can divide a neighbourhood.

One Canadian mother of a one year-old was beside herself when the baby's grandmother, also known as The Mother-In-Law, cut the baby's hair without the mother's consent. I am not the 'Canadian mother' by the way, but I can hear her pain.

The cultural background to the snippet incident is that Baby's First Haircut is a big event in Canada. The child is placed on a high stool, usually in the kitchen, and a fresh towel dons her tiny shoulders. The feathery locks are lovingly snipped, usually by a nervous but excited mother, and then saved for posterity, pressed in the baby book along with other *momentous* milestones in the child's life. Before, during and after photos are taken, usually by an equally nervous but excited father. There is a gift for the child such as a cupcake or little toy, a sort of 'reward' for bravely making it through this essential rite of passage into toddlerhood.

Well, that is the way my Canadian girlfriend explained it to the obviously not Canadian grandmother, also known as The Mother-in-Law. After listening patiently to this lesson in Canadian culture from her daughter-in-law, the grandmother, also known as The Mother-in-Law, and the widow of a war veteran who has seen a lot of suffering in life said, "It's just hair, ain't it? It was hangin' in her eyes."

Who is Mrs Grandma?

Due to the complicated geography of a multicultural family, it is heartbreakingly true that many GloLo families do not see one or even both sets of grandparents and other extended family members on a regular basis. Hence GloLo children often end up being 'introduced' to Grandma, Grandpa, aunts, uncles, and cousins over and over again. There is a rather skewed understanding of the filial bond. Whereas Grandmother & Co are *ecstatic* to finally see GloLo Junior, something like 'My grandchild! My progeny! Light of my life!' roughly translated into any language, GloLo Junior is hiding between his mother's legs, fearing for his safety amongst this pack of hysterical tall people, whimpering, "Who is Mrs Grandma?"

Modern technology has fortunately eliminated this problem for anyone with an internet connection and willing to go on video camera without professional hair and makeup. Family members can gather 'round the computer screen with its soft, blue glow, just as they once gathered 'round the fireplace to share stories together. It is the globalisation of family love.

Edward and Angel installed a large screen just for this purpose. Edward explained.

"My mother, who is 78, is in Dorchester, with my brother nearby. He set up the equipment she needs to video conference with us. At least once a week we sit together and have a proper family gathering. She's even picking up Spanish from the kids," Edward chuckled softly.

Education and discipline

The burden parents impose on themselves to educate and discipline their child in such a way that they become upstanding, law abiding, taxpaying citizens, never mind concert pianists, star athletes, brain surgeons who cure cancer and scientists who stop global warming, is huge.

Just as the print on this chapter was drying, Amy Chua excited and shocked parents everywhere with her book *Battle Hymn of the Tiger Mother*. Chua basically splits parents into two categories. There are 'Chinese mothers' who also come from other countries but are all very strict and demanding with their offspring and there are 'Western parents' who are not strict, and too lenient in fact, and non-demanding. Without giving away the plot of this autobiographical journey through motherhood, one style of parenting prepares children for a life of 'personal bests' and success while the other group allows their children to follow a path of mediocrity and under-achievement.

Although attitudes toward education and discipline are highly personal, the framework for personal preference is cultural. *Battle Hymn of the Tiger Mother* depicts the polar opposites of parenting styles based on the 'Chinese' and 'Western' cultural orientation.

From morning until night time, parents are constantly making decisions about GloLo Junior's upbringing, from what to eat for breakfast, what to wear to school, household chores, pocket money, table manners, choice of toys and games played, hobbies, sports, friends and 'no dessert until you've eaten your peas / finished your homework' type attitude and even sleeping arrangements. Amongst all the multicultural couples I met who have children, education and disciplinary style are the most frequently mentioned areas where they admitted to having great differences.

Muddy shoes

Remember Mexican Martha and Swedish Björn who we first met in *Chapter 3 – Profile of a GloLo*? Spanish and Swedish is not the only difference in the way they talk to their children.

"We each have our own way of talking to the children," Martha, the Mexican engineer told me. "Whereas Björn will calmly say, 'Jan, is that a good idea to play on the sofa wearing muddy shoes?' I will say, 'Get off my sofa!'."

"Martha threatens that they will turn to stone if they don't get off the sofa," Björn interjected. "She thinks I am too soft with the children and I think she is too harsh."

Awareness of the cultural differences on parenting is somewhat different than *acceptance* and living with the differences, particularly as it concerns GloLo Junior. The wonderful advantage of GloLo parenting is learning from both cultures and using what is best for the family.

"As multicultural parents, we could take what we learned from our upbringing and create a new style of parenting that is not so culturally determined. How we function together as a family is something we created ourselves," said Martha. I asked for an example.

"My family is very hierarchical and patriarchal with the men heading the family and making all of the decisions," she said. "Björn's family has a flat hierarchy. Our new family is a mixture of these two styles. I have flattened the hierarchy and Björn has increased the hierarchy. We are the parents and together we are the head of the household."

"The children accept it. Sometimes they say that the other mothers are less strict but they know I could be much stricter. They talk to their cousins in Mexico!" Martha concluded.

Yet sometimes the joy of multicultural parenting leads the family into a cultural gridlock. Gender specific education, religious practices and sports are three particularly hot topics in GloLo families. The Same But Different couple, Güner and Fahri, who we met in *Chapter 1 – Global Alliance Strategies*, had heated debates about the necessity of education for their daughter Ela. Fahri, the traditional father who grew up in Austria has future plans for his girl, including arranged marriage, which did not match what Güner, his modern Turkish wife, envisioned.

"He did not think her education to be important because he saw Ela marrying young and becoming a homemaker," Güner told me. "I had Ela enrolled in the local girls' soccer. It took a lot of discussion. Ela could not continue soccer because Fahri considers it a man's sport. She takes ballet lessons. She is the only Turkish girl in the class. And she will finish her full education in Austria."

Güner and Fahri's story exemplifies the cultural aspect of wanting the best for their children. Fahri forbid his daughter from playing 'rough' sports because, from his cultural framework, it is not ladylike and it would decrease Ela's chances of being taken as a wife. He wants her to have the best chances.

"Our divergent ideas of the best life for Ela is a typical conflict within the community," Güner added. "I want her to be modern and independent, whereas Fahri hangs on to traditions. We are a multicultural Turkish family."

Language

'They pick it up so easily at that age' they pipe, 'the wee ones are like sponges', and 'I wish my parents had taught me' is the background chorus of the bilingual child.

The GloLo toddler in our household is growing up bilingual, or even trilingual if you count the influence of the Romanian babysitter, which will be significant if I do not finish this book soon. The GloLo toddler tries out new words like it's a game of chance and daring. Her tiny little tongue is training for two Olympic events, English and German, or *German* and English as my husband insisted I write, simultaneously.

Languages spoken within the GloLo family are usually based on pure emotion rather than practicality and even geography. If you are a GloLo parent whose mother tongue is a unique dialect of a remote tribe somewhere in the jungle without an internet connection or any Facebook friends, you might forego GloLo Junior the language of your forefathers. On the other hand, precisely because the dialect of the remote tribe is so unique, you may feel strongly about 'preserving' the language and culture.

The political climate of the time can also affect the family language(s) of choice. Remember my Canadian mother, branded a Communist and put under *Perogie* house arrest for cooking Ukrainian dishes in the British household? Speaking Ukrainian, her mother tongue, in the 1960s was like an act of treason in Canada. The Cold War was in full swing and anything that came from east of Bratislava was *Communist* and Communists, and all of their languages, were a threat to Canada. My siblings and I were born in this political era, so that pretty much determined our unilingual upbringing in the *Capitalist* language English.

2.5 languages

It is very common for GloLo children to grow up with 2.5 languages. Often GloLo moms and dads do not speak each other's native language, so they speak in a third language together. Fortunately for me, the third language is often English, so I could conduct interviews with couples from all over the world.

Martha from Mexico speaks Spanish with their children and Björn speaks Swedish, however they speak English together, the language they met in and their so-called 'love language'. Hence the children have 2.5 languages at home.

"When we lived in Switzerland, the children also had an additional language, German. It was no problem at all, except that helping them with their homework was not always possible. We even had David, our eldest son, who was 12 at the time, help us with some administrative papers in German. He really liked being the family translator."

Secret language

Bilingual children can also be very naughty with their superior language skills, particularly when they speak a language that a parent does not understand.

"When the twins are angry with me, or when they don't want to go to bed," Georgia told me of her English and Greek speaking seven year-old twins, "they speak Greek. Although I have been listening to Greek passively for years, I understand very little. It's like a secret language they have. I once recorded them on my phone for Sandros (her husband and the girls' father) to hear. Apparently they were chanting, 'you can't make us, you can't hear us, no one can stop us'. The cheek!" She laughed heartily and continued.

"It's nice for the girls to have their own little world, as long as they are not offensive."

Every once in a while, a unilingual radical will shout out that children in bilingual families will suffer 'brain damage' from hearing two languages, as did happen to a girlfriend speaking Spanish to her son, right here in Vienna, home of Freud and all, but fortunately scientific studies have proven that brain damage is not a risk of bilingualism. I could even further that by saying that scientific studies have actually proven that bilingual children become *smarter* from the exertion of learning two mother tongues, but that would sound like I was bragging about my own brilliant bilingual daughter, which clearly I am not going to do.

Religion

Historically, religion has been known to cause a war or two, and this is no exception in the GloLo interfaith family. Even interfaith parents who claim that they are 'not religious' usually develop strong faith-based opinions when you throw a baby into the marriage. Non-practising followers are suddenly adorning religious symbols to their baby's crib, lighting candles to protect their little souls, and contemplating gender-based medical procedures that sound really painful. It may surprise the parents themselves.

In *The Complete Idiot's Guide to Interfaith Relationships*, which is a better resource than the title might suggest, author Laurie Rozaki advises parents to talk candidly about religion and religious expectations *before* the baby arrives. What she says is, "religious debates and 3am feedings do *not* go together well." *Italics hers*. I know from 3am feedings with my own daughter, and remember it is not usually a one-off kind of thing, it's usually more like a *series* of 3am feedings, that I would pray to any deity and promise all kinds of future sacrifices as long as it would have led me back to my bed and the salvation of sleep. I was having an interfaith relationship with myself in those desperate hours.

Somehow the arrival of the next generation stirs up an awareness of and desire for cultural continuity. Grandparents, in particular, find new hope in carrying on their values and traditions within the family. Where they may have failed or been disappointed in the spiritual choices their own children made, that would be you, GloLo Junior gives them a second chance to fulfil their religious duties within the family. GloLo parents can get caught in the middle of inter-generational salvation and tug-of-love.

Irene and Jeff are an interfaith American Canadian family who struggled between sports and religious education.

"We wanted David to have a *bar mitzvah*," Irene explained, "even though I think 13 years old is too young to really make that kind of decision about your religion and your life and the commitments involved. Jeff wanted David to play hockey. Preparation for the *bar mitzvah* conflicted with hockey practice and games. We were torn between the importance of hockey and the importance of religion."

I asked how they resolved the issue.

"The hockey coach agreed to change some of the practice times. Most of the other parents were fine with the changes but a few complained. A few Christian boys were preparing for Communion. So the families were trying to balance religion and hockey."

It further proves the point I made earlier. Hockey is religion in Canada, isn't it?

Cockroach in hell

In interfaith families where religion plays a strong role in daily life, children may be confused by what they learn from each parent and each religion. When a religion is exclusionary and allows no flexibility for interpretation of scriptures, children may get caught in the cross-fire of contradictory messages from each faith. The consequences of breaching adherence to religious teaching, an eternity in a burning hell, for example, is a lot to deal with when you are eight years old, or any age really.

Walter, a young Hindu Catholic boy whose parents were educating him about his mixed religious background was found crying by his mother.

"He had misbehaved and was feeling particularly remorseful," his mother told me. "When I asked what was wrong, he answered, 'you will never be able to find me. I will be a cockroach in hell, you won't recognise me'.

Walter was mixing reincarnation with eternal damnation. His mother continued.

"I am not sure what was more unsettling, that he thought that he was going to hell or that he was so certain that I would be there with him," she added wryly.

The upside of an interfaith upbringing, as we learned in *Chapter 6 – Religion*, is the regular celebrations, and the gifts of course. If combined well, an interfaith family has an on-going party of spiritual celebration.

Who am I?

If we recap the issues quickly, GloLo children are faced with identity labels such as language, religion, ethnicity, race, pet names and multicultural parents as well as the standard hormones and pimples. Under these circumstances, how does a GloLo child develop her own identity? Joel Crohn, author of *Mixed Matches*, which we have referred to earlier in the book, writes "Born of parents who were raised in different worlds, children of interracial, interethnic, and interreligious unions begin to learn at an early age that identity is as much a matter of decision as of destiny."

Ideally, GloLo Junior will rejoice in his global constellation of self, but remember, we are talking about young, impressionable and often changing minds here. Likes and dislikes, opinions and attitudes, not to mention T-shirts, can change faster than you can say Twitter.

From half to whole

Multicultural children will often refer to themselves as being, for example, 'half French and half Vietnamese', which reflects that they feel literally half of something and therefore not whole. Children often feel a bit clumsy in both cultures. It takes a particularly self-confident youth to identify with and embrace another cultural framework as his own, particularly if he has no memory of the country.

Miriam is the mother of Jens, her Swedish-Lebanese 14 year old son.

"Jens never felt very Lebanese. He had visited only once when he was four years old. Finally, we managed a visit last year and we both noticed how he talks about Lebanon much more. He had a project in school where he chose to study Lebanon. He has developed a sense of pride about it," she said with a sense of her own pride.

It is difficult for parents to share their culture with their foreign born children and find the right balance. It is a new generation for starters, with a different value set, it is a new country, and one you may not always understand completely, and it is a mix of culture, language, religion or colour, never mind the awful music that is never as good as the groovy tunes of a generation ago. Some GloLo children may feel overwhelmed by their cultural heritage, with duties and loyalties to family and religion, that they may not feel there is much room left to create their own identity.

A multicultural, bilingual, interfaith family tried so hard to teach their son about his family cultural background that he complained of 'cultural burn-out'. He was nine.

"We had him in language lessons, religious schooling, and then the various religious traditions throughout the year. One Saturday afternoon, my husband said to Peter, 'let's play football, we are Italian.' My son said, 'no, I'd like to be me this afternoon'. I realised that we overloaded him with our cultures. Since then, we allow him to choose what he wants to do."

Further, as rebellious as children can be, they have divided loyalties to their parents. Children may feel that by associating with one culture, they are also favouring one parent more than the other. They may identify more with the parent from the dominant culture, which is usually the country where the family lives, or with biracial children, the parent who is most similar in appearance. By consciously choosing one culture or religion over the other, children fear that they are therefore rejecting the parent of the other culture or religion.

Remember Slovenian Petra and Ethiopian Dahnay? They have already shared their experience being the 'only mixed race family' in their town in *Chapter 7 – GloLo Colours* and *Chapter 10 – Location, Location, Location*.

"When we go about town," Petra explained, "the girls stick close to their father, who they look like. But when we were in Addis Ababa, the girls shifted and always held my hand. I think they are supporting whichever parent is in the minority position. They are highly attuned to this type of situation."

Cultural superheroes

GloLo children face a unique set of challenges and opportunities. Ideally, a multicultural child will create a synthesis of their parental heritage and become a sort of cultural superhero. They learn open-mindedness and tolerance from day one while they listen to their parents debating about cloth versus disposable, and who, what, where, when on feeding. They learn early that *the way* in life is actually just one of many equal possibilities. They experience that being part of a majority group in one place means being part of a minority group someplace else. They see that they can pray to one divinity while respecting another. They know that discriminating against someone based on their skin colour is hurtful and unfair. They hear that language can lead to secrets as well as to sharing and understanding. Children are the future, they say, and GloLo children are little ambassadors for the future of world peace.

♥

Top 10 clues that you have GloLo children

1. Your child started collecting frequent flyer miles when she was 3 months old and flies half way around the world at least once a year but still complains that you 'never go anywhere on vacation'.
2. Your child told the teacher at school that the history lesson was 'prejudiced, biased and failed to recognise the inherent rights of the indigenous peoples at the time of the conflict'.
3. Your child colours the map of world with a big heart and a connecting line between the countries where his parents are from.
4. The bookshelf in your child's room is groaning under the weight of Cinderella, and other fairy tales, in multiple languages.
5. Cinderella's face has been coloured a darker shade with crayons and tuffs of black wool have been glued over her blonde hair to make her 'look more realistic'.
6. Your youngest child, who is five, corrects your pronunciation at story time.
7. Your seven year old child wrote a letter to world leaders requesting an end to war so that Grandma would be safe in her home.
8. When you go to the photo studio for a family portrait, the photographer says in a surprised way, 'I was expecting the Smith family at 10 o'clock, which group are you?'
9. Your grown child met a new love interest who is different in nationality, ethnicity, colour, language, and religion and the only thing she tells you is, 'you will love him, he's just like Daddy'.
10. Your child became the 44th president of the United States.

Happy Holidays

The only way to write this chapter with any *authenticity*, let's say, was to go on a holiday myself. That is the life of a bestselling author, you see, always ready to *immerse* oneself in work. So here I am reporting *live* from the south of France. The lapping of the Mediterranean Sea along the shore and the scent of lavender *are* distracting, however if F Scott Fitzgerald could make his career writing at a desk in Antibes, I too shall persevere. And if the location has any influence on the writing, this chapter, like the whole book actually, promises to be a classic.

Before we dig into the nitty-gritty of happy GloLo holidays, however, it will be necessary to expand the English language once more, as if the addition of 'GloLo' as a noun *and* an adjective wasn't already enough. In a GloLo relationship, there is a distinction between holidays and vacations. I know, in the dictionary they are the same, but please bear with me for a moment. We need to look at each of these issues separately and, as ever, *within the GloLo context*.

'Holidays' within the GloLo context, therefore, are big national or religious events. The date of the holiday, sometimes called a public holiday or bank holiday, is determined by the state or church where you live. Perhaps a messiah was born, a nation state was founded, snakes were banished, or a king or queen, dead or alive, has a birthday. Often you get a day off work and the whole country celebrates. The festivities are optional, however, and you can just enjoy your paid 'holiday'.

A 'vacation', by contrast, is a time of respite and a period during which the normal daily routine of school and work is suspended. A vacation is determined by you, or if you are a happily married man, probably by your wife. You, or likely your wife, also decide where to go for a vacation, even if you decide to sit in your own backyard. Sometimes holidays and vacations 'collide', as one GloLo couple put it, when you take your vacation 'during the holidays'.

This chapter therefore includes two sections:

- Holidays around the world
- GloLo vacations

Holidays around the world

Holidays, as mentioned, are determined by the state or dominant religion where you live. The greeting card industry has also made a significant contribution to the holiday business. In a multicultural, meaning multi-*national* or interfaith relationship, GloLo partners may experience discrepancy, shall we say, in the joyfulness and meaningfulness of said holidays and the holiday season.

Remember Oksana Leslie, the *How to Survive in International Marriage* author, who was identified in *Chapter 2* as a Mail Order Bride? Oksana expressed how she felt about some of the star-spangled American holidays. In her charming Russian English, she wrote, "Having a wife from another culture can be frustrating sometimes. Who would not get excited about decorating a house for Halloween? I would not. Who would not care about the 4th of July holiday? Your Russian wife would not."

She brings up two important points. Firstly, it can be frustrating for the GloLo Host. If you have celebrated an annual event, like Halloween or the 4th of July for example, your entire life, you likely have a lot of positive associations and memories of past events. National and religious holidays reinforce culture, don't they? The 'cultural continuity', the family bond and the friendly camaraderie, let's say, give you this sense of being part of something bigger, to risk a cliché, and *to belong*. And that is exactly the problem for GloLo couples. Holidays can emphasis the cultural gap between you and your GloLo partner. So while you are having the time of your life, revelling in your national, ethnic, or religious heritage, your partner may be having some kind of cultural out-of-body experience.

Remember American Stella, who refused her Swiss boyfriend's marriage proposal because she thought it was for 'administrative reasons'? Didier finally managed to convince Stella to let love rule and they have been married ever since (a New Fangled Wedding apparently). Stella told me about her experience at the *Basler Fasnacht* carnival in Switzerland.

"I had been out of the country during the carnival time for the first two years I lived in Switzerland. I just heard the stories from Didier and it sounded really exciting. The whole town participates," explained Stella, referring to the three day carnival event held every year in the Swiss border town of Basel.

"When I finally did see *Fasnacht*, it freaked me out to be honest. I think of a carnival as a fun event. The Basel carnival is eerie. It starts at four o'clock in the morning and everything is silent. Didier kept 'shushing' me whenever I spoke. The masks and costumes are scary, and the piccolo music is irritating. It wasn't even fun, it was just weird," she complained.

Didier saw the holiday more philosophically.

"It is very American to associate a public holiday with fun, laughter, balloons and a band," he said, pumping his arms like a marching band. "We Swiss are not so jolly. We have the bands but we have fun in a different way. I think it was important for Stella to see that at *Fasnacht*."

"That's true," Stella readily admitted. "I was expecting the carnival to be as it would be in the States and to be fun according to my idea of fun. However it was interesting to see how the city transforms itself. I never would have thought that sleepy Basel could change so dramatically."

And that is the second, fortunately wonderful thing about holidays. It provides an opportunity to learn about your partner's culture and even your partner. It can be a day when you fall in love all over again.

Remember English Carole who 'swore like a trucker' and her Canadian diplomat husband Kevin who was teased about his 'provincial accent' by his British in-laws? Carole told me what she learned during the Canada Day celebrations in Ottawa, the capital city.

"It was adorable," she began, "little kids were waving Canadian flags, their cheeks were painted red and white, Ryan even wore his 'I am Canadian' T-shirt," she said. "The crowds were happy and proud. I always thought that Canadians lack a true nationality, and that

Canada was just a knock-off of the British Empire really, however on Canada Day I saw that even if the culture seems to be just a collection of other nationalities, the people are proud of that mix. That is what Canada stands for and it impressed me deeply. I fell in love with Ryan all over again."

I asked Carole if she would like to live in Canada.

"Well," she laughed nervously, "I'm not one for the cold really, and Kevin is a diplomat so I presume we'll be on foreign soil most of the time. It's lovely here in the summer though," she recovered somewhat, "so I'd like to visit again."

State determined holidays are usually quite rigid in the sense that they are celebrated uniformly across the country or region. The Queen's birthday cannot be changed after all. Religious holidays, by contrast, are usually not as uniform as state holidays. There are national variations, family traditions, historical folklore and even 'interpretation of the scriptures'. Christmas, for example, is not always Christmas.

The Protestant turkey

I grew up believing Christmas was on December 25th. I also believed that Santa Claus, a fat, jolly man in a bright red suit, was universal and that he brought presents to children *all over the world*. He rode his reindeer-powered CO_2 neutral sleigh through the night of December 24th while we were asleep. When we woke up, usually very early on the morning of December 25th, Santa had drunk the milk and eaten the cookies we left out for him, and, more importantly from the perspective of a seven year old, he left gifts for everyone under the Christmas tree. In Austria, Christmas or *Heilige Abend* is celebrated on the evening of December 24th. *Christkindl*, a blond, slightly cherub-like angelic looking child, brings the gifts the same evening. He comes *invisibly*. Christkindl was 'invented' during the Reformation in Europe during the 16th and 17th century (you know, the *Protestant* reformation). He was a replacement of sorts for the previous guy who was St Nicolas. You can already see where this is going.

Well, one year I was grumbling (I thought to myself but apparently not) about the 'cultural oppression' of my Austrian family who were ignoring my Canadian-Santa-comes-on-the-25th heritage. Further, to add insult to injury, Austrians, who really know how to put on a proper feast when they want to, typically eat fish on the 24th. Not just any fish, mind you, but carp. And that carp comes to the pre-Christmas household *alive and kicking*, where he then lives out the last few miserable hours of his life in the bathtub, where he is supposed to clean the river silt from his gills apparently, until he meets his final destiny on the chopping block in my mother-in-law's kitchen.

My mother-in-law, a fantastic cook even if she could not convince me that carp is a fine meal, sensed my lack of enthusiasm, some would say rudeness but never mind, concerning the Austrian Christmas dinner. She explained the Catholic origin of the meal, something about the monks ending a 40 day fast apparently, and believe me, it would take 40 days of fasting to make that carp taste good, and then she asked me how 'the Protestants', by this she meant me and all Canadians, celebrated Christmas and what 'the Protestants' ate for the Christmas meal. I reminisced about the ten kilogram (no exaggeration) oven-roasted turkey my mother cooked every year, starting at five in the morning on Christmas day, the stuffing with sage, thyme and chopped celery, to give away my mother's secret ingredient, the creamy mashed potatoes and the not-too-thick-nor-too-thin gravy that covers the meal like a wave of yuletide joy. And don't get me started on the pies. The food chapter has already been written, so let's get back to this story.

The next day, the 25th of December, or Christmas in my Canadian 'Protestant' world, I smelled something savoury coming from my mother-in-law's kitchen. I kept myself occupied in the living room, however, with a moving celebrity Christmas special on TV and a generous stash of my mother-in-law's twelve varieties of Christmas cookies, including my favourite *Vanillekipferl* which are covered in powdery icing sugar. (It is not that I never enter my mother-in-law's kitchen, mind you, but I was still reeling from the sight of that poor carp looking up at me in his final moment, *begging for mercy*, so I was keeping my distance.) It was only when the family was seated for dinner that I noticed that the table had been formally set and was *even fancier* than on the evening of December 24th. My mother-in-law proudly entered the dining room carrying before her a platter on which there was a beautiful bronzed turkey, the most perfect looking Christmas turkey I have seen in my life. It could have been used for a photo shoot in *Gourmet Today: The Turkey Edition*. It even had white paper frills around his feet.

"Today," she beamed at me, "we are having a Protestant turkey. Merry Christmas, dear daughter-in-law."

It was the tastiest darn Protestant turkey you can imagine.

Is Christmas cancelled?

Remember Sheida and Andràs, the GloLo Black American-White Romanian couple who we met in *Chapter 3 – Profile of a GloLo* and *Chapter 7 – GloLo Colours*? Sheida and Andràs basically celebrate two separate events. Both happen to be called Christmas.

"We have been to Romania once for Christmas and I will never go again," Sheida began the story with her trademark take-no-prisoners style. "I love Christmas and Romanians don't know how to celebrate it right. There was *no* entertainment, *no* football on TV, *no* After Christmas sales. I was like, what, is Christmas cancelled this year or something? It was totally depressing."

Andràs stifled a laugh, as did I to be honest.

"In my country, we have a different way to celebrate Christmas. We are a poor country and we don't have things like in America. In Sheida's home, and I think everywhere in the US, every TV and radio and light in the house is switched on. The microwave is spinning, the phone is constantly ringing. It's noisy and total chaos. In Romania, Christmas is more about spirituality and time with family."

"And I am not going back," Sheida repeated for good measure.

Intercontinental Christmas

A GloLo couple can make good use of both the different interpretation of and the varying significance of religious holidays. A German-American couple I know dine with her family on the evening of the 24th and then on the morning of the 25th, they jet over to New York where they arrive in time to have Christmas dinner with his family.

"We celebrate Christmas on two continents," Antje explained. "My parents are happy we are with them for *Heilige Abend*. Jack's parents are happy to have us at Christmas. Travelling at peak season is expensive and stressful, so sometimes we are not that happy, but so far we have avoided any family Christmas tug-of-wars."

In a GloLo *interfaith* relationship, the different dates of religious holidays provide the luxury of being able to attend all major celebrations, within geographic limits of course, thereby avoiding that dreadful 'your folks or mine?' discussion that plagues monocultural couples several times a year. Some GloLo couples, like Cokie and Steve Roberts, the married authors of *Our Haggadah*, covered in *Chapter*

6 – *Religion*, celebrate *every* Catholic and Jewish holiday, and they do so with enthusiasm. However many GloLo couples elect for 'none of the above' religious holidays. Remember from *Chapter 3 – Profile of a GloLo*, that GloLo spouses often have a low affiliation with their national or religious culture? They tend to be low on 'religiosity' and hence many big holidays fall into the 'no big deal' category.

"We've agreed to skip them all," a Danish GloLo husband told me. "While everyone else is running around completely stressed out from shopping, cooking, and arguing with their spouse making a big deal about nothing, we use the day to go sailing or ice skating. Now that's what I call a holiday."

Happy ~~birth~~ name day to you

Birthdays are not usually public holidays or religious events unless of course you are very, very famous. For most of you though, your birthday is just a private affair with family and friends. Yet all birthdays are not equal.

On the one cultural extreme, your birthday is a Big Day. The date is marked in big, bold letters, usually in red, on the calendar and references to the Big Day are made starting several weeks in advance. It starts with 'oh, you have a birthday soon, don't you?' followed by two or three reminder questions such as 'oh, your birthday is getting closer, isn't it?' and then something about 'next week' and even 'tomorrow'. On your actual birthday, calls start coming in very early in the morning. It is a bit of a competition to be the first to call someone on his birthday. Then a 'surprise' bouquet of flowers is sent to work, followed by an evening dinner, usually planned, with family and friends, possibly including a 'meaningful' gift, like super-powered binoculars for birdwatchers or concert tickets for music lovers.

The other extreme is where your birthday is not really celebrated but rather acknowledged. The acknowledgement can even be an oops-sorry-I-forgot-your-birthday greeting card, which arrives two weeks too late. You might receive a joke gift from your spouse, like super-powered binoculars that leave black circles around your eyes for birdwatchers or a CD with hit songs from your birth year for music lovers. You can see how mixing these two birthday cultures into one GloLo relationship can really blow out the candles on the proverbial birthday cake.

Althea and George are a Greek-British couple who met in a GloLo cliché on Crete, a Greek island and popular tourist destination. It was a whirlwind romance that went from zero to married-and-living-in-London within eight months.

"I had to get back to work, it was that simple," George, a dapper looking event manager, explained. "So I brought Althea home with me," he grinned, "my souvenir from Crete." He laughed heartily at his own joke and continued.

"Althea was mostly at home in those first few months, you know without knowing anyone here. So one day, I came home from work rather late and she had this big surprise waiting for me. She had cooked a lovely meal and had a gift. She said 'Happy Name Day George'. Well, I'd never heard of Name Day and thought it was something she found on the internet or something, you know, because she had so much free time."

The plot thickened as George continued to talk.

"My birthday followed a few weeks later and nothing much happened really. I was working a lot. It was the same for Althea's birthday. I brought some flowers after work, but nothing flash. With any other British woman, I would have been in the doghouse, but Althea didn't seem to mind. But then came Name Day," he said in an Armageddon-type voice, and Althea swatted him playfully.

"I didn't even know about Name Day," he said defensively, "so how was I to know it was Althea's name day, Althea Day? Well, the doghouse would have been a luxury that night I'm telling you," he grimaced at the memory.

Althea finally gave her side of the story.

"We live in England. We speak English. I have to learn all about English culture, drinking tea all day, hot water here, cold water there," she said with mounting frustration, referring to the water faucets in British bathrooms that separate hot and cold water, which is pretty annoying actually. "What about learning Greek culture? Name Day is important. I told you that."

"I felt like a real fool," George admitted and lowered his eyes in shame. "Luckily though, I'm an event manager," he perked up, rubbing his hands together. "Althea's next Name Day is already in the making. It's going to be absolutely smashing."

I am not sure if Name Day celebrations are supposed to be 'smashing' actually, but it brings up a couple of salient points. Firstly, as a GloLo spouse, sometimes it takes a while to learn and understand the value and relevance of culturally prescribed celebrations, particularly if you are living outside your home culture. Secondly, even when the holiday or celebration is accepted as 'legitimate', there will inevitably be some 'cultural interpretation' of that holiday. My husband, for example, loves Thanksgiving (the *Canadian* Thanksgiving mind you, not the American one). In the 'pilgrim spirit', he sparks up the barbecue I told you about in *Chapter 9* and grills turkey. Turkey *filets*, mind you, which are for the Thanksgiving *burgers*. We invite friends from Austria, from Canada, and as many other countries we can think of and, to be honest, it looks nothing like Thanksgiving in Canada, but it is always *absolutely smashing*.

♥

Top 5 clues that you have had a GloLo holiday

1. Your Imported GloLo spouse asked why you are not going to work today.
2. Your Imported GloLo spouse calls the holiday 'post-imperialist nonsense'.
3. When you try to teach your GloLo children age old holiday traditions passed down through generations, he or she asks, 'if it's so important, then how come Mommy/Daddy doesn't do it too?'
4. Your spouse says, 'if we celebrate _______ (insert name of your national or religious celebration here), then we should also celebrate _______ (insert name of the equivalent, usually much bigger, national or religious celebration of your spouse's culture here).
5. Your children tell you that the gifts at _______ (insert name of your spouse's national or religious celebration here) are way cooler than _______ (insert name of your national or religious celebration here).

Vacations

When you think about it, there are two types of GloLo vacations. There are 'travel vacations' when you select a destination on the map where you will go to explore the region, absorb the culture, try new foods and, in my case, flop on the beach and eat too much ice cream. As natural born jetsetters, GloLo couples tend to prioritise 'travel vacations'. Remember Spanish Salma and Austrian Christian from *Chapter 2 – When Heinrich Met Saanvi*, who met in an airport lounge and then quit their consultant jobs to settle down in GloLo domestic bliss? Salma said that every birthday, Christmas and anniversary gift is 'a plane ticket to somewhere'. So even once they had settled down from the working jetset lifestyle, they still maintained their jetset status.

In contrast to a 'travel vacation', there are 'visiting vacations' when you return to your native country or the native country of your GloLo spouse, and you visit family and friends. Both a 'travel vacation' and a 'visiting vacation' are considered a vacation, however it does not always feel that way.

As mentioned at the beginning of this chapter, I am currently on a 'travel vacation'. Well, it is a 'working travel vacation', of course, as I am busy writing a bestseller. But when I take a short break every once in while, I can swim in the Mediterranean, or just splash about on the shore with the GloLo toddler, and browse the many, many markets with their piles of lavender sachets and colourful woven baskets, which are far more fashionable than you would think. In the evening, I drink rosé wine with my GloLo husband, which also tastes much better when you are on location, if you know what I mean. Pictures are taken, memories are created, souvenirs and yes, even a couple of woven baskets are purchased. Well, you get the picture, we are on vacation. However there are consequences.

Firstly, my Canadian family is wondering why I am on vacation in France rather than on vacation in Canada. This is nothing against France of course. Canadians have a strong history and high appreciation of the French *je ne sais quoi* culture and food in particular, even if we never have quite mastered the language. So what is it then that has them a bit rattled? Well, they have not seen me, their progeny and pride and joy (I think), in almost a year. The internet has thankfully enabled regular and cheap contact, including video calling so we can actually see each other (my mother even puts on lipstick when she goes 'on TV') but there is nothing like being in the same room together, is there? I mean, how else can I eat my mother's should-be-world-famous blueberry pie?

Secondly, and let's be honest, much more significantly, the reason for my family's displeasure is that they have not seen the GloLo toddler, their progeny and pride and joy (I know for a fact), in almost a year. They have missed many toddler milestones over the past 11 months, so it is difficult for them to understand why I am denying them another two weeks of toddler milestones while frolicking in France rather than in Canada.

Thirdly, my parents in particular do not understand the economics of the travel vacation. Why waste money on hotels and restaurants in France when we could vacation with them *for free*? (They are children of the war generation remember.) Somehow the cost of the trans-Atlantic flight, what with sky-rocketing fuel prices, extra luggage charges and now the be-a-good-global-citizen CO_2 compensation are not part of their calculation.

Fourthly, my family does not factor in the jetlag which is a result of the six hour time difference between our respective places of residence. Remember my theory that jetlag is a major, if unrecognised, plague in today's globalised society? If a vacation, even a working vacation, is a 'time of respite', then sometimes you just want the respite without being exhausted for one week after arrival *in both directions*. All my mother is thinking is that she has not seen the toddler, *her progeny and pride and joy*, in almost a year. Surely we can take a nap and shake off the jetlag. It is not going to kill us after all.

Finally, my family are kind of wondering why, if I have not seen them in almost a year, I would extend this period of anxious separation even further by wasting my vacation time in a foreign country. Yes, well, that is a tough one to answer. The truth is that sometimes a 'travel holiday' is more *regenerative*, shall we say, that a 'visiting holiday'. Even if a GloLo couple typically have jetsetting in their DNA, sometimes there is the need to take break to 'get away from it all'.

It seems like a rather personal list, but this is not a 'memoir' remember, it is a book about GloLo couples the world over. So I checked with a couple of GloLo friends and asked if their experiences were the same, particularly the fifth point, the 'travel holiday' – 'visiting holiday' issue. Was I being indelicate, I tentatively asked?

My dear friend, X, let's call her, replied bluntly.

"I work 60 hours a week and you expect me to go back to _____ (insert name of her small, not that glamorous mid-western home town here) and waste my vacation hanging out in my mother's kitchen? Oh no, London, Paris, Rio, here I come. I need a *real* vacation."

Thanks X, I was just wondering. It really does seem that when you plan a GloLo vacation, you choose between keeping your spouse happy, making your mother happy, or being happy yourself. All three is rarely possible.

Claudia and Arvind, the German-Indian couple who have provided so many personal anecdotes for this book, told me what happens when you try to mix a 'travel vacation' with a 'visiting vacation'.

Living rooms of India

Arvind, a born storyteller, spoke first.

"The further away a German goes from home, the better," he said animatedly. "The more exotic, the better. It should also be an outdoor experience, preferably dangerous. It's supposed to be a holiday and Claudia wants to summit mountains and sleep in a tent. It's much nicer having tea in my aunt's parlour."

"Arvind doesn't understand why I want to explore and be challenged on a vacation. We work so much. When we take a vacation, I like to really do something different. I don't need to go to India to drink tea. I can do that in Germany," she explained.

"It's the only chance to see my family though," Arvind said, turning to me for support. Both Arvind and I are the Imported GloLo spouse you see.

"But every time we visit India, the family seems to have grown. We go from one Indian living room to the next. I come home completely exhausted and fat from eating so much, and I haven't even seen India."

Claudia had one last grudge to bear.

"It is also boring, the same stories are told every year," Claudia complained. "That's why I need to sit on a mountain peak and just hear the silence."

Memory lane and nostalgia

Claudia brings up an important point that many GloLo couples struggle with when they have a visiting vacation, which is the family trip down memory lane. When visits with family are once a year or less, get-togethers have a reunion-like quality. Family history is regaled, old traditions are upheld, and there is often a nostalgic yearning for yesteryear *when we were all together*. If you are the GloLo partner tagging along, it means that much of the vacation conversation is about a time before you existed within this family. It can be alienating and possibly hurtful for the new spouse.

"I do like hearing the stories," Claudia stated in her defence. "I love to hear about Arvind as a boy. I love to learn about his family history and their culture. It's just that I feel left out. The past, when I did not exist, is glorified. Where does present and future play a role? Where do I fit in the family?"

Yet she is not alone in feeling alone. Visiting home after long absences and long years in a GloLo relationship can be emotional. The disconnect between you and your friends is typical of anyone who has lived in a foreign country for a period of time. You have fewer shared experiences and therefore less understanding of your respective situations in life. You are confronted with images and memories of the past while being suspended in time until you fly back to your new 'home' with your GloLo spouse.

"It can be depressing," Arvind said, "to see how much has changed, and to see how your home has moved on without you. My friends don't understand my life in Germany and I don't really understand theirs any more either. I always feel a little bit lost at home, a bit like a foreigner actually. It reminds me that my life is with Claudia and our marriage is our home base."

One more thing...

As frustrating as Claudia finds the journeys to India, she is fortunate that she and her Indian family all speak English. The visiting vacation is even more difficult when you or your partner do not speak the family language. Remember English Lindsey and Japanese Mahito, who already experienced a few language and information hiccups when his parents visited them in London? Two months after Mahito's parents returned to Japan, Lindsey and Mahito flew to Tokyo for *Obon*, a Buddhist event where families commemorate their ancestors.

"It may sound nasty, but thank goodness it was a short trip," Lindsey began. "It felt like I sat cross-legged on the floor forever, smiling and nodding my head. I didn't have a clue what was going on the entire week. Even though I specialise in languages, Japanese is not my forte. I felt like I was sitting in the middle of foreign film, without sub-titles unfortunately."

I asked if Mahito translated for Lindsey and his family.

"My English is not so good that I can translate everything," Mahito answered softly. "I have to find the words, and then make it simple for everyone to understand. It was difficult. I was sorry for Lindsey. She did not have such a nice vacation."

I asked if Mahito enjoyed his vacation.

"Me? No. Too much translating, visiting family, talking about dead relatives," he sighed. "When we flew back to London, I said, 'Lindsey, I need a vacation'."

We all laughed.

"We took a mini-break and managed to squeeze in four days in Malaga," Lindsey piped up. "We went swimming and just soaked up the sunshine. It was glorious."

♥

Top 5 clues that you have had a GloLo vacation

1. You have a really bad case of jetlag and an impressive collection of air miles without having seen anything new in the world.
2. Your head is exploding from 12 consecutive days of simultaneous translation between your GloLo spouse and your family and everyone still feels 'left out of the conversation'.
3. If you see another pot of tea and plate of cookies…
4. When you flew 'home' from your vacation, you stood in the 'foreigners' line for immigration.
5. You feel that you really, really need a vacation right now.

Conclusions on happy holidays

There is a saying that you never really know someone until you have travelled with them. You get to see them in a different context and under different, sometimes even stressful, circumstances. In the GloLo case, the saying could be amended to read 'you never really know someone until you have travelled together half-way around the world to visit Mommy'.

When you experience national public holidays and religious celebrations together, it is an opportunity to learn more about your GloLo partner. Lindsey said that watching Mahito with his family during the Japanese Obon helped her to realise how far he had travelled to London, not just geographically, but spiritually and intellectually.

"It was not an easy trip, but I saw further into the Japanese person he was and the international person he has become. It was like peeking into his soul," Lindsey said with contemplation.

Some would argue that a GloLo marriage is a permanent holiday or vacation. There are endless language issues, cultural misunderstandings, customs and rituals that seem quaint or sometimes bizarre, and the food on the dinner table is sometimes difficult to identify, never mind swallow. Yet, everyone knows there is nothing as romantic as a holiday romance.

Sadly my holiday and this book are drawing to an end. Before we say farewell, let's take one last look at the globalisation of love and see what conclusions we can draw.

Epilogue

What should the final words of *The Globalisation of Love* be, other than 'tell all your friends to buy this book' I mean? Each chapter in the book could, some would successfully argue *should*, be its own book really. It was fun, and gruelling, researching the topics and learning about the intricate complexities of the globalisation of love. I am hesitant to try to summarise it all and draw grandiose conclusions in a few pages when really there is so much more to say, but the GloLo toddler will be starting college if I don't finish up soon.

If we look at the globalisation of love in its most raw and naked form, as we have done throughout the pages of this book, we can say with certain confidence that there is significant evidence to support at least one theory about this modern social phenomenon. At the risk of sounding like a snooty intellectual, then, a GloLo relationship rocks your world.

Rocks your world

Virtually all GloLo spouses I interviewed, even those who, oops, did not get to the happily ever after part of the romance, said how they felt 'enriched', 'blessed' and 'privileged' to be part of a multicultural relationship. By virtue of your chosen bedfellow, you are exposed to new and different things. The phrase he or she 'opened up a whole new world to me' is meant quite literally, including international travel, new attitudes and belief systems, foods, household habits, language, customs and celebrations. And the exposure to new and different things kind of rocks your world. By constantly challenging your existing values and assumptions about life, a GloLo relationship provides an on-going opportunity for self-reflection and for learning about yourself and your own culture.

But let's not sugarcoat *how* a GloLo relationship rocks your world. The 'whole new world' your partner opened up to you may be a world of cultural confusion, language hurdles and historical family feuds that have nothing to do with you and Mr or Mrs GloLo Right. And the 'challenge to your existing values and assumptions' may want to make you want to stick pins into a voodoo doll replica of your GloLo spouse too.

Yet exposure to new ways of life and cultural frames of reference help you realise that the person you are is a choice. You can actually change your identity and culture. Many GloLo spouses develop a kind of 'cultural merger personality' by picking and choosing the good bits from both worlds. You can draw on the strengths of each GloLo culture at times when they are needed. You can share your new and improved culture with family and friends.

Being a GloLo spouse kind of launches you from being 'lil ol' you into becoming a *global citizen* too. All those pretty lines and colours on the world map start to blur. You cross them first thing every day when you kiss your GloLo spouse good morning. Being part of a global community means that more things fall into place in the world. You gain a better understanding of the inter-connectivity of the world and start to think about the larger ramifications of international politics, religious conflict and natural disasters that happen half way around the globe. Suddenly it has a deep and personal relevance because your GloLo spouse is from the very place you hear about on the six o'clock news, you have family there, and you were just there for your last vacation in fact. Even a big sports victory can rock the foundation of your GloLo household. When a Canadian does well in a ski race, I am telling you, the whole dynamic of our household shifts and my husband is much nicer to me. He realises that even though Austria dominates the *current* international ski scene, there may be a day when Canada reigns supreme. He cannot afford to be smug.

Ultimately what happens in a GloLo relationship is that the things you grew up with and the culture that you believe in so strongly that you think it was all your idea in the first place is questioned by your GloLo partner, your soul mate, the one you love the most, the one *you chose*. You don't really think about it when you meet your international man or woman of mystery for the first time, do you? Even once you are an established GloLo couple, you don't realise that this every day cultural merger transformation is rocking your world.

Ambassadors for world peace

A second snooty intellectual theory would be that GloLo couples, by virtue of their chosen bedfellow, inadvertently become ambassadors for world peace. It sounds kind of lofty and self-congratulatory but when you think about it, it's true. Sharing your new and improved culture, not to mention cooking recipes, with family and friends opens up a whole new world to them too.

GloLo relationships weave the foundation for a world that is connected by families and children who have a different ethnicity, heritage, colour, language, religion and nationality. GloLo couples enhance cultural integration and peaceful co-existence. And not to put excessive pressure on GloLo children, but those little cultural superheroes only know a world where multiculturalism and tolerance for different ways of living are the norm.

Yet there is no right way to do it. Every couple seems to find their own GloLo way of managing that intricate balance between 'your culture', 'my culture' and the thing we have created in our marriage. Each couple comes with their own individual patchwork of 'cultural stuff' that may change over time too. Different events in life and different stages in life may awaken strong familial ties and a longing for traditions and cultural continuity. It is perhaps, nay, definitely, more challenging than a monocultural relationship but few could imagine how it would be any other way. And despite the cultural, language, religious, and ethnic differences, despite the uniqueness of the globalisation of love, GloLo couples demonstrate on a daily basis that peace between different countries, cultures, and religions is possible. GloLo couples and GloLo children are ambassadors for world peace

There may even be a third and final snooty intellectual theory. It follows what the environmentalists have been saying for decades actually; we only have one planet to live on so let's take good care of it. We only have one planet to share so let's play nicely together. There may be wars, ethnic conflict, religious strife, racism and prejudice, but each and every GloLo couple is proof that there is a world of romance happening out there. There may be the odd border skirmish in the GloLo refrigerator or a night or two on the GloLo couch every once in a while, but we all can *and do* get along harmoniously. I guess you could say this is a grandiose conclusion actually. World peace, like the globalisation of love, begins at home.

Now it's time for a GloLoTini. Let's toast to world peace and the globalisation of love.

The End

♥

Top 10 clues that you are a GloLo spouse

1. You read this book with your spouse and laughed quite a lot actually.
2. You read this book with your spouse and cried quite a lot actually.
3. You wonder how the author knew about your personal and private relationship issues.
4. For each and every topic covered in this book, you said, "I knew that!"
5. For each and every topic covered in this book, you said, "you could also include ______ , ______ , and ______ " (insert several related issues here which you know from personal experience).
6. You know several other GloLo couples with whom you want to share this book.
7. You have several non-GloLo family members and friends with whom you *need* to share this book.
8. You know that world peace begins at home... starting at breakfast every morning with your GloLo spouse.
9. You complain frequently about the challenges, the frustrations and the difficulties of having a GloLo spouse.
10. You would not trade in your GloLo spouse for the world.

References

Black Women in International Relationships: In Search of Love and Solace, Kellina M. Craig-Henderson, Transaction Publishers, New Brunswick, USA, 2011

Cross-Cultural Marriage, Ed. Rosemary Breger and Rosanna Hill, Berg, New York, 1998

Cupid's Wild Arrows, Ed. Dianne Dicks, Bergli Books, Weggis, Switzerland, 1993

Dating the Ethnic Man Strategies for Success, Faizal Sahukhan, PhD, Trafford Publishing, Vancouver, Canada, 2009

Don't Bring Home a White Boy and other notions that keep black women from dating out, Karyn Langhorne Folan, Gallery Books, New York, 2010

How to Survive in International Marriage, Oksana Leslie, Author House, Bloomington, Indiana, 2004

Guess Who's Coming to Dinner: Celebrating Interethnic, Interfaith, and Interracial Relationships, Brenda Lane Richardson, Wildcat Canyon Press, Berkeley, California, 2000

In Love But Worlds Apart, Ed. Grete Shelling and Janet Fraser-Smith, Author House, Bloomingdale, Indiana, 2008

I Got the Fever, J.C. Davies, DoubleWide Publications, New York, 2011

Intercultural Couples, Terri A. Karis and Kyle D. Killian, Routledge Taylor and Francis Group, New York, 2009

Intercultural Marriage Promises and Pitfalls, Dugan Romano, Intercultural Press, Boston, 2008

Interracial Intimacy, Rachel F. Moran, The University of Chicago Press, London, 2001

It Ain't All Good Why Black Men should not date White Women, John Johnson, African American Images, Chicago, 2004

Joining Hands and Hearts, Rev. Susanna Stefanachi Macomb, Fireside, New York, 2003

Lust in Translation, Pamela Druckerman, Penguin Books, New York, 2008

Mixed Matches, Joel Crohn, PhD, Fawcett Columbine, New York, 1995

Navigating Interracial Borders, Erica Chito Childs, Rutgers University Press, New Brunswick, USA, 2005

Swaying Essays on Intercultural Love, Ed. Jessie Carroll Grearson and Lauren B. Smith, University of Iowa Press, Iowa City, 1995

The Complete Idiot's Guide to Interfaith Relationships, Laurie Rozakis, PhD, Alpha Books, Indianapolis, Indiana, 2001

Your Intercultural Marriage, Marla Alupoaicei, Moody Publishers, Chicago, 2009

What Children Learn From Their Parents' Marriage: It May Be Your Marriage, but It's Your Child's Blueprint for Intimacy, P. Siegel, Harper Collins, New York, 2000

Why Black Men Love White Women: Going Beyond Sexual Politics to the Heart of the Matter, Rajen Persaud, Karen Hunter Publishing, New York, 2004

Lightning Source UK Ltd.
Milton Keynes UK
UKOW031316301011

181199UK00002B/5/P